A Cairngorm Loop on the Hoof

A circular horseback journey around the Cairngorms

Claire Alldritt

A Cairngorm Loop on the Hoof

Map by Claire Alldritt

Copy-edited by Sari Maydew

Text design by Wild Seas Formatting – www.rikhall.com

Cover Image: Ardverikie, unknown photographer

ISBN number 9798364589781

Horse Trails with a Bear and a Spotty Bum
www.bearandspottybum.com

Follow on Facebook
www.Facebook.com/hoofinaroundthehighlands/

Illustrations by Leandra Sutherland

The Author
Claire Alldritt

Photo by Jessica Crighton

Claire has always had a passion for outdoor adventure. This started at a young age, with both parents being involved in the Scout and Guide movements resulting in many weekends spent under canvas, whittling sticks, peeling spuds, and cooking over an open fire. In adulthood, this led to adventure travel in many different countries and wild places around the world.

Closer to home in Scotland, the adventure is constant; when Claire says she is just 'popping out' with a rucksack over her shoulder, don't expect to see her for a while. Her fascination to see where a trail leads to, or what's just around the next corner, feeds her constant desire to explore.

Recognising the importance of adventure for all, Claire runs a charity (Outfit Moray) in her spare-time that provides the opportunity of outdoor activities to disadvantaged and vulnerable young people near where she lives.

Horses have always featured in Claire's life, but work commitments as a petrophysicist (someone who studies rock properties for the oil industry) and then as an outdoor sports instructor required a different focus for a while. A better work-life balance as a paramedic, enabled a return to all things equine and the realisation of her childhood dream to own horses.

Mixing a love of the hills with owning horses, plus a craving for exploration, challenge, and adventure - led to a sport she likes to call dobbineering. She regularly carries out this gentle kind of mountaineering with horses in the Scottish Highlands, exploring the glens and an occasional hilltop but especially the history of the places and routes travelled through.

This book is dedicated to John, a dear friend who departed too young. His passing was a reminder that life is too short, and it ignited the fire under my one-thousand-mile dream.

Acknowledgements

Thank you to those who read and enjoyed my first book *From East to West by Saddle is Best.* Your positive and encouraging feedback inspired me to do it all over again.

Much gratitude also, to Jackie Harris for providing a peaceful place to write and for introducing me to a new group of friends at Buntait - not least, the wonderfully colourful character, Mo.

Many thanks to all those who provide stopping points and hospitality whenever I'm on the trail. Team Swogi and I couldn't do this without you. During the Cairngorm Loop: Davie at Glen Feshie, Dominic at Glen Bruar, Andrew at the Lude Estate, The Glenshee Eco Lodges, Glenprosen Estate, Hector and Sharon at Glenprosen Hostel, The Blackwood family in Glendoll, and the rangers at Mar Lodge.

I was delighted that Leandra Sutherland agreed to get her crayons out again, despite being in the middle of a house build and running a new business. A talented woman who creates the most wonderful illustrations – thank you.

Thank you, Yvonne, for supporting all my adventures, for being a fantastic friend and trail partner, and not least for being there when I need to call you from the trail.

Once again, I find myself indebted to my husband Dave for all his support, love, encouragement, and head groom duties. You tolerate so much, but please don't stop.

Claire Alldritt 2022.

Contents

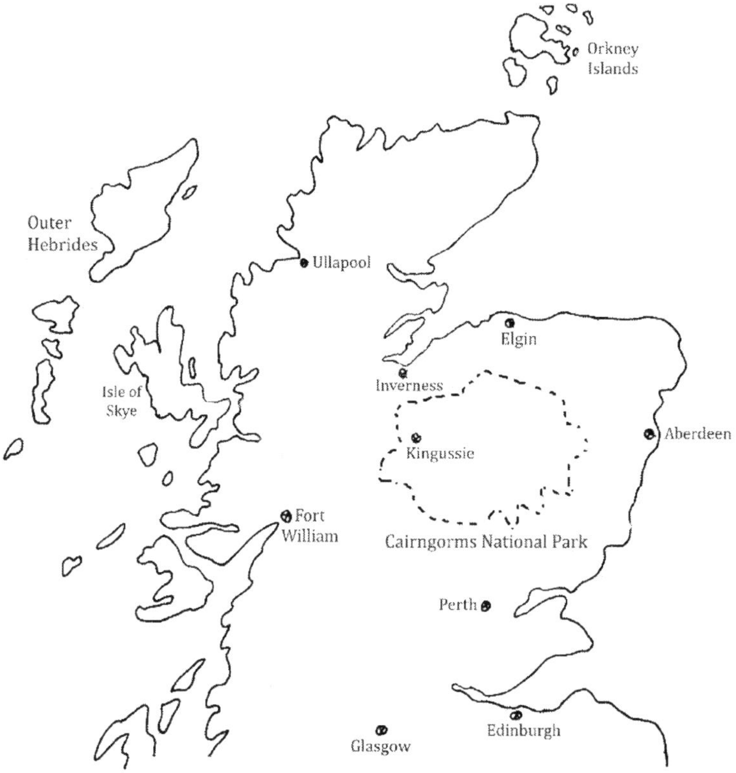

Location of the Cairngorms National Park

The Love of Dobbineering

Dobbineering – a made-up term - can be described simply as 'heading off into the hills with your horse.' It's travelling for as long and as far as possible, winding your way between the peaks and ticking off the occasional hilltop too. This gentle kind of mountaineering, backpacking with a horse to see where the trail may lead, also includes camping out under the stars and often requires two horses (one as packhorse) to carry all the equipment.

Dobbineering starts with the building excitement of design, logistical preparation, and the proposal of routes, with no set trails or guidebooks to assist - only the paths found on a map to tempt your travel. Then follows the recce to search for suitable trails, calculating your personal capability, your risk-tolerance, and finding your own way. Your own way, not just through the hills, but the unique approach of how you interact and travel with your particular horses and the specific equipment you choose to use.

I love the mountains and I love horses, so to combine the two, to form dobbineering, feels like a completely natural activity to me. The oneness with nature acquired by prolonged time in the hills appeals, but there's another bonus - the deeper connection achieved with horses by living, breathing, and moving together - creating such a unified team. Unspoken communication develops and you learn to understand what every twitch of ear, facial expression, flick of tail, shake of head or slightest movement of body means. I begin to communicate in a similar manner, granted without ears to waggle or a tail to flick, but I have been known to shake my hair to make a point or two!

I use my voice, facial expressions, and body language to direct my companions – nothing else is required when both human and equines tune into the same objectives and move together as one. They observe me for subtle cues, as I do them, so that it seems like they read my mind - and I theirs. I love becoming part of the herd as we journey together.

My curiosity is stirred by the historical significance of places passed through. Who lived here? What was their life like? What made them leave? I enjoy traversing through hills on routes which have been used by people and animals over hundreds of years, with wonder aplenty at the why and how. A strong sense of travelling back in time develops as I attempt to rediscover and explore horse-travel skills from the past. In the modern era, dobbineering is classed as unusual, a novelty, or a great adventure - but I'm just an average person with ordinary horses revisiting what once was the norm of everyday life.

This old style of travel is still a challenge however, and I love facing what others might consider impossible (for one wee gal with two big horses) and that the rewards when found are incredibly well-earned. It's hard work and the romantic notion of riding your horse off into the sunset is far from the reality. The truth is dirty, it's smelly, it's exhausting, and it's relentless - but this makes it feel so fulfilling, so deserved, and so special.

I find the rhythm of the horse's movement addictive, step after step and day after day, alongside the daily routine of pack up, move on, make a new camp, repeat. This combines with the rhythm of nature - the cycle of sunup, sundown, and the stars moving across dark skies at night.

My horses seem to thrive on the physical and mental stimulation of the daily challenge. Their willingness to please confirms that they enjoy their 'job' and the new sights and sounds around every corner as much as I do. Their muscle definition, their strength, their dexterity, and the shine of their coats after many days on the trail are magnificent. I breathe deep the smell of horse, mixed with leather and the scent from the land, the earthiness of fresh rain and heather or the sweet smell of pine and gorse.

The serenity of the slower pace allows absorption of landscape, flora, and fauna in all its glorious detail. My eyes soak up every change in colour with the shifting clouds, the shapes of the sun's shadows, the ripple of land caused by a passing breeze, the river's sparkle, and the sprinkling of rare mountain flowers - bright amongst the darkness of heather.

There is a contrasting sensation of feeling so small and so vulnerable in the vast mountains, as we move through the glens and over the peaks, against that cosy feeling when settling in for the night, held safe in the arms of a craggy outcrop or hollow of land. Always present is the comfort of my companions striding along beside me and the sound of their munching, contented sighs, and snores drifting through the flysheet of the tent in the middle of the night.

I love the step away and pause from 'real world' pressures - the living in the moment. There is no room to worry about anything other than the here and now. Above all else, I love the peace and restfulness that dobbineering brings to my mind and to my soul.

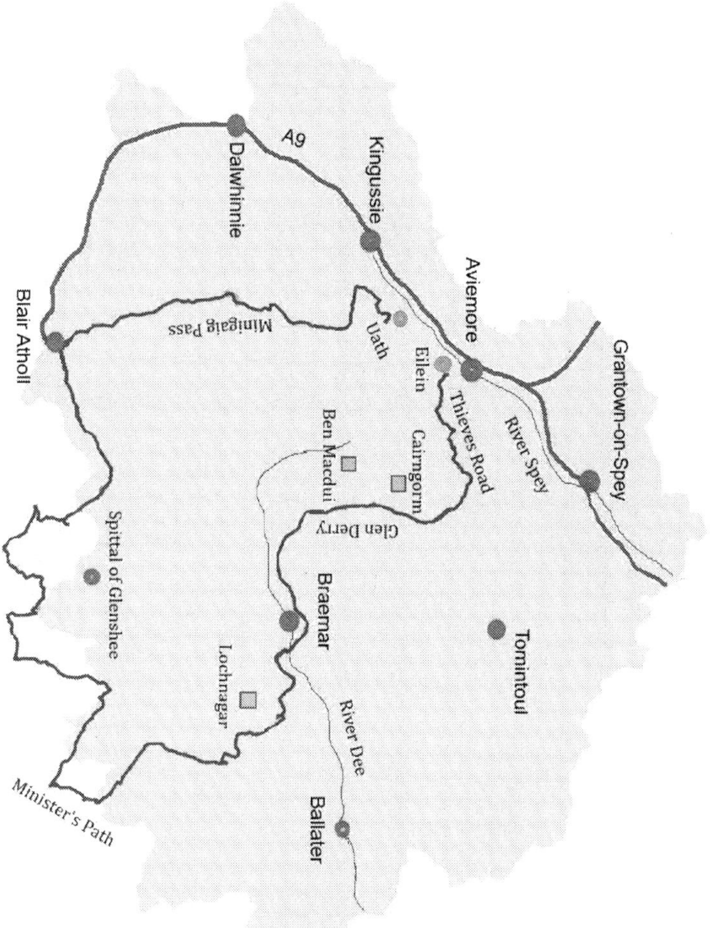

My Circular Route Through the Cairngorms

Starter's Orders

Day -1: The Night Before

It was a warm enough evening and in mid-June there was still a large amount of daylight remaining. The grass was speckled with colourful daisies and buttercups, all dancing happily in the slight breeze. It was a cloud-filled sky, but the clouds were white, empty of rain and progressing over the surrounding mountains with speed. The cloud's shadows cast below were creating an illusion of gullies and outcrops skipping across the slopes.

My tent was flapping gently, its beat mixing with the rhythmic rip and tear of grass as Yogi and Swift's teeth devoured the tasty shoots. The peace and quiet was a welcome tranquillity at the end of a tiring day, but I was fighting back a building cascade of overwhelming emotion.

Sitting on a patch of grass at the head of my favourite glen, I'd travelled here with my much-loved equine companions. It might have seemed like an innocent (and serene) moment to some, but to me it felt like a monumental achievement. It had been three whole years since we'd last managed to be in a similar situation. Thoughts of the struggle to get back to where I was sitting now were filling up my brain, my heart, and - I do confess - my eyes a little with tears.

This was my first proper solo dobbineering adventure since being diagnosed with Lyme disease (LD), and Yogi's first since he'd been diagnosed with Equine Cushing's disease (ECD). Yes, we'd been long-distance riding within those three years, but mostly 'riding designed easy' with a second rider, other companions, and organised support along the way. The routes chosen were flatter and closer to civilisation, and although I'd had some amazing and adventurous times with wonderful people, it wasn't what I classed as true dobbineering.

True dobbineering involves exploring remote places, up in the hills, reliant on only the kit you've decided to carry.

"Oi!" said Swift. "You mean the kit you've decided that *I* should carry."

"True my love, but you do carry it so very well," I replied, desperately hoping to off-set any early mutiny from my famously moody mare.

She smiled smugly to herself as she mooched a little closer to see if the grass was any tastier near where I'd pitched my tent.

"Any chance you could move your tent, by the way?" asked Yogi. "The grass does look greener under there!"

I rolled my eyes in response to this unreasonable request – the horses currently had a whole field to explore, yet here they were both choosing to hang out in the corner I'd claimed as my own.

The plan of adventure this time was a circular route, anti-clockwise around the Cairngorms, starting and finishing in my favourite glen - Glen Feshie. The route would take in historical drovers' routes, ancient byways, heritage paths, and many interesting features that I would, no doubt, discover as I went along. It would involve two weeks of travel, through glens and over hills, and - to match the remit of true dobbineering - was planned to be remote with wild camping for most of the way. I would meet a support crew for replenishment of stocks at roughly the half-way point, and collect a box of stores positioned in advance towards the end of the trip. Other than that, I would be alone with my two equine companions.

I have a habit of planning my trips the old-fashioned way - by spreading out a series of overlapping maps across the floor. The last major undertaking was planned in a galley kitchen, and I ended up riding all the way across Scotland from the east coast to the west in, roughly speaking, a straight line. Now living in a different house with a more rounded kitchen space (and undertaking a circular route), I couldn't help but contemplate whether my dobbineering adventures would continue to be influenced by the shape of the room which contained both the kettle, and the chocolate.

Whatever the shape of the route, this trip would be a test for both Yogi and I - to see if we were properly back on track. Yogi was doing well with a good response to his daily medication and no sign of lameness or discomfort for over two years. I was doing better but couldn't say I was fully back to my old self yet - not anywhere near. Supposedly, I'd been cured of Lyme disease eighteen months ago by a series of oral antibiotics, but in reality, setting off on this adventure, I'd only been out of hospital for six weeks following a return spell of migraines, fever, uncontrollable hypertension, and cardiac arrhythmias.

In his book *A Walk in the Woods,* Bill Bryson describes Lyme disease as "a disease for the person who wants to experience it all." He lists maladies such as "headaches, fatigue, chills, shortness of breath, dizziness, and shooting pains in the extremities, then marching on to cardiac irregularities..." He lists more symptoms, but I'll stop there, because *there* is where I was at, at this moment in time, the cardiac irregularities.

Not all medical professionals believe the concept of Lyme lying dormant and therefore the possibility of relapse. I, conversely, had a deep suspicion that Lyme had made another appearance and that treating my cardiac anomalies on their own wasn't going to fully address the source. I'd been discharged with medication that was designed to encourage my heart to behave and although it was helping, it wasn't alleviating all my symptoms.

This Cairngorm circular idea had been in the concept stage before hospital admission, but the prolonged spell 'inside' and partial recovery had curtailed the recce part of my regular planning routine. As I watched the horses graze, I reflected that the minimal pre-adventure planning *and* my heartbeat were both going to be highly irregular for this trip.

With ongoing symptoms and a lack of time for detailed preparation or full route recce, I'd almost called the whole thing off. However, with three years of 'taking it easy', I had this overwhelming need to test myself despite the present circumstances. This was hard to explain to the rational part of my mind, knowing that I was unwell with something that could potentially become serious in the remote hills, yet I couldn't bring myself to back down.

Perhaps Avril Lavigne sums it up best in her song "Anything but Ordinary." I'd had such a long period of watching everything I did, what I ate, what supplements I needed, how much energy I used, how much rest I took. I was tired of it all and needed to shake things up a bit - I was needing to 'walk outside of the lines' to 'go to the extreme in order to feel alive.' I craved to experience "Anything but Ordinary" for a while.

Normally my first day worries would focus on the health and well-being of my horses and of keeping them safe during the obstacles and days ahead. This time though, I had a new worry, one I wasn't accustomed to; a worry about myself and my own well-being. I was suddenly acutely aware of my own fragility, and this was a new concept to struggle with at the start of a two-week trek – one that was potentially full of physical challenges and hazards ahead.

Sitting in the field in the head of the glen, I tried to move my mind away from concerns of a cardiac nature and away from what might be crawling around in the grass (with the trouble another Lyme-carrying tick might bring). I instead thought back to the start of the trip when we'd arrived on the lochside of Uath Lochans the previous evening.

We'd arrived the night before the start date to ease ourselves (the horses and I) into life on the trail. The horses were corralled on a threadbare patch of grass, but as they were both on the plump side and relatively out of trail condition, a meagre night was considered beneficial (by me alone in this trio, I might add). I was having an opposite experience, by indulging in the luxury of glamping in the horse lorry and cooking myself up a huge portion of curry. Still trying to regain the weight I'd lost on the undeniably effective (but unquestionably non-tasty) hospital food diet, I didn't hold back on portion size.

Sitting on a picnic bench with a full belly and a beer in hand, I was attempting to coerce my huge pile of kit to behave itself, become more orderly and somehow compress itself to a size that would fit into the saddle bags. Most items were complying apart from the mound of human food heaped on the far-right corner of the table. That particular pile might have to reduce in a most disagreeable way as far as my shrunken stomach was concerned - by leaving some behind.

I was just applying the finishing touches to the packing process when a 4x4 pickup bounced across the car park, and its driver jumped out of the cab with a cheery "Whoo Hoo! How's it going?" I was astonished to see my friend Yvonne standing before me, miles from where I expected her to be, which was at home - an hour's drive away.

"Thought I'd surprise you with some company on your first night, to settle your nerves," exclaimed Yvonne.

"It's a fantastic surprise and so good to see you!" I didn't verbalise my full appreciation as I knew it was entirely unnecessary; my huge hug said it all.

Yvonne had been a frequent dobbineering trail-partner over the years and completely understood early-trip anxieties and how they take a day or two to shake off. Any distraction during this necessary and unavoidable process is always most welcome, particularly when undertaking a solo challenge.

We threw the now fully prepared bags into the lorry, set up the second bed, and as Yvonne got comfortable for the proposed pyjama party that would inevitably delay my intended bedtime, I spread out some hay within the horse's corral. The wind had dropped, the midges were out, and Swift and Yogi were demonstrating their usual coping strategy of pacing up and down in an effort to outrun the little blighters. Much like Yvonne arriving for me, the hay arriving for them would help to distract them from their (midge) anxieties.

"Hmmm ... yum ... thanks," said Yogi, immediately stuffing his face and mostly forgetting about the buzz around his head.

Swift continued to pace and looked at me with suspicion. "Is this us back on tour then?" she asked. "I saw you packing all those bags and they looked heavy. Can I have some clarification as to who is packhorse and who is ridden on this particular excursion? How far is it this time? By the way, you'd better organise more breeze or I am going home, these midges are torture!"

I spent a few moments answering her questions, offering reassurance, and swatting the handful of cleggs (horseflies) that had come to join the party. Poor Swift really wasn't happy. Her questioning mind was working on overdrive, and insects happen to find her particularly tasty no matter what repellent I try to apply to a horse who doesn't want to let me. The hay distraction would only be effective for half of Team Swogi but Swift had at least started to eat a little.

I should explain early on that Swift and Yogi prefer the collective term 'Team Swogi'. It's a celebrity name combination, a supercouple if you like, that they devised after an interview by BBC Radio Scotland. Modelled on the Brad Pitt and Angelina Jolie combination of *Brangelina*, they felt a joint name was an easier way of dealing with the popularity and attention their fame would attract. I didn't think this team terminology would catch on if I'm honest, but seemingly, over the years, it appears to have stuck fast.

I retreated from the midge and cleg fest to join Yvonne back in the lorry. We settled in amongst the pile of pillows and the depth of duvet that Yvonne had firmly established on the spare bed and whiled away a few hours, a few drams, and a few worries - reliving funny yarns from our experiences on long-distance horse trails so far.

It wasn't long before the yarns slowed and the yawns commenced, and I clambered up to my Luton bed in a relaxed state for a less fretful sleep than I would have had if it wasn't for the thoughtfulness of a good friend.

Melting Moments

Day 1: Glen Feshie (Distance 19km, Ascent 437m)

I awoke early, full of trepidation and excitement, but I wasn't in any hurry. Today could be as long or as short as I cared to make it. We were starting from my favourite place in Scotland and possibly in the whole of the world - Uath Lochans. Previously, I'd lived a short drive away from here and I knew the woods and the trails like the back of my hand. It was a regular choice for cycling, running, dog walking, and horse-riding. Today we could take a direct route to our evening's destination or choose to play a little with favourite trails and mini diversions. Either way, I wouldn't need to look at the map.

Yvonne was still buried deep under her pile of duvets and blankets, and I admired her philosophy of 'only slum it when you have to.' I packed up my thin sleeping bag as silently as I could and compressed it down to fit neatly in the last remaining space in the saddle bags, then left the lorry as quiet as a mouse to go for a little homage.

Not far around the corner was a peaty platform next to the dark waters of the loch. I'd spent many amusing moments here watching my dog Danny enjoy a swim. This little spot in our household is known as Dan's swim hole. Dan had passed away some eighteen months ago (at the grand ole age of thirteen-and-a-half), and I always take a little reflective moment here if I find myself on the lochside.

My thoughts moved on from soft fur, floppy ears, and shaken sprays of water (amongst squeals and smiles) to the weeks ahead. On one hand I wished that Yvonne had arrived last night to announce that she was going to join me for the whole trek. On the other hand I needed to go alone. This was a reasonably challenging route I'd set and I'm not sure Yvonne would enjoy it as much as I would. Putting that aside, I was in any case feeling a need to push my limits and test my resolve, and that's often something best done solo.

This wasn't about proving anything to anyone else, but it was very much about proving something to myself. I've always had this inner need to be challenged on a regular basis. Not just with outdoor sports and adventure, but my job, my volunteering, my 'something new.' The challenge over the last three years had been of a different nature, and I desired to get back to a more typical type. I'm not sure where the normal comes in though, of taking two horses over hills and through glens for two weeks on your own, but then I've never been particularly good at mainstream.

Although this route would be demanding at times, I hadn't ignored my current state of health entirely. It was planned with short days; fewer remote overnights (most of the time) and a large amount of external pressure had been removed. Other than my husband and a handful of friends, I hadn't told anyone else what I was doing - so there was no burden to complete it. At least that's what I tried to tell the 'I must always finish what I started' ethos lodged firmly in my brain.

Usually on a trip like this, sponsorship would have been sought for donations to a charity of choice, but for that to be an effective fundraiser it generally involves a lot of attention. The pressure then to complete becomes immense. For once I'd listened to my husband's advice not to undertake this adventure for anything or anyone other than myself.

Waking up this morning with heavy fatigue – a regular, unpredictable, and unwelcome LD guest – I knew he had been correct (but women have a pact to never tell their husbands this, right?). So, his words in my head were a comfort as I dragged my weary bones away from the lochside to head back to the lorry – "You only need to do as much as you want to, you can stop at anytime and I'll come and collect you."

Back at the lorry Yvonne was up and about. I gave more hay to Team Swogi (as hungry, opinionated horses are not pleasurable companions) and cooked up a leisurely breakfast for us humans. Despite this unhurried approach, it didn't seem to take any time at all to be packed up and ready to go and I was soon waving goodbye to my good friend who offered to deconstruct the corral as I set off on my way.

The keys for the lorry would be hidden and a local friend (Mike) would come and collect it later. It would probably be safe enough sitting in the woods for two weeks until I returned, but I was concerned that someone might think there was a missing horse and rider somewhere and then contact the police. Mike was primed to return the lorry to where he'd found it on the day of my planned completion. Or, as I reminded myself, whenever I called him if I decided I needed to stop early.

As I settled into Yogi's stride, I looked at my watch and was surprised to see it was nearing lunchtime. The morning had flown by, and this was certainly an unusually late departure for life on the trail.

"I'm packhorse again then," grumbled Swift, behind me.

"I'm afraid so, my love, as I need an easy time this trip."

"Did you see how much curry she ate last night?" asked Yogi, looking around at Swift behind him. "Believe me, *you* have the easier job!"

Swift by far was better at being towed, as Yogi tends to weave behind her. He thinks that the packhorse role doesn't have a job description and totally switches off from things happening around him. He spends his time mooching from side to side of the trail for snacks. He also stops abruptly when needing to poo or pee, causing a dropped rope and three or four circles whilst I try to convince Swift that we really should go back for him.

Despite her grumblings (which she does about most things in life), Swift actually seems to love the role of bag-carrier. She doesn't have to make up-front safety decisions about the route ahead and can spend her time snacking along behind Yogi and me. No weaving from her thankfully, as my gal has an uncanny knack of munching on the move (even in trot) without putting any strain on the tow rope. Often, she will follow behind without a rope attached anyway, whereas Yogi may not always choose to come with us if we tried that with him. Not if he'd found a particularly tasty patch of grass.

Yogi is a chestnut (ginger) Highland Pony x Thoroughbred. He's of average height at 15.1hh, but of an unusual build. The Highland pony part of his heritage settled around his midriff, giving his body a strong and stocky appearance, whereas his legs and head embraced the slender, more delicate Thoroughbred side. When trim and fit, he takes on the look of the Arab breed of horse and many people ask if that's what he is.

When not in work, he soon rounds into a contented plumpness and those who don't realise he has a native origin have been heard to suggest that a crash diet might be in order. His love of picnics and snacking, alongside his friendly nature and furry embrace, has earned him his extended nickname of 'Yogi-the-Bear' or just 'The Bear'.

He never stays plump long however, as he has a keen and forward mental attitude to life and throws himself into a return to work with enthusiasm (particularly when faced with a hill). His Thoroughbred turbo-boost setting for periods of upness is legendary - proving that his ancestral mix isn't limited to appearance alone. His mind has a lively, enthusiastic, and excitable Thoroughbred core which is encased in native Highland food obsession.

I couldn't have collected two more different horses into my herd, as Swift in comparison is all lean and lovely from ears to toes and is as laid-back as they come (most of the time). She is an Appaloosa x American Quarter Horse, with a small slither of Knabstrupper way-back-when. The influence of this latter drop of blood in her family tree is surprisingly sizeable, or at least, I should say, incredibly tall.

Swift stands at 16.2hh and whilst there is nothing unusual in her build or proportions, she makes up for this in her clothing. Her coat consists of a base of reddish-brown accessorised by a silver collar of mane, a silver trim of tail, and an array of pretty, white broaches, pinned at random, but mostly over her bottom. Her individual style has earned her the affectionate term she is often referred to of 'Spotty Bum.'

Fashion-sense isn't the only thing that Swift has unusual ideas or strong opinions about, as she generally applies the bizarre and tenacious to all aspects of life. Swift is most particular about the way in which things should be done – especially if those things are intending to occur anywhere near her personal space. She is a joy and so incredibly light to ride (absolutely push button), but permission must be granted to be allowed to get to that stage of the relationship, and this will only happen after rigorous quality assurance examinations. I'd spent years taking exams in Swift etiquette, body language, emotional mastery, psychology, tactical negotiations, and mind reading skills. Luckily, I'd now passed them all - although several required refresher courses from time to time.

They say that animals are like their owners, which is slightly disconcerting with two such differing characters as my chosen companions. The thought of having a split personality is an interesting one and something I may consider exploring in a future period of self-insight and enlightenment.

Reaching the end of one of the three smaller lochs, I asked Yogi to take a right turn. This trail would take us away from a direct route to camp at the end of the day, but would take us up onto a ridgeline from which there are spectacular views. I love the views from the top, and the horses enjoy playing with the rolling trail.

There are numerous undulations on the way to the final summit. It's a game of 'how slow can I keep them' on the downhills, before allowing them to explode into action at the end of the hollows for an 'as fast as you can to the top.' It's difficult to get them to stand still after this excitement – to take in the view across the waters of the lochans, and beyond to the magnificence of the mountains that line the way to Glen Feshie. However, they do enjoy having a quick munch of the silver birch trees beside the trail, which keeps them still for a short period of time.

The dark waters of the Uath Lochans are coloured by the peaty soils that surround them. They probably aren't very deep, but it's impossible to tell through the mirk. The lochans are remnants of the last (Devensian) glacial period in the UK, which began approximately 33,000 years ago. At its peak, about 10,000 years later, the ice sheet would have covered all of Scotland and as far south as the Midlands in England.

During the final melt about 11,500 years ago, large blocks of ice were dropped and abandoned at the glacier's face, and as sediment-filled waters flowed from the glacial retreat, the blocks became surrounded by deposits of sand and gravel. Eventually the isolated ice-cubes would succumb to the heat, melting away to leave depressions that later filled with water - thus forming predominantly circular lochs called kettle holes.

The more well-known Loch Morlich is formed in a similar way, but although its beauty is a tourist's honey pot, it's the Uath Lochans (or the secret lochans, as they are also known) that are the bee's knees. Their secret not only lies in their hidden location, but in their indentation on the land. Viewed up high on the Farleitter Crag (a huge roche moutonnée – another glacial feature), the lochans look like a gigantic bear's paw print stamped firmly within the trees. Also, up on the Farleitter Crag stands a lonely, polished erratic - smoothed and rounded by the glacier before being spat out like a pea from a pea shooter, to perch dangerously close to the sharp face of the north-eastern edge.

It's here that I like to pause to admire the second view that the height of the ridge offers - across Loch Inch and right down the Spey Valley. Thankfully, there were silver birch trees growing there too.

"I can't wait to get there," said Yogi. "Those leaves are very tasty."

"Well take your time, we are all unfit and you sound like a steam train."

I knew this reply would fall on deaf ears when Yogi was faced with an uphill, but it was always worth a try.

Team Swogi were still giving it their all on the ups of the undulations, but I could see that Swift's heart wasn't quite as committed as Yogi's. It wasn't long before she brought the team to a standstill with a request for a break.

"Just ... gasp ... need to ... heave ... catch my ... wheeze ... breath a minute..." She panted this statement out, glaring at Yogi and looking to see if she could disconnect his turbo-boost somehow.

The Pea from the Pea Shooter

Yogi was standing with his sides heaving too, and the fact that he wasn't nibbling the heather at his feet was a clear indication of his general lack of fitness. An unfortunate consequence of me having been out of action for a while, but it wouldn't take either of them long to get back on track.

The benefit of dobbineering is that it's mostly carried out at a walk, so, as long as you don't overdo things distance-wise in the first few days, you can often just pull a horse out of a field and get on with it, without weeks of fitness training first (although that of course is always preferred and advised).

Apart from the birds-eye view of the lochans, which I was now admiring in a rhythmic fashion paced with Yogi's panting, the other advantage of adding this circuit was that it would give me the chance to remember what it was that I'd forgotten to pack. The exit from this trail wasn't that far from where we'd started, so it wouldn't be much of detour to nip back to the lorry (if necessary) before we set off up the glen for real.

As we continued up to the summit and admired the Spey Valley view, squeezed between the huge erratic and the tasty silver birch, I really couldn't think of anything I'd left behind. I did, however, need to adjust the weights in Swift's bags as they were tilting to the right.

It's important and necessary to get the bags of the packhorse balanced to perfection and I'll often use a set of sensitive kitchen scales to ensure this, but over the years I've become accustomed to what piece of kit matches another for weight. The scales, therefore, hadn't been placed in the lorry for the final packing session yesterday, but as I was carrying more human food than usual, I suspected that this was causing the issue.

I transferred a packet of rice and a sausage and bean casserole to a left-hand bag. I figured that this combination had the correct proportion of carbs, protein, fat, and fibre to balance things out a little. I would watch carefully as we started to head up the glen to see if the adjustment had resolved things.

Dropping down off the ridge, we turned right onto a tiny single-track trail that wove through young trees. Each time I come here these trees have grown a little. Some now block the view to the left to the largest loch that forms the palm of the bear's paw, some also bend their branches over the trail. The head height was perfectly passable for a human on two feet, but three feet higher on the back of a horse, my head was having to duck and dive to avoid an incidence of concussion.

I was managing the branch dodging just fine, but not the entanglement of spider's webs that nobody else had cleared this high up. The skill of the silken weave across this sizeable expanse for a creature often less than five centimetres in span is impressive, but it's also a sticky, sensation-rich experience across your face that isn't overly cherished.

As I wiped the final remains of the layers of thin veils from my face, Yogi broke into a trot to celebrate the tiny section of upness at the end of the trail. We would be back on a wide forestry track for a good while now.

Sweeping around the western edge of the Inshriach Forest, Team Swogi were striding out well. I suspected that Yogi assumed we were out for our usual circular day-ride and that conserving energy for tomorrow wasn't considered necessary. I knew Swift had me sussed, but she seemed content to match Yogi's pace.

The trail through the woodland runs in a south westerly direction, parallel to the Badenoch Way - an eighteen-kilometre path from Dalraddy to Ruthven. This short trail had stood alone for many a year with no greater purpose than to be an interesting and pretty route, but in recent years the Speyside Way had swept it up in its westerly extension.

The Speyside Way, now one-hundred-and-forty kilometres long (or thereabouts), runs from Buckie on the Moray Coast to Newtonmore and is another long-distance route that Team Swogi and I had once enjoyed completing. This was one of my 'riding made easy' routes over the last three years, undertaken with good friend Ellen and supported by another friend Fiona and my husband Dave.

No packhorse used on this excursion, Ellen had sat and past all the required Swift examinations with flying colours and bonded with her well. This had allowed me to settle into a comfortable ride carried by Yogi, or as comfortable as I could get with my achy-joints and foggy-brain, as I continued my battle with Lyme.

We completed around two-hundred kilometres of riding/walking, diverting from the official route to places we knew (and loved) from time to time. We also stopped at every ice-cream shop and pub along the way - purely for medicinal reasons, obviously. Accommodation took the form of friend's houses, bunkhouses, or the back of my converted campervan which magically appeared at the end of each day, thanks to our incredible support crew.

Ellen and I finished our route at the inaugural meet of the Golden Hoof event. An event set up in memory of Cameron Ormiston - a pony trekking pioneer and renowned Highland Pony breeder. The event is for people (and horses) who enjoy long-distance riding or carriage driving to arrive at the same time, in the same place, to socialise together. A trophy is awarded to the team voted to have had the most fun getting there.

Possibly due to the large number of ice-creams and whiskies sampled in our 'getting there', Ellen and I were delighted and honoured to receive the trophy awarded for the very first time.

With Ellen on my mind today, I made a hasty left-hand turn. Her love of thin trails through trees suddenly influenced my decision to try a trail I'd never been down before. I knew where it started and was pretty sure I knew where it came out, but I didn't know what lay in between. It felt good to explore and to have some curiosity quenched.

I pulled out a coffee flask that Ellen had once gifted, to toast my good friend. The toasting continued as I contemplated that it wasn't only Yogi and Swift who had carried me through the last few years. Good friends, family, and colleagues supporting me in various capacities (as I regained some health) deserved a moment of appreciation too.

The toasting soon turned to swatting, as here, deep in the trees, there was no sign of a breeze and it wasn't long before about a thousand flies were circling around each of our heads in a black buzz of annoyance. We were all glad to finally emerge into an open section with a funnelled wind moving down a break in the trees. All of us that was, except Yogi, who had spied a section of bog ahead (his nemesis).

I was pleased that the clever design of a track system at home had almost cured Yogi of his bog phobia, and I only experienced one temporary refusal before I was able to coax him through the small soft section, and up onto the board walk that facilitated a less sinking exit. Swift as usual followed on, not batting an eyelid at the bog nor the wooden planks, but she did roll her eyes and release a big sigh at Yogi's initial dramatics.

Previously this would have been a sizeable obstacle for a Yogi-brain to contend with, but the track system created back home had fulfilled a tertiary objective that I'd never had in mind. Made with an extra internal fence, the system forced Team Swogi to move around the outside of the land we had, rather than living on the grassy fields in the middle. These two horses had to work and walk for their keep! The increased movement meant that they maintained a greater background fitness, but this was the secondary objective.

The primarily purpose was to facilitate management of Yogi's ECD (a pituitary problem that affects how horses process sugar). For effective control of this condition, unfortunately and much to Yogi's displeasure, he would be low sugar for life. With hay available 24/7 in substitute for sugar-filled grass, the track-system kept Yogi's Highland belly as trim as possible. The only grass available was small nibbles at the side of the track or in limited sections of the middle that I could allow them access to when deemed appropriate.

Only a few metres wide, the track passed through woodland, mossy ground, hardcore sections, and three areas of bog. Yogi and Swift had to pass through these too if they wanted to obtain shelter, get to water, or find hay hidden in various places. Regular passing through of challenging terrain had created two horses that were surer footed, more confident, and more decisive over uneven ground than I'd ever had before - a bonus feature in addition to the track system's original intentions.

The thin trail popped out where I had expected and after another half kilometre of tree shelter and fly accompaniment, we finally emerged at Baileguish. We weren't in true Glen Feshie yet, this was the floodplain of a pre-valley (Coire Fhearnasdail). To reach the sides of the River Feshie, we had another two kilometres or so of trees to go through.

Here though, in the open, there was a strong wind rippling the long grass and there were three fords of a burn to cross – a forked tributary which eventually joins the River Feshie four kilometres further north-east. Team Swogi were glad to be away from the flies and I let them have 'munchies' of the long grass for a while.

The grey stone of ruined buildings stood out against the bright green of the lumpy grass. The wide gravel track winding through the glen could be seen fading into the heather on the other side of the flat expanse. At the end of the heather, it vanished into a boundary of dark trees which marked the start of the western edge of the Cairngorm Mountains.

Baileguish is an abandoned township meaning 'township of the pine trees.' The first part of Fhearnasdail means alder, but with neither of these trees evident now, I can only assume they refer to the materials from which the township and the next settlement along (Corarnstilmore) were constructed from in the 1600's as the land was cleared for crofting life.

These two settlements were the most persistent in the Glen Feshie area, providing crofting, cattle grazing then sheep grazing through the agricultural progression of the highlands - enough to support several families at least. According to the 1881 census, it had still been inhabited by a small population of seven adults and two children.

There was a new network of paths since I'd last been here, and with clear ways to ford each of the tributary arms, we made Swift progress across the valley. By which I mean, at each ford we had to persuade Swift not to drink the stream dry nor to sploosh-splash the remaining water out all over the banks. She likes to play with the water with nose and feet, splashing the water around her. Despite her maturing age on paper, this is a girl who clings to a childlike relationship with water.

We were soon drying out and through the trees on the eastern side of the valley to the tarmac (private estate) road that leads to the head of Glen Feshie. I was incredibly grateful that the gate to the woodland had been left open, as its always a tricky one to manage from the back of a horse. My thigh bones were aching (a common annoying Lyme symptom), and I was still feeling fatigued, so I was glad not to have to dismount to deal with the gate.

We didn't have far to go now. It was only another three-and-a-half kilometres to where we could ford the main river to camp on the other side, and this distance would be easy riding on tarmac. I'd have preferred to use the aptly named 'Pony Bridge' to cross the River Feshie sooner to stay on off-road trails, but unfortunately the trail on the far side had been badly eroded by spates of the Allt Garbhlach Burn. It was still passable by horse(s), but only just and was thin, steep, loose, and tricky - not what I wanted on day one of my journey. So, even though I usually avoid tarmac as much as possible, I was happy to take the straightforward option today.

With Yogi striding out on easy ground in a place he knew well, we were soon at Carnoachuin. This was another site of old shielings dating back to the 1600's, but replaced now by the houses and barns of the working estate. Here all three of us bumped into Thomas, the factor of the estate – I think there was more surprise on his part than ours as he wasn't used to meeting me on horseback. I didn't know him well, but we recognised each other from frequenting the same local bar when I used to live in this area and, as we chatted, I asked him if the bothy was finished yet and whether it was worth us fording the river.

The Glen Feshie estate is currently owned and maintained by a landlord with an objective to allow the land to regain a more natural ecological state. The project started in 2001 to restore peatlands, wetlands, and native woodlands and has been continued by successive owners. The deer population is held at a much lower level than other sporting estates to encourage the Caledonian Pine woods to become re-established along with other native plants. There has been a massive amount of investment to infrastructure and the latest project, I knew, was a complete renovation of the Ruigh Aiteachain bothy.

A bothy is a basic hill hut, used in the past as a temporary shelter when grazing cattle or sheep in the hills or by estate workers/shooting parties. These days they are often frequented by hill goers looking for emergency refuge from wind, rain, or midge. Most are windproof, weather tight, and midge free but few have any facilities to speak of other than four walls and a roof.

This one, however, was posh by bothy standards with a wood-burning stove, a composting loo, and a primitive filter system for a trickle of fresh stream water. It's one of my most favourite bothies to stay in, so I was disappointed with the news that this bothy was still currently closed and restoration not yet complete (although I fully appreciated the investment to ensure its use for many years to come).

"The grass is tasty too!" said Yogi, looking longingly over the river.

"I like the trees to scratch on," stated Swift. "My Spotty Bum will enjoy a good scratch after those itchy midgy bites from last night."

"Might we be able to stay in the field on this side of the river?" I asked Thomas, ignoring my companions.

There didn't seem much point in crossing the river just to camp, eat grass, and scratch a spotty bum, when all these things could be performed on this side too. Besides, our route tomorrow would continue up the glen on this side of the river, so we'd have to tackle the ford again in the morning to get back over here. With permission granted and gratefully received, I'd steered Team Swogi into the grass-filled field. I wouldn't have to build a corral tonight, which was an advantage for fatigued and achy me.

It was like I'd never been away from the camping lark and in no time at all, I'd set up my tent. To protect the saddles and equipment I also constructed a tarp shelter against the stone wall. It was only four o'clock as the horses had made good speed today, and the whole evening stretched ahead of me. Sitting on the grass amongst the daisies, buttercups, and possible ticks, I knew that despite my fatigue, I needed to go and do something to distract - rather than sit mulling over emotions and apprehensions that always feel most strong in the first few days of a trek.

I wandered around the field and found a gate at the back with a path leading up the hill, that wasn't on the map. With a cat-like curiosity, I huffed and puffed my way up the steep slope to see where it led – the horses weren't the only ones who needed to exercise their lungs a little. The answer to my interest wasn't particularly far, the path stopped abruptly at what appeared to be some sort of weather station.

I'm no expert on these things but there were a couple of square grey boxes, a coil, lots of wires, and a pair of 'Micky Mouse' ears at the top of the pole. Least that's what they reminded me of – two circular cups, designed to catch the wind.

Gazing back down to the field, the horses looked like tiny mice and my tent and tarp were almost invisible, camouflaged against the grass and wall. Across the valley, the sandy path network stood out, but I couldn't see the bothy it led to through the scattering of trees in the river valley. The sprinkling of trees continued up the lower slopes of the mountains – the steep sides rising abruptly and magnificently to their bare rocky tops. That side of the river was alive with the bright yellow flowers of gorse, still hanging in for summer, although no doubt having lost the full strength of their sweet coconut smell.

I strolled back down to make myself some dinner and did so with the companionable sounds of laughter and hilarity wafting over from a barn next to the field. In a moment of social-seeking (quite unlike my usual self), I went and knocked on the door. I guess the walk to the weather station hadn't been distraction enough.

There was a moment of sudden silence behind the green door. Someone laughed out loud, followed by the fervent barking of a dog and a scuffle in the door's direction. I was greeted at first by a wriggly Border Terrier, then shortly after by Davie and Ivan - two friendly but slightly tipsy gamekeepers of the estate.

Their welcome was warm; I was bade inside, offered a very large dram, and a given a guided tour of the kill they were celebrating. Any explanation on my part, as to why I'd chosen to knock on the door, didn't seem important (which was just as well as I was still unsure myself).

The kill was a Royal stag – a male red deer with twelve points to its antlers and a status worthy of salute. Now hunting isn't my thing (unless armed with a camera), but I could recognise the knowledge, marksmanship, navigation skills, observation, and patience required for such a craft, so I put my personal views aside. There was also respect and admiration evident for the mighty beast and at the end of the day, in the absence of natural predators to curb deer populations, there is a requirement to manage the estate's ecology. This was their job, and it was a job well done today.

The initial large dram was followed by several others; there seemed an endless supply and I was soon providing my own fair share of laughter within the happy crowd. My intended route for tomorrow was brought to the table, alongside a couple of maps and another bottle of liquid gold. Davie suggested a different trail – strongly, with animation, and many hand gestures. He promised a drier underfoot route than planned and I knew Yogi would approve.

In all honestly, it didn't matter to me which path I tried, as by now I'd had a fill of whisky and would have agreed to any trail. Both led to the same objective, and I'd not had time to recce either one of them. Tomorrow would be a try it and see kind of day.

I was thankful for the Keepers' warm welcome, advice, and entertaining company, but felt I had to call it a day and stagger back to my tent before I could no longer do so! This was one way to distract from worries – just kill off the brain cells causing them.

The Pony Express

Day 2: Glen Feshie to Bruar Lodge (Distance 21km, Ascent 828m)

I hadn't expected to sleep all that well, it being my first night in a tent for a very long time, but the whisky blanket had been cosy and I'd slept like a baby. Surprisingly, despite the large measures of last night, I felt full of energy this morning; although I did require some paracetamol to settle my slightly sore head. It was still too early to set off (judging by the horizontal positions of Team Swogi), so I decided on a pre-breakfast excursion. I felt that no trip to Glen Feshie could be complete without a visit to the bothy on the other side. Besides all else, I was curious to see how the renovation was shaping up.

I left Yogi and Swift still in slumbers, curled up not far from my tent, and explored upstream to find the shallowest crossing point as the footbridge no longer existed. It had been washed away in floods many moons ago, and although vehicles and horses could ford the river it would have been knee-deep water for me. I rock hopped across the gravel section, underneath where the bridge used to stand, and followed the path to the bothy.

The bothy's name, Ruigh Aiteachain, means "stretch or shieling of the junipers." In the past, during the spring/early summer months of the year, it would have been the site of a yearly migration as cattle were moved up here for grazing. Their humans (usually the womenfolk) stayed in roughly constructed shelters, whilst the homesteads further down the valley were repaired and crops harvested before a return to winter. The early use of this area for cattle grazing is confirmed by names of nearby features, such as Druim nam Bo and Lochan nam Bo - meaning ridge and loch of cattle.

Later, around 1830, this small clearing in the trees was adopted and cherished by Duchess Bedford (the youngest daughter of the 4th Duke of Gordon) who established a series of huts here. Roughly made from turf they may have been, but she was known to describe them in letters as her "little paradise" and invited the distinguished of society to spend time there. Hunting parties as well as fine dining and balls were staged, and guests accommodated in the basic huts or tents.

One of the regular visitors, English artist Sir Edwin Landseer, is rumoured to have drawn his initial sketches here for his famous *Monarch of the Glen* painting that appears on the bottles of Glenfiddich whisky. That's not the only sketchy speculation though, as portrayal of an undercover relationship with the Duchess exists too.

One thing that was written in stone, however, was his decoration with frescoes of deer on a chimneystack - described in *Queen Victoria's Highland Journals* from 1861: "The huts, surrounded by magnificent fir-trees, and by quantities of juniper-bushes, looked lovelier than ever; and we gazed with sorrow at their utter ruin... We got off and went into one of the huts to look at a fresco of stags of Landseer's, over a chimney-piece."

Landseer must have been quite the talent as he was a favourite artist of Queen Victoria's, too. She tried to protect the frescos by building a wooden hut around the chimney stack, but the hut was later destroyed by a falling tree. Like the 'Bedford Huts' themselves, the chimney's bare stone is all that remains.

I'm not sure whether it was these historical connections that convinced the current Laird to invest in the present hut in this wonderful location, but the restoration certainly looked to be thorough. I couldn't wait for the stone bothy to be open again as I totally agreed with both Duchess and Queen about the special feel of this wee place - although my taste in art (and artists) differs.

The Duchess I'm sure would be thrilled to know that many still travel here to enjoy her "little paradise." Some are even known to throw elaborate parties - with the estate's help and permission, I might add. I'm sure she was spinning in her grave (in time with the tunes) when a friend of mine held a significant birthday here. The Ceilidh was wild, relentless, and 'stripping of the willow' continued until sunrise as did much joy, merriment, and admiration of this beautiful place.

Back across the river, Team Swogi were back on their feet, and it was time to get on our way. I made breakfast, dismantled the tarp, collapsed the tent, brushed the backs of the horses, picked out their feet, applied their hoof boots, and packed everything into the saddle bags. I'd saved time this morning by not having a corral to collapse and pack away. After popping their saddles on and lifting the bags up onto an objectionable Swift (she objects to most things happening within her personal space), we were ready to go in just an hour.

As we set off past the estate houses, I was immediately transported back in time with only one short request.

"Pass on my regards to Dominic when you see him later," shouted keeper Davie as he waved me on my way.

Dominic was the keeper of Glen Bruar, and since I was planning to camp near Glen Bruar Lodge tonight, I would see him when I reached the next main valley. This innocent passing on of well-wishes felt strange, as though I was the Pony Express of the 1800's with an important telegram to deliver. The two keepers hadn't met for quite some time as the distance by road was much further than the direct line over the hills. It was an instant reminder of how communication channels used to be, not all that long ago.

I half expected a servant boy to come running down with a bundle of letters for an express delivery as I passed the entrance to the Victorian Glen Feshie Lodge.

"I'm not carrying any more stuff," said Swift, glaring up the track to the lodge with a mare-stare that would surely tremble the limbs of any such boy.

"I don't mind being express," said Yogi. "But back then, didn't horses get nose-bags full of oats to maintain energy levels?" he added, somewhat hopefully.

I steered Team Swogi onto the wider and lower path, nearer the river, and in a kilometre or so we passed a silted-up pond. This is believed to have once been a 'floating dam', whereby water would be retained then suddenly released to aid the floating of timber down the River Feshie and onwards to Garmouth via the River Spey, a distance of forty-five kilometres.

The main period of deforestation and timber sales here happened between 1787-1830, as a ship building business was established on the Moray Coast during the Napoleonic wars. I'd kayaked this river in periods of spate, and although it is a wonderfully scenic run, it was an experience I'd describe as a 'bum scrape' with numerous rocky rapids to negotiate. I can't imagine logs being floated down it at all but maybe there was a deeper and cleaner channel back then.

Soon we'd reached the ruin of Ruigh-fionntaig, the site of a shooting lodge from c1825 overlaying old shielings from the 1600's. A single tree, standing tall in a triangle of paths, marks the spot of those lives-gone-by with the layers of history entwined in its roots. This tree and its triangle of paths also marked the point between three valleys, like a toll house at a junction, where you might pay your dues and stamp your ticket before being allowed to proceed in your proposed direction of travel.

To the east, Glen Feshie stretches through to the Geldie Burn and onwards to the watershed of the River Dee – an old drovers' route through to Braemar. Straight ahead was a steep path up to Meall Tionail Lorgaidh (meaning gathering hill). What kind of gathering I'm not sure, but another nearby hill (An Sgarsoch), is thought to have been used as an old tryst or cattle market. The gatherings held on this exposed hilltop on the Highland/Perthshire boundary were in an effort to avoid a surprise attack by reivers (cattle rustlers).

Our chosen path would take us to the west through Slochd Mor, and onwards to join the Minigaig pass, but I felt the need to pause for a while. I'd now be heading into uncharted territory – a way through the hills I'd never tried before and one I'd not had time to recce. I was now totally reliant on the word of a friend, the recommendation of a tipsy gamekeeper, and my own hungover map-reading skills. Savouring the familiar form of the bowl of Glen Feshie, I felt both dwarfed and protected by the sheer mountainsides and so I lingered a little longer.

Team Swogi were quite happy with the delay. As I admired the beautiful array of tree greens on the steep sides of the glen, highlighted by the morning sun, they did the same with the fresh stalks of grass immediately in front of their noses. Their appreciation was more in taste than sight however, as their eyes appeared to be closed in delirious delight.

There were no signs of any other equines today. I remembered another time here with Yvonne, when three free-roaming Highland ponies had come thundering across the glen at our approach to the toll tree. Moving our own four horses on to try and avoid any conflict, the three had dropped happily in-line behind us as we worked our way along the trail.

If it hadn't been for recruitment of two enthusiastic walkers (and their walking poles) who waved frantically to scare the Highland ponies back to the riverside, I think they may have followed us all the way on our long-distance ride. It's one thing delivering mail and messages by Pony Express, but I'm not sure the gamekeeper in the next glen would appreciate express delivery of three extra ponies!

Plucking Team Swogi from their pasture of pleasure, I turned them to the right to head up the unfamiliar gully. Not much navigation was required so far. The track was wide and solid and was unlikely to get itself lost as it had nowhere else to go other than upwards, squeezed as it was between the steep gully sides. It opened out slightly at Lochan ant-Sluic and, glancing back down to Glen Feshie, I was surprised to see how far we had ascended in such a short time.

"Maybe you didn't notice," said Yogi, "cos my turbo-boost speed walk is super-fast when going uphill."

"Can we go find those Highland ponies to carry all this heavy gear instead of me?" asked Swift, glancing back down the glen.

I didn't tell her that we'd only done about one quarter of our total height gain for the day, and judging by the sardine-like arrangement of contours in four kilometres time, the steepest was yet to come. Yogi would be happy, but I knew Swift would grumble.

However, we had come to the fork in the trail and a decision needed to be made. Did I follow the advice from a friend, another long-distance rider, and head to the right? Or did I heed the merry suggestion offered by keeper Davie last night and head to the left for a possibly drier trail?

"Less bogs to the left, did you say?" mumbled Yogi as he set off with determination, taking the decision for the whole team upon himself.

We ascended to the top of Meall an Uilt Chreagaich 'hill of the craggy stream' on a good 4x4 track with long views across a barren, brownish (and no doubt boggy), heathered expanse to the peaks in the distant west. There was a strong breeze blowing and the sky was packed densely with a woven blanket of white clouds.

In no time at all, it was time to jump off for the steep descent to the small flatland that lies between the watersheds of the River Feshie to the east and the River Tromie to the west. It felt strange to be standing on the source of the Feshie, knowing that it heads east for eight kilometres or so before looping back on itself to head west again. After this large sweeping diversion, from which it gathers support from many a burn and bog, it then follows the more familiar northerly course through the main glen.

As I found a place to cross a burn with Team Swogi, I looked up in dismay at the hill ahead. In less than a kilometre's length, we'd be climbing one-hundred-and-sixty metres of height. I've scaled steeper with Swift and Yogi, but it felt extreme today, with a dicky-ticker, a slippery slope, and a horse who won't stop for a rest until the peak, or the end of a trail is reached.

It was too slippery to ride, and I didn't think Yogi was fit enough yet to carry me up something this vertical anyhow. As usual he pressed his turbo-boost in preparation for upness, and I knew Swift and I were going to struggle to keep up.

I slipped his lead rope through his stirrup to give me an emergency brake for when he ignored my verbal command to stop (the turbo-boost tends to affect his hearing somewhat), then grabbed hold of his tail. This might sound cruel, but 'tailing' is a recognised technique for getting around the steeper grounds of the Highlands, a method passed down from stalkers with much mountainous experience and used often by Endurance Sport riders.

I'm not sure I'd ever attempt it with Swift, given her lack of pleasure at personal space invasion and her athleticism with her back legs. However, Yogi didn't mind one bit. In fact, focussed on the peak as he was, I'm not sure he even noticed. He hauled me up and I hauled Swift and as a team we'd reached the first of two false peaks. We were all blowing hard, but Yogi still wanted to press on with a job he considered to be only halfway done.

I was grateful to see a guy striding down to meet us, as this temporary distraction diverted the Bear from his upward mission – and gave us all a little breather.

"Well, I didn't expect to see a horse all the way up here," the walker exclaimed.

"There's two of us *actually!*" responded a slightly annoyed Swift, as she poked her head around from behind Yogi's bottom (a diva never likes to be ignored).

"Oh, there's two of them!" he went on to say, before asking me a torrent of questions.

Whilst I contemplated that I appeared to be the only one who could hear my horses talk, I tried to answer his questions as well as I could between my gasps of exertion.

As often on adventurous journeys, we were being viewed as a fascinating curiosity; one that is out of place, brave and bold, rather than a blast from the past - old fashioned but exactly where we belong. In response to his questions, I explained where we'd started, where we intended to finish today, and the overall plan for the next two weeks.

The guy couldn't quite believe that horses were able to move around the hills and questioned whether we'd make it all the way through to Glen Bruar safely, despite the historical context of the pass involved, which was constructed originally with horses in mind. I'd met this kind of incredulity many times before, often mixed with respect and approval but sometimes with scorn and disbelief. I had the distinct impression that this chap was in the latter party, so his disparaging reaction to the full plan of a Cairngorm circumnavigation wasn't entirely unexpected.

"And you're doing this all on your own?"

He actually peered behind Swift's spotty bum to see if there was another person (presumably male) hiding there. I make this stereotypical supposition with the knowledge that I could be wrong, but I'd met this type of attitude time and time again. Whether whilst intending to become a paramedic, kayak huge rivers, ski a black run, reverse a trailer, or travel through mountainous terrain with a tonne of horse - some men don't think women are capable enough for these sorts of things all on their own. These are the type of *people* I chose not to hang out with, and thankfully, they appear to be on the decline.

With renewed resolve to succeed (despite my perceived handicap), I released Yogi's handbrake and we were off to the top of 'Two-too-little' - the name I decided to give the hill we were climbing as it didn't have one of its own. Standing at 912 metres high it was only 2.4 metres short of a Munro title (a list of mountains in Scotland at least 914.4 meters high), and to add insult to injury, its sister mountain ten metres lower and less than a kilometre away was named on the map. They were both part of the same ridgeline, but you'd have thought that the higher peak, with the trig-point cherry on top, would have been the one to receive a christening. It was at least recognised as a Corbett (a list of Scottish peaks between 762 and 914.4 meters) in compensation and consolation - although deviously sharing its little sister's label.

Now, despite my recent encounter and the feeling of self-assurance and inner strength, I still as a *person* (not only as a woman) have moments of self-doubt, and I was feeling this sensation now. I was totally reliant on my navigation skills going forward to keep myself and my horses safe; with a spur of land to follow down off the hill and a thin trail to pick up heading south. This trail was possibly the only safe passage through the peatland plateau but with little to no features on which to focus a bearing.

The weather wasn't settled and concerns about losing my way if the clouds came down were playing on my mind. In historic times, the thin trail I was searching for had had a bad reputation for claiming victims due to the uncertainty of weather on its bleak and blustery heights. Nevertheless, its name, the Minigaig, means 'Smooth Gaick'.

The Gaick name in general refers to the area of land between Badenoch and Atholl, but the 'Gaick Pass' label is commonly used these days to describe the way through the upper reaches of the River Tromie, passed Gaick Lodge, and traversing three beautiful lochs before arriving at Dalnacardoch.

Looking back in time however, there were three routes through the Gaick expanse. The most westerly one mentioned just now, a second in the middle - the 'Rough Gaick', which branched off at the Allt Gharbh Ghaig and formed part of Comyn's Road, up over the hills to descend in a south-easterly direction to Blair Castle – and then the third most easterly, the 'Smooth Gaick' which ascended the Allt Bhran and over the plateau to emerge via Glen Bruar. Whichever of the routes chosen, they all linked the River Spey of Speyside to the River Garry in Perthshire and connected the inter-community trading opportunities of Badenoch and Atholl.

The Minigaig remained an important trade and drovers' road throughout the 19th century, but once General Wade had built a more robust pass through Drumochter, completed in 1730, the Minigaig was more commonly used only as a summer route. It's easy to understand why, as this vast plateau reaches a height over eight-hundred-and-forty meters and would often be covered in snow or blanketed in disorientating cloud during the winter months.

With the featureless plain and confusion in bad weather, it's also easy to see how the pass earnt an enchanted reputation, with numerous stories of fairies and mythical creatures imparted by those who travelled or stalked game along it. However, given that somewhere along its length there was once a covert hut that sold illicit whisky, the bewildering clouds might not be the only thing causing disorientation and hallucinations.

Illicit whisky production flourished for fifty years or so before legislation changed in 1823 and legal whisky became a competitive price. Before that time, it wasn't uncommon to see fake funeral processions with illegal whisky hidden in the casket or suddenly pregnant women going to market with bottles stuffed up their jumpers, their real children used as lookouts. No wonder that myth was commonplace, and nobody trusted what they saw with their own two eyes!

Intending to join the smooth option for crossing the Gaick, we carefully descended from 'Two-too-little' via the heathered spur of her sister. My bearing didn't have to be all that exact as I'd intersect the Minigaig somewhere along its length. However, since the pass looked thin on the map, I didn't want to blink, miss it, and step over it - to disappear into the peat hag expanse never to be seen again. Okay, so my mind was getting a little carried away here, but I did pace out the exact metres and looked for a precise drop on my altimeter watch, just to be sure.

I was delighted to arrive on what appeared to be the pass, at the right pace number, correct height, and a little white cairn. As I took a rough bearing to the south-east, I was even more delighted to see a second white quartzite cairn ahead.

It would be easy to be lulled into a false sense of security with these markers leading the way, but I remained alert as the cloud appeared to be descending. It wouldn't take much to leave us floundering in swirling mist on a featureless terrain, with the cairns hidden from view, and the fairies free to cause mischief unseen.

I used the little white cairn as a mounting block and jumped back up onto Yogi, and then used the gap between his ears as reference for the compass bearing. Not a traditional navigational practice, but there were very few other features on which to focus. Yogi was fidgety and tense, with his head full of potential encounters with bogs, fairies, and mythical beings, and was not in a listening mood (so his ears weren't being used for any other purpose anyway). All he wanted to do was get to the end of this peculiar path.

The Bear was on a mindful mission but was suspicious of every puddle, patch of peat, and malleable moss, so was mostly jogging along on tiptoes. The ground looked solid enough so long as you stayed on the trail, but to the left and right it appeared spongy and particularly dangerous for those of us with a foot-size to body-weight ratio that made us prone to sinking.

"My Thoroughbred-Highland mix is the wrong-way-round for this!" wailed Yogi. "I've neat feet and a braced waist - I'm sure to sink to the brink!"

"Just stay on the trail and follow the cairns, the pass is solid enough."

I gave his neck a good rub for reassurance, but he remained wary of his surrounds and was not helped by Swift, who was making bog-sinking sucking noises behind him for her own entertainment.

The surrounds were a mix of tufty grass, patches of heather with cottongrass sprinkled through it, sphagnum moss, squares of slimy waters, and smears of dark-brown peat. The pass at times ran in a hollow through all of this and I could imagine the numbers of feet and hooves (and more recently tyres) through time that had caused this indentation. Across this kind of terrain, it would be hard to establish then maintain a clear path on your own - it requires the collaboration of many feet undertaking regular passage.

Fording the Caochan Lub (meandering streamlet) looked interesting, and it took a while and a fair amount of meandering of our own to find a suitable crossing point that all three of us were happy to take. The horses were reluctant to jump down steep banks into the water and I was on foot, trying to keep my feet dry. We also needed to exit on the far side in a good place to pick up the trail that ascended in a thin manner up a sheer-sided slope - the reason I was on foot in preparation. Eventually we came to an 'all for one and one for all' agreement - that we'd all be getting our feet wet.

I persuaded Team Swogi to enter the streamlet via a gravel bank further away and resigned myself to walking along its waters for thirty metres or so before exiting on the far side with a squelch, a little jump up, and a difficult scramble up the sheer slope on the opposite side. We got a little separated in this process, but since all were heading roughly in an upwards and correct direction, I let this widening of team dynamics happen then regathered the clan at the top.

After that it was plain sailing from cairn to cairn, boggy in places, but easy enough to follow. I started to navigationally relax and just follow the cairns, as the further along we progressed on the plateau the nicer the weather was becoming. Finally making its mind up, it settled into a windy but gloriously sunny day and the thick blanket of cloud, no longer descending, was folded back to air the blue sheet underneath.

The trail turned to gravel just before the descent into Glen Bruar, but it was apparent that people had taken a mix of routes down off the 'soggy harper's breast' as the track became less distinct over the edge. I'd heard of tennis elbow, golfer's elbow, and housemaid's knee, but I'd not heard that harp playing could impact your health too. As I wondered about the quality of hill-name translation from Gaelic to Anglo-Saxon, I wandered about looking for the trail - as I'd strayed off it somewhat.

Picking it up again for the steep, rocky, and twisting descent, Yogi's turbo-boost (normally reserved for upness) appeared to be stuck on full throttle for this tricky down-hill section. He just couldn't wait to get away from the bog monsters and fairy tales of the eerie Minigaig pass.

Swift, who was by now well into her afternoon snooze window (generally around half-past-one), was bored of bog-monster impersonations and was descending at a somewhat slower and daydreamy pace. The damage had been done by the mischievous minx though and Yogi remained flustered.

The only way I could manage the conflicting speeds of the differing duo was to be a piggy in the middle and let Yogi lead the way. I was now using the tailing technique, usually reserved for steep uphill, to try and slow him down. It was arm-stretching, it took concentration, and it was not an easy task.

As a result, when we reached the first sizeable patch of grass, where a side burn tumbled into the glen's river (the Bruar Water), we all required a rest. Team Swogi tucked into the grass while I lay down to enjoy the sun on my face and eat a bit of late lunch. We only had around five kilometres to go to our intended wild camp for the night now, and all of this would proceed on a wide 4x4 track.

The feeling of reaching an easier stage, after negotiating a hard one, is difficult to describe. It's certainly a different feeling than when travelling with other humans or without equine friends. Team Swogi may carry the bulk of the physical load, but the responsibility of making sure my two equine companions stay safe and well falls heavily on my shoulders alone.

There is a sense of relief, achievement, and celebration - alongside a self-granted permission to push any future concerns from your mind, and fully enjoy the next wee while. Safe navigation of the Minigaig had played most noisily on my mind (a downside of reading too much about its fierce reputation), but for now it was done and fairy-dusted - so I could relax for the rest of the day.

I call these my 'Mars Bar moments', a treat I carry with a strict, one-a-day weight allowance (in terms of both me and the saddle bags). I'm not one for sitting still but the full appreciation of the luxury of chocolate on the trail must not be done on the move; that would be sacrilege! It's my restorative 'take-a-break' moment, just with my preferred brand of sweet.

The days coming up would have sections of concern too, areas that I hadn't fully recced for example, but this had been the first big test of the journey. I knew there would be more to come but challenges at the earlier stages of any dobbineering adventure always feel more abrasive - as mind, body, and soul aren't yet fully aligned to the constant management of risk.

Adventures such as these are such a step away from life at home, so it takes a while to become comfortable with the non-stop consideration of undertakings, and the responsibility of keeping my companions safe. As the journey unfolds, the assessment of risk becomes routine, the travelling rhythm becomes more in-tune, and there's a quieting of the 'what ifs?' This gradual adjustment allows the ratio between fretting and fulfilment to tilt towards the latter.

I'd moved on from Mars Bar to apple and Yogi had moved on too. Spotting the trail continuing down the valley, he'd set off on a 'mission to somewhere and somewhere fast' on his own. I was left to rapidly pick up my packed lunch, and Swift had to stuff as much grass into her mouth as she could as I asked her to tag along too.

Having to apply a turbo-boost of our own, we soon caught up with him on the other side of the high wooden bridge that spanned the tributary. I stuck my thumb out and Yogi politely waited for me to hitch a ride. When I say he politely waited – he at least let my bottom land in the saddle before he immediately continued his onward objective.

The track was wide and rocky with a soft grassy middle. It stretched down the valley, accompanied by the tumbling waters of the River Bruar to our right. The sun was still shining strongly, causing retina-burning reflections to explode like fireworks from all the puddles on and around the trail. There had been more rain than I'd appreciated last night, tucked up as I had been in my tiny tent (snoring under the whisky blanket). No wonder the Minigaig had been a little on the soft side.

Yogi was delighted to have fairy-free firmness under foot and was striding along happily, with no input required from me. I was still enjoying post-challenge and post-chocolate endorphins - totally along for the ride and grinning from ear to ear. The hour passed quickly, as time always does when having fun, and we were soon approaching the planned end of day.

Helped by a small dam, the Bruar Water had spread out here, filling the valley base with a wide expanse of rippled water and reed grass. On the other side, the patchy green slopes of the hills rose steeply. Also on the other side was our planned camp spot for the night, making use of an old sheepfold just up the valley from Bruar Lodge.

Or at least, that had been the plan, but things were looking very different now to when I'd mountain-biked in for a recce. The river had completely changed its course and not only did the sheepfold look to be on an island now, but the banks on this side of the river were steep, gravelly, and concealed unstable cornices. These were just hanging there, lying in wait for the weight of a hoof to initiate a collapse and cause a rocky avalanche down to the river.

There must have been some flooding here or a manual channel alteration for hydro works. Either way, there was no way to the sheepfold from this side now, not without considerable effort, which seemed pointless due to the amount of grass at our disposal on this side of the valley.

We continued down to the lodge, crossing its sloping grass frontage, and I wondered if anyone might mind me setting up a corral in the dip, a little out of sight, but still very close to the buildings. We ambled around the corner of the lodge to knock on a door to ask and came face to face with a massive black cow standing casually in the driveway.

"Waaahhh!" shouted Yogi.

"Eeeeeek!" squeaked Swift.

Together, they about-turned as fast as they could, did three bouncy canter strides, then spun again to see if the cow had followed. Thankfully, they'd done this in perfect unison and somehow, I'd managed to remain on board.

"Hellooooo, I'm – mmmmoooo! Flora," said the cow as she gazed dopily at her potential new guests and continued to chew some cud.

"Seems friendly enough," whispered Swift, all head-high, ears pricked, and on high alert.

"Will you get a load of those horns," said Yogi, in awe and wide-eyed fear. "They must be six feet across and extremely sharp and pointy."

He followed his statements with a long slow whistle, a snort, and two backward steps.

I was just about to jump off, as Flora looked docile enough and Yogi required the added confidence of me on the ground, when I heard a second "Hello." Confused, I naturally assumed there was a second, more-timid cow, hiding behind the first.

Peering around the expanse of black fur, I found a man standing with a smile on his face. Luckily, he appeared to be relaxed and friendly too and said, "I've been expecting you."

This was the gamekeeper Dominic, who lived behind the lodge. We'd met on my recce when I'd asked permission to camp at the sheepfold and he immediately made us feel extremely welcome now. With the sheepfold out of reach, Team Swogi were offered a small paddock for the night at the back of the buildings. It had a high fence all the way around (for the silly Bear to feel safe from friendly Flora) and water in the centre.

Dominic chased Flora from the driveway, then the ducks and chicken out of the paddock, and by the time I'd untacked the horses and made them comfortable, he was back with the offer of a bed in the summerhouse for me. I hadn't even had time to scope out a discrete place to pitch my tent. With no corral to set up, no water to fetch for a thirsty Swift, and no tent to pitch - I was in for an easy over-night stay.

Flora the Friendly Highland Cow

I settled into the summerhouse and cooked some food on my stove, but soon found myself swept up in the embrace of a busy house, full of kids, dogs, TV noise, and sweet-tasting homemade wine. It was shaping up to be yet another entertaining and more sociable night than I was expecting in the back of beyond.

Delivering my Pony Express telegram from Glen Feshie as promised, I again received some route top tips for the following day. It was becoming apparent that the best way to ride in the hills was to travel from gamekeeper to gamekeeper to take full advantage of their local knowledge. I was grateful, too, for the bonus hospitality I'd received so far - easing my travels in more ways than one. To pay my way a little, I promised to let Dominic's daughter Rosie and her friend Rebecca have a ride on Yogi as we set off in the morning.

The homely embrace and the lively chatter were hard to leave, but I was starting to fall asleep. I made my excuses and said my good-nights, then made my way back to the summerhouse. It wasn't far to go, but within a few steps I discovered that I was struggling to walk. Not due to the amount of homemade wine (although no doubt that didn't help), but my left calf had, out of the blue, become painful, solid, and swollen. I couldn't remember at any point during the day twisting in an unusual way to cause a strain or tear, and I hadn't felt any discomfort when I'd arrived at the lodge.

Sometimes being a medic means you know too much, especially if you have an imagination as enthusiastic as mine. Combining my sudden onset of swollen-calf symptoms with the continued cardiac irregularities – I diagnosed that I was at significant risk of this being a DVT (deep vein thrombosis). Nevertheless, I did what I would strongly advise no patient of mine to do, and hobbled over to say goodnight to Team Swogi, then went to bed to see how it was in the morning.

Caper-Ceilidh

Day 3: Bruar Lodge to Old Blair (Distance 14km, Ascent 240m)

It had been surprisingly chilly overnight for June and as I poked my head out of the comfort of my sleeping bag, I could see my breath. I tried an exploratory flex of my left ankle, pulling my toes up towards my shin, and was relieved to find that my calf felt very tight but was not as sore as last night. Trying a downwards flexion was a complete mistake though, as the cramp was immediate and painful, causing a very rapid egress of sleeping bag and exposure to the cold surrounds. "Brrrrr!"

Hopping around the summerhouse, I concluded that my calf wasn't as hot nor as swollen as it had been last night, and I was able to walk okay, although with an obvious limp. *That would do,* I thought, *the show can go on...*

I threw some warm clothing on and experimented with my new uneven gait, up to check on the horses who were standing content in the corner of the paddock with floppy bottom lips. A slackness in the jaw vicinity generally indicates a happy and relaxed horse, and these two looked like they might trip over theirs if asked to move forward this morning.

Yogi had his butt up against the side of a chicken shed, the protection giving his mind extra reassurance. When out in the wilds, I always try to cater for Yogi's insecurity needs by building the corral somewhere that has an integral butt protector. Whether a tree, stone wall, or part of a building (no matter how ruined), he is much more settled if he can park his butt somewhere safe through the night; safe from all the things his fretful imagination suggests might harm it.

Swift is a lot more self-assured and will totally relax, flat out, often displaying proper REM sleep even in unfamiliar places. Like a ladybird, maybe she is confident that the aposematic colouration on her behind offers a warning, and provides additional protection by discouraging predators.

I hobbled back down to the summerhouse to begin the morning routine with my standard, on-the-trail breakfast of porridge (made only with water), a handful of nuts, and a mug of Earl Grey tea. It was a very short day ahead, one which could probably be done before lunchtime if we pushed on a bit. The shortness was designed to cater for ongoing ailments elsewhere in my body, but my lower left leg was quite happy with the arrangement too.

As I filled my coffee flask for the day ahead, I lingered over a second cup of tea. Watching the hens and ducks cluck around the pen beside me, and bees buzzing at the flowers in the garden, I thought that maybe I could get used to sitting still if I tried really hard to quiet my ‘up and at it’ mind. The monkey on my shoulder won out in the end however, and I packed up in record time.

I’d just collected a sleepy Team Swogi from the paddock and tied them up at the side of the barn when the girls arrived. They watched, asked shy questions, and giggled a lot as I tended to feet, put hoof boots on, and tacked-up. Once ready, Rosie and Rebecca played a brief game of ‘rock, paper, scissors’ to see who’d win the first dibs of Yogi. Rosie’s rock blunted Rebecca’s scissors, so as I parked Yogi at a rock of his own, Rosie clambered aboard. Yogi still had a loose lower lip so wasn’t looking particularly sharp himself yet.

I shouted, "Cheerio and thank you!" and the girls yelled, "See ya later!" to Dominic, then the five of us set off across the grass along a raised embankment. This looked to be the best option for making our way through an initial section of marshy ground. It was solid under foot and hoof and seemed to follow a man-made bank of earth and stone - that was until it ended abruptly, vanishing into a boggy swamp without a clear way through.

Suddenly awake, Yogi panicked, spun around (and around) and neatly wrapped up Swift in her own lead rope like a joint of beef trussed up for roasting. Ms Swift was most displeased and uncharacteristically decided to panic too.

"Whoa! Stand back! Hold on tight!" I hollered.

Rebecca jumped out of the way and Rosie somehow managed to stay on board, despite a few back feet leaving the ground. I was glad about this, as it wouldn't have been a great start to the day to return a broken child (or two) to my kind host only five minutes after we'd left.

I sorted out the tangle, calmed Team Swogi down, and went back the way we'd come to try a better route. Rebecca didn't seem all that keen now to claim her turn on Yogi - he was going to have to work hard in the next ten minutes to reconstruct his reputation of reliability.

"Wasn't my fault," sniffed Yogi, shuddering. "You know how bog messes up my mind, it rudely caught me half asleep too."

"Numpty!" said Swift, direct and to the point. Her mare-glare spelt out the rest of what she couldn't say in front of the children. She did not appreciate a tow rope under her tail one bit!

We found a better way through the second time around, closer to the main river, with only a couple of narrow boggy ditches to traverse. Yogi stepped over calmly, more awake now and seeming to understand the precious young cargo he carried. Swift, still unnerved by the offence of rope under tail, decided to jump each one behind us.

After a kilometre I knew the track would steepen, which would mean a switch to turbo-boost from Yogi, so I needed to let Rebecca have a turn before that kicked in. Seeing that the Bear was more settled now, she swapped with Rosie and bravely jumped on board. As we started to climb slightly, I turned around to assess how far the girls would have to walk home on their own and saw Flora standing proud, off to one side.

I hadn't seen her on our approach, so, although I knew she was a friendly sort, it was an eerie feeling suddenly being escorted off the premises by her strong, silent, and seemingly wise presence. She struck a lonely and dark silhouette against the green slopes behind.

"Safe travels!" she bellowed suddenly, causing Team Swogi to rapidly raise their heads.

"Cheerio!" shouted Swift, her head raised as she whinnied her reply.

"See Yogi, I told you Flora is nice," I said.

"Maybe without her huge scary hat on," said Yogi. "Let's just keep moving."

Yogi and Swift were both generally good with cows and had stood fast amongst stampedes and bovine bouncing displays numerous times before. We'd rarely seen a cow with such a large and pointy hat this close up before though, and it was Flora's fashion sense that Yogi had reservations about. I placed my hand on his neck to keep him calm as there was no need for Rebecca to experience similar acrobatics to those that Rosie had endured.

Today's route was following the tail end of the Minigaig pass down into Old Blair. This section wasn't surrounded by so much myth and legend. The path was also more distinct and would shortly change to a wide

4x4 track for the rest of the day, with only a couple of trickier spots to negotiate before this change happened. We were approaching one of those now, where the path cut through the Allt nan Dearcag burn.

As a walker this would pose minimal concerns, but the track cut through the burn in a manner that wasn't fit for hooves as it exited in a patch of bog.

"Definitely not fit for *my* hooves then," said Yogi, shaking his head.

It was a simple diversion to take a sharp left turn on the other side of the hill and arc back down to the trail in a few hundred metres time. This, however, was in an upwards direction, which meant application of a Yogi turbo-boost and therefore time to say good-bye to the girls.

We said our farewells and I hoped their thirty-minute walk back to the lodge was worth their fifteen-minute rides on Yogi. As I prepared for limping on upwards (I'd not get on until we'd completed the diversion), I watched the girls descend the track and gave them a wave to see them on their way.

It's a shame that this sort of trust and freedom isn't so commonplace for the young these days. There are possibly more dangers in society to be aware of, but there's also a huge amount of cotton wool wrapping being applied. All childhoods shape the adult you become, and I very much appreciate how adventurous mine was from an early age.

When still in primary school, I'd sometimes spend the day at my friend's house. Her parents left us to play in the brook/burn at the bottom of the garden (something my parents would have been happy to do too) - except we didn't always stay. Often, we'd set off down the brook in our wellies, sneaking past the garden of the nunnery unseen, through a tunnel under the road to emerge close to 'Joey the Swan' park.

The only thing that stood between us and the swings was a traverse of a wide-girthed drainage pipe, suspended up high over a channel with a circle of spikes to carefully squeeze by, designed to keep stupid fools from balance-beaming across the pipe like we did.

We'd spend a couple of hours, or as long as we dared, playing in the park and generally doing our own thing. Exploring paths, climbing trees, peering into the deep water-filled pits of the water treatment works - ruined and abandoned, with insecure fencing and numerous risks. Then the nerve of being caught would overshadow and we'd scurry and hurry back the way we'd come, emerging in the back garden hungry and thirsty with parents none the wiser.

I also used to set off with our dog Duke, after school, for hours on end on my own. Exploring every field and footpath within reach of the house. We lived in semi-rural Cheshire, so these adventures took place in the realms of natural and man-made hazards and my parents didn't know exactly where I'd gone.

I observed nature, I felt the thrill of solo exploration, I experienced fear, assessed risk, and learnt my limitations. Exposure to healthy risk is such a key part of growing up, but sadly, it's not as safe today for child or dog – at least that's how it appears in media.

With 'Stranger Danger', increased traffic, and fear of litigation amongst other anxieties, most children confined to the house now, play inside rather than out. They interact less with nature; they play drastically closer to home (or adult supervision) and spend more time than you'd think possible in a week on digital entertainment. Whilst I was negotiating spikes on the pipe, playing hide and seek outside in the dark, or catching frogs in the garden – the majority of kids today don't even get their hands dirty!

The most recallable and treasured memories I have of childhood are moments of independent 'play' – away from adult supervision, exploring the world around me, and learning from the experience. I find it incredibly depressing that in the main, this kind of upbringing - which provides so much in terms of resilience, risk management, self-confidence, and an affinity to the natural world - died with my generation, and that young people nowadays miss out on so much.

The trail after the diversion was thin and through heather. I jumped back up on Yogi and from my elevated position I looked back down the glen. The girls were no longer in sight - still making their way back to the lodge, they'd become merged with the land and were indiscernible specs in the distance. This provided perspective of the grand scale of the glen.

Behind me, the sky was full of white clouds with the river snaking back and forth across its floodplain below them. Its sparkling line wound its way up to the head of the glen, disappearing within the slopes of the hills we'd descended yesterday. Ahead, the sky was blue; and although rough under foot, the trail was clear and uphill. Yogi happily got on with his job for the next kilometre or so and Swift had to jog to keep up.

We descended a soggy channel towards the next tricky stream. With a difficult negotiation of twists and turns and a few large steps down at the end, I didn't at first notice the building on the other side of the water. It was a stone and slate construction, with one small window and two doors facing us, one of which looked to be displaying the Mountain Bothy Association (MBA) logo. The MBA is a charitable organisation that maintains one hundred or so of these hill shelters, all upkeep and preservation carried out by volunteers with permission and support of the owners. It is always a delight to happen upon a bothy, versus being given an introduction and directions to one.

As an MBA bothy, it would be listed on their website, but I don't seek them out along my route unless I'm looking for a place to stay or for options in case of emergency. Many others, not under the MBA's care, aren't listed online anyway. Their secret locations are gently cosseted by those in the know, passed on quietly by word of mouth to persons deemed trusted to respect them.

Bothy enthusiasts, in their quest to find unlisted ones, may search the small squares marked on an Ordnance Survey map - trying to find a particular shelter surrounded by tale and legend, only to find a shack in ruin at the end of a long day's walk. Finding one intact and open, or happening upon one by accident like this, feels thrilling. I can't help thinking that this is perhaps just how it should be.

This river crossing looked worse than the last and I struggled to find a way to cross, as every access point along the bank on this side involved a large step down into the water. Team Swogi are never keen on this as an idea. The only slope into the water was a long, rocky slab but I knew that, with a little persuasion, I'd be able to convince Yogi to give this a try and then Swift should follow behind. However, I also knew the wet and rocky slab wouldn't provide much grip and things were likely to get a little hectic for a moment or two.

Yogi calmly followed me to the start of the slab and, with only two minor objections, he worked out what I wanted him to do and then slid all four feet down the rock to land with a splash in the riverbed. I threw his lead rope after him as he strode through the stream and neatly jumped up the bank on the other side. Swift was a little less graceful and her lanky legs a little less organised.

She was slightly panicked that Yogi was leaving her behind, as he'd continued up the track on the other side - clear in his mind on where the trail led next. Her four feet went in four different directions, but as soon as they all landed in the water, they immediately bounced out and onto the far bank. Boy that girl can jump when she wants to!

I splashed my way out of the stream, forgoing dry feet for a limping dash to catch up with Yogi as I wanted to look at the bothy before continuing our route. I escorted him back down with the temptation of grass to eat, to help him forget the onwards trail for a moment.

"Hmmm... tasty grass," he said, as I plonked his nose near a large tuft beside the door.

"It's lovely over here too," said Swift. "Can't believe you walked on past it, your trail obsession is a pain in the..."

"I'm just nipping inside for a moment." I interrupted. "I won't be long, so *don't* leave without me."

I made this last statement whilst making direct eye contact with Yogi.

Inside the bothy was dim in comparison to the sunshine outside, with only two small windows providing light to the singular room. Someone had at least tried to brighten the place up a little by whitewashing the walls and it looked like a comfortable and cosy spot to spend the night.

There were a few old chairs, a table, and a wooden sleeping platform to help insulate from the cold of the stone floor. A small fireplace, raised up on a bed of bricks, took centre place. It looked proud in its ability to turn a cold wet evening into one of warmth and cheer. With a quick flick of flame, its magic could gather all present in a red glow and a snug embrace, as they shared tales, song, and laughter surrounded by the reach of its spell.

I carefully closed the door behind me and looked around the corner of the building. Here was a tantalising trail advancing up a narrow valley which was luring me to explore its destination. That would have to wait for another time, however, as we were heading in the opposite direction around the base of Càrn Dearg Mòr in a south-easterly course to Old Blair.

The trail rose steeply from the bothy and Yogi strode out with his usual enthusiasm for upness. It didn't take long to get to the top of the rise, and as we contoured around the hill a long view opened up to the craggy ridgeline of Farragon Hill. The ridge formed a distant yet strong silhouette in comparison to the green lands around us, which were brightened by the midday sun. We soon descended the slopes of Carn Dearg Beag and crossed a concrete bridge over a stream, to arrive at the Lady March Cairn.

Cairns are used to mark various things. To guide your route (like the white quartzite ones on the Minigaig pass); to mark a burial or protect a grave; as a commemoration; to warn of the edge of a ledge; or to guide a boat safely into harbour. They are also used to mark the top of peaks as a celebration of a successful climb, and it's become customary to carry a stone from the bottom of a hill to place it on top of the cairn at the summit.

The Lady March Cairn is a commemorative one and, given its size and sturdy construction, it seems the lady was very well thought of indeed. Amy Mary Ricardo gained her Lady March status when marrying Charles Henry Gordon-Lennox (the Earl of March) who was the 7th Duke of Richmond, the 7th Duke of Lennox, the 2nd Duke of Gordon, and a descendant of the illegitimate son of King Charles II. I bet he couldn't list all those titles off after a glass of fine port.

It was the Duke of Gordon title and ownership of Gordon Castle in Fochabers that provided the March's connection to Scotland. Each year the whole family would travel up to stay for three or four months, socialising with the elite (King George V was a regular visitor) and partaking in shooting, fishing, stalking, or countryside walks and picnics.

On one such picnic, the cairn was initiated with a small pile of stones. From here it grew and was later formed into the bold and robust pear-shaped structure seen today. The Cairn's significance was without doubt expediated by the sad, unfortunate, and early demise of Lady March in 1879 at the age of only thirty-two.

The impressive cairn marked a bend in the trail and our final descent for the day down into Old Blair. With woodland surrounding us on the final approach to the village, it was an abrupt exit from the cover of trees to arrive at a busy crossroads. It was the tiniest crossroads you could imagine, so the liveliness was a bit of a surprise for all three of us. Not least because the road ahead, the one which I was planning to take next, was full of smoke, dust, noisy machinery, men in hi vis, and to top it all - a large, red 'Road Closed' sign. *There goes the plan then!*

Unsure how far the diversion might take us from the intended route, I stopped to ask one of the hi vis men if the road was still passable for 'pedestrians.'

"No way. You can't take horses down there. The road is being completely re-surfaced, and the machines will scare them," he answered. "You'll have to go around."

"He's right, you know," said Yogi. "I don't like the look of those big contraptions at all. They might resurface me by mistake."

"Meah!" snorted Swift, bumping the man with her nose. "I don't like mile-increasing, energy-wasting diversions - surely, we could just sneak past?"

"I don't think so my love, it does look a bit hazardous. We will have to find another way – especially since you've just completely terrified the person in charge of the stop-go sign!"

I was trying to stifle a little giggle as the man was looking up in awe at Swift's towering figure, absent-mindedly rubbing his bumped arm with his opposite hand. He was also looking rather pale.

"Go that way." He pointed, stammering, and scampered back to his work. "Round by the Castle."

I waved and shouted out a thank you, but I don't think he noticed.

Steering Team Swogi south towards the Castle as instructed, I paused to let them munch the long grass at the side of the road while I had a look at the map. The diversion only added a couple of kilometres to today's journey and since it was only a short day anyway, this didn't really matter. What did matter however, was that we'd now have to ride through the grounds of the popular Blair Castle.

Popular that is with visitors arriving by the coach load, tour guides with umbrellas, and pipers - piping the visitors into the castle with a welcoming, merry tune. I wasn't too sure which was the lesser of the two evils to be honest; the road works, or the unpredictability of a hectic tourist hotspot.

On the approach to the castle, I knew my concerns were justified. I could hear a piper in the distance and Yogi already had his head held high in maximum alert mode. Having lived in the Highlands before moving north, my horses had encountered bagpipe playing before - at a distance though. I couldn't recall a time that we'd ventured as close as we were about to do so.

Sure enough, standing by the entrance to the castle was a piper in full regalia, merrily puffing and squeezing away, tapping a foot as he welcomed visitors inside. Between us and him were numerous tourists asking to take our photo. I think they thought we were all part of the castle's historic display.

Yogi was torn between pausing for a pose and continuing the jig he'd started to do (not quite in time with the music I might add). Since Swift was also now doing a "Dashing White Sergeant" behind us, the jig won, and I decided to turn left over the bridge to give us more distance from the tunes.

"What on earth *was* that dreadful noise anyway?" asked Swift, as she shook her long ears to rid them of the sound.

"Well basically it's a guy squeezing the inflated skin of a dead sheep. He blows lungs-full of air through it and makes different notes by covering various holes on the chanter," I explained.

Swift was speechless at my reply, and I realised too late that it probably wasn't the best time for honesty. Yogi launched into "The Military Two Step" upon hearing my description, and I wasn't sure if I'd be able to calm him down when suddenly he came to an abrupt stop and Swift bumped into him from behind.

"Never mind the noise and that poor sheep," he said, "what's that *thing* over there?"

Over the bridge, we'd hopped and skipped into some sort of fete. There were square white tents dotted along both left and right of the track, each advertising or selling their individual wares. The first on the right was a Guide Dogs for the Blind stand, no doubt intending to fundraise for this fantastic cause during the day's event. A little way in front of their tent stood a solitary Golden Retriever decked out in his bright reflective harness, to draw in the crowds. This Golden Retriever had Team Swogi's full attention.

"It's just a stuffed dog," I said, in what I thought was a calming manner.

"A s-s-s-stuffed dog?" stuttered Yogi, as he did a quick 'Do-si-do' to swap places with Swift.

"First they skin sheep and now they stuff dogs – lets get outta here!"

The horses began an integrated side-step formation that any Ceilidh caller would have been impressed with. As the side-step took them past the Retriever, they spun one-hundred-and-eighty degrees, allowing them to never lose eye contact with this dangerous beast. They then continued down the track, slowly backing away.

The tourist crowd scattered as I muttered my apologies to everyone who had to move out of the way, and I noticed that nobody was requesting any photos now.

"Do stuffed dogs bite? I'm sure I saw it move," said Swift, her neck now stretched higher than any giraffe I'd ever seen.

Still moving in unison, a pirouette followed, and we clattered away out of the castle grounds. *Well, that went better than expected,* I thought...

Bagpipes and Stuffed Dogs

Blair Castle dates from 1269 and originally consisted of a single tower. The Earl of Atholl owned the land at this time but it was his neighbour, John Comyn (the Lord of Badenoch), who built this tower for himself. Taking advantage of the Earl being away on crusade, he was trying to expand his empire into the adjoining estate. Needless to say, the Lord was evicted from the Atholl Estate on the Earl's return and the Earl quite happily incorporated this 'gift' of a tower into his own castle. It's still known as Comyn's Tower to this day.

Over the years the castle was expanded and redesigned, the décor and style influenced by the tastes and fashions of the time. It eventually emerged in its present form in the 1870's and hasn't change drastically since. Bonnie Prince Charlie of course stayed there several times throughout the Jacobite uprisings, but it was a visit from Queen Victoria in 1844 that left behind a unique claim to fame.

The Queen granted permission for establishment of the Atholl Highlanders, a private army with a singular purpose to protect the Earl. They remain to this day, the only private army in Europe (but please note – this is a pre-Brexit claim).

Team Swogi calmed as we left the castle by the long tree-lined driveway. Deep in thought about their close escape of potentially being stuffed or converted into musical instruments, they didn't even look up when several tourist coaches thundered past. I checked my map and took the first left turn, heading through some trees. We had just over one kilometre to go now, and this track through the trees would deposit us (I hoped) back on the road being resurfaced earlier - but on the other side of the workings.

My expectation was correct, and we arrived at the road next to another large, red 'Road Closed' sign indicating that the left option was a no-go zone. I directed Yogi to the right, away from it, and onwards to our field for the night. Our field was situated on the edge of the Old Bridge of Tilt and had been donated in fair exchange for a contribution to the church roof fund.

The Lude Estate had kindly welcomed us to stay for the night and had even mowed a patch of ground within the knee-height grass of the larger field. This service was most appreciated by someone who was travelling with a Cushing's horse, and suggested they knew the ins and outs of a horse's digestive system. I assumed, therefore, they wouldn't mind the numerous deposits of 'outs' that would appear in their field by morning.

I jumped off Yogi, untacked them both, piled the bags at the edge of the shorter grass, and set about constructing the corral. As always during construction, I left the horses to mooch about, grazing with the length of their lead ropes trailing along the ground. Generally this system worked well, as if they wandered away they'd eventually stand on the lead rope and stop themselves from straying too far.

I hadn't considered that they might stray too close though, as that had never been a problem before. So I was astonished to find myself wiped out from behind by the electric tape hitting me across my knees. The astonishment continued to build at a hasty rate, as I was pulled along the grass, behind a rather alarmed Bear!

As I accelerated across the ground, I tried to work out how this unusual situation arose, and more importantly - how I might extract myself from it. Yogi had obviously stepped over the tape mid corral assembly, snagged the tape around his hoof boots, and it was not letting go. Taking a fleeting glance over my shoulder, I could see that Swift was safe and well out of this tangle. I on the other hand was in the midst of it all, and was rapidly gathering grass stains on the back of my jodhpurs as I was dragged along.

"Whoa!" I shouted. "Whoa!"

Never have I more appreciated this voice command that I'd trained both horses to do, and had reinforced time and time again. Yogi stopped dead, but spun around to face me, tangling himself more in the tape. I knew I wouldn't have long before the effect of the command wore off and I sprang to my feet to grab his lead rope – despite my two burning calves.

Yogi was in two minds; I could see it in his fearful face. He wanted to run from this scary white tape, but also wanted to 'Whoa'. He also knew that in all likelihood a human would be required to unpick him from his pickle. I ran my hand down his neck and repeated the command in a soothing voice to try and keep him still.

Keeping hold of the end of the lead rope, I reached round his ample behind and unhooked the tape from his heels.

Phew! I thought. That had been a close call. On every trip, no matter how experienced you are, you always learn something new. Especially with unpredictable horses as your tutor. This would be chalked up as another bad judgement, turned into a worthwhile learning experience. Leaving the lead ropes on had proved to be a sensible move, but never again would I leave hoof boot removal until after the corral was built.

Yogi was quivering a little but otherwise fine. The tape hadn't caused any cuts on his heels, and now that it was removed from his boots he was keen to return to the grass. I was fine too, apart from a few grass-stains and possibly bruised legs. However, my heart was beating fast, and an adrenaline rush like this wasn't exactly what my cardiologist had recommended.

I led both Yogi and Swift well away from the corral area, removed their boots, and kept a much closer eye on them this time as I ran the electric tape around my portable poles to create a sizeable grazing space. It was only mid-afternoon, and they'd need plenty of nibbling to keep them entertained until morning.

Once they were safely contained, I pitched my tent and in its private quarters lowered my jodhpurs to view the extent of the damage that I could feel behind my knees. As expected, a mass of purple bruising was already forming at an alarming rate. Still, I supposed, at least *both* calves were an achy matching pair now.

I knew Team Swogi would be thirsty after today's travel as it had been sometime since we'd found any reachable or suitable water. Our host had mentioned that they'd drop off some containers of fresh water, but I'd obviously arrived earlier than expected, as these hadn't yet been delivered. Never feeling comfortable until all Team Swogi's needs are met, I tentatively set off towards the loud rumble of a river I could hear, hidden behind the trees at the edge of the field.

The river was rumbling for a reason as it crashed and splashed its way through a deep gorge with shear sides that prevented any way down. I attempted instead to descend to the depths of a tributary, but after nearly sliding in, I decided there had been more than enough excitement for one day and Team Swogi would just have to wait.

Luckily, they didn't have to wait long and when I returned, as promised, two large containers of water were delivered by Andrew (the owner of the estate). As Swift got stuck into her sploosh-splash routine that precedes a long slurp, I politely enquired about a free refill service as it might be required. I have to confess to feeling a little awkward, asking on Swift's behalf, as I was slightly taken aback by this personal service, delivered by the Laird himself.

However, nothing seemed too much trouble and he was kind enough to not mention my dishevelled, grass-stained state. I thanked him for putting us up and we chatted for a while about horses and my circumnavigational plans. As he turned to leave, I was wished a safe onwards journey and welcomed back anytime.

All horse needs now met, I settled in for the evening and cooked dinner, but not totally at ease. The field was overlooked by several houses in the village, and despite being made welcome by the Laird himself, I wasn't accustomed to wild camping in such an un-wild setting.

I'm a strong believer of a 'leave no trace' policy, and tonight this felt more imperative than ever. I also felt I should apply a second policy of 'remain unnoticed', so I tip-toed around my little camp as quietly as I could. The evening was still early, but since it had started to rain, I said goodnight to Yogi and Swift, then retired to my tiny tent.

Three Bald Kings

Day 4: Old Blair to Loch Crannach (Distance 24km, Ascent 824m)

I opened the tent in the morning to find that we'd have an overcast start, but it looked as though it might brighten up later as the clouds weren't amassing in a rain-threatening way. I cooked my porridge and looked forward to today's ride, a beautiful route with incredible mountain views (so long as the clouds lifted) and a tranquil camp at the end of the day.

I was trying to make the day sound easy and appealing, but with limited time to recce, there were a few unknowns to come. I knew the start was fine, and the finish too, but another long-distance rider had suggested that a river crossing in the middle might be a little tricky. Taking a deep breath, I focussed on the present.

Yogi was happily munching in the far corner of the corral, seeking out any remaining morsels that he'd missed in the last sixteen hours. Swift, however, had already given up on the corral's contents and was concentrating instead on what could be reached outwith.

She was standing before me, with her head stretched over the electric tape as far as she dared, and was pleading for porridge with deep, soulful eyes that followed my every move. The steady tick of the corral's energiser was loud enough to hear, but the risk of a shock was one worth taking, apparently, as far as oats were concerned. Her soft nostrils vibrated gently - the snuffles offered as fair swap for slurps of my spoon.

"No chance gal, you've still got plenty of grass left for *your* breakfast!"

Tempted as I was to go and sit somewhere less scrutinised to eat my breakfast, the surrounding soaking wet grass full of dew wasn't that appealing. I stayed where I was and tried to ignore Swift's begging behaviour as I scraped every ounce of oats from the bottom of the pan. I washed up, packed my stove away, and after temporarily misplacing my spork, I realised that camp deconstruction would have to be done with care today, to not lose items in the thick carpet of grass.

I took the tarp down first and laid it on the ground dry side up, then as each dry bag was filled with its designated contents, I placed them there. Neat rows formed, laid out with military precision, and ordered by saddle bag position. Left side of Swift here. Right side of Yogi there. I stood by the end of the tarp with everything present and accounted for – "Ready for inspection, sir!" I was confident that this approach had left no essential items lost in the grass, but I hadn't realised that it would recruit additional troops. Packing the saddle bags, I dismissed a dozen slugs who had joined forces to try to mount their charge.

Slipping headcollars on, I tacked up then let Team Swogi think they'd escaped the corral. The grass outside would taste sweeter this way and it might sweeten Swift's mood, as she was seriously sulky, still holding a grudge over uneven distribution of grain. Learning from yesterday, I'd left hoof boots off for now, as my calves were still smarting from the mistake and my pride was too. Any failure can make you feel a little unwise, but more foolish still would be to let the lesson slip by.

As I hobbled around, deconstructing the corral, I mumbled appreciation to my sturdy leather boots and chaps that were keeping my feet and lower legs dry. The chaps were apologetically rubbing on the bruises borne from yesterday's bind however, which were now a beautiful blend of purples and reds, with a little hint of yellow just beginning to appear. I anticipated that for me today, walking should be kept to a bare minimum.

Regardless, after hoof boot application, I set out beside Team Swogi as usual, to make sure we were all warmed up and that bags were staying where they should. The start of the day was on a small tarmac road, leading to Loch Moraig and a route into the hills behind. As the road began to steepen, Yogi increased his pace, so I led him over to a fallen tree at the side of the road and jumped on.

I couldn't enjoy the comforts of saddle and the leg rest for long though, as just around the next corner was a cattle grid, and its side-gate proved too difficult to open from above. The gate wasn't hanging well and needed to be lifted, but the bigger challenge was the wire bound tightly round it, alongside a complex knot in a length of blue rope.

As my battle with the gate commenced, I was frequently interrupted, not by impatient horses, but by vehicles driving passed. The road was much busier than expected, and since the verges were narrow, Team Swogi filled the road. Squeezing their bulk past several cars was beginning to take its toll, and as the next car rattled the grid, it rattled their nerves too. We were all wound up just as tightly as the wire around the gate.

Finally, through and on our way again, we were sheltered from a breeze by woodland to our right and admired views over to Glen Tilt to the left. In another kilometre I spied a mound with a stone on top and since the team had stepped off the road to let another car past, I pointed Yogi up to it to take a closer look. It was a memorial stone – *"To commemorate the raising of the royal standard and to honour the courage of Montrose and those who loyally fought alongside him."*

Montrose (James Graham the 1st Marquess who lived 1612-1650) initially favoured resistance to the rule of King Charles I in Scotland, but he swapped allegiance and became a Royalist as the Wars of the Three

Kingdoms developed. These wars between Parliamentarians and Royalists were violent protests against Charles I who attempted to apply the same religious policies all across the United Kingdom.

He granted a large amount of power to bishops, imposed taxes without consulting parliament, and even dissolved them from time to time, believing as he did in the divine right of kings (basically that the rule of a king was God's will, and any objections may constitute a sacrilegious act). The argument was always more about power than religion, but ill-feeling rapidly rose surrounding the King's Catholic tendencies and the political authority King Charles had given to the bishops.

Montrose, a key player in all this warfare, is remembered for his spectacular victories. He often took his opponents by surprise with a tactical brilliance still admired by military personnel today. In the end, Montrose had backed the wrong side as the Parliamentarians eventually emerged triumphant. King Charles I was found guilty of high treason by parliament and was beheaded in 1649, followed not long after by Montrose who was hung, drawn, and quartered.

Oliver Cromwell became Lord Protector of a united commonwealth of England, Scotland, and Ireland, but only for around a decade. After Cromwell's death, with politics in crisis once again, Charles II in 1660 was invited to come back from France (where he was hiding in exile) to take the throne. The earlier victory of the Parliamentarians paved the way for Britain to develop into the constitutional monarchy we know today.

The breeze was beginning to blow the clouds away and sunshine was intermittently poking through. I could hear numerous lambs bleating away, desperately trying to find their mums in amongst a swathe of same-coloured wool. They'd just moved fields and it sounded like a frustrating process for my fellow Aries to unravel. From only twenty-four hours after birth, lambs rely predominantly on voice differentiation to recognise their mums, focussing on timbre, amplitude, and frequency. In a field full of calling comrades all doing the same, the confusion would last a while.

Accompanied by their calls, we soon arrived at the next cattle grid and my heart sank at the collection of gates next to it. Why fill the gap with one well hung gate when you can fill it with three over-lapping, tied together by wire and rope? *Sigh!* As I jumped off again to untangle the mess, Yogi and Swift enjoyed clearing the grass at the side of the road. Thankfully the earlier traffic had subsided now, and they were left in peace to trim the verge.

There was a large herd of cattle on the other side of the gates so I could understand perhaps why the farmer wanted to make them so hard to open in such a popular spot. However, most walkers and mountain bikers would just use the cattle grid and not open the gates beside (potentially leaving them insecure). They certainly had no insecurity issues now, busy as they were performing a Fort Knox impression.

Feeling some empathy with the field of sheep, it took me some time to untangle the confused combination and as I removed the last piece of twisted wire, the three gates all fell to the ground in a heap. Not one of them was hung on a hinge and two of them were extremely heavy - these of course were the two that were most in the way.

Struggling, I dragged the two gates to the side and led Team Swogi through. I just hoped that the cattle didn't stampede, collecting Yogi and Swift up in their excitement, whilst I was distracted by rebuilding the fortress. It doesn't take much excuse for young cows to have a romp and two horses eating their grass would probably be enough.

My frustrations continued as it took a while to re-position the gates, balance them so they didn't fall, then secure them closed with the wire and rope. I found a more efficient design, so didn't replace all the tie-points I'd undone, but it would still be difficult for the next rider through. I hoped though that they wouldn't lose the thirty minutes it had taken me.

"Personally, I enjoyed that gate," mumbled Yogi, with his mouth full of lush grass.

"Those thistles right next to it were particularly tasty," agreed Swift.

The cattle showed excitement as we continued along, but kept their frolicking at a polite enough distance for Swift and Yogi to remain indifferent. The bellows and snorts weren't quite in harmony with the sheep's bleats, still audible from across the valley, but their bouncing hooves provided an interesting rhythm to accompany the discordant refrain. Despite the racket, it was nice to think that our passing presence had somewhat brightened the cattle's day.

I knew it was a strong probability that on the far side of the cows there'd be another cattle grid and, as predicted, in less than another kilometre we reached it. This side-gate wasn't possible to open from up top either, despite Yogi being an efficient gate opener these days (after many years of training). It was at least hung on hinges, had an easy bolt mechanism, and only required a hard shove-lift manoeuvrer to swing it open. However, this on and off wasn't helping my sore calves any and as the next gate wasn't far away, I decided to stay on my feet.

The unofficial carpark next to Loch Moraig was filled with the cars and vans that had passed earlier in the day and it was an easy deduction that the hills would be busy with walkers. Our route, staying relatively low in the glens, was unlikely to be their focus, so I anticipated a quiet trail as we left the tarmac road behind at the next gate. Loch Moraig, an artificial loch, is dammed at its south end to create a stretch of water from what used to be marshland. Its waters were dark and still, and the edges ill-defined as it shallowed to meet the land around it in a haphazard way.

As we sauntered up the trail, tall pine trees hid the loch from view and my focus turned to the remains of an old settlement (Cean na Moine) on our right. A lighter pattern of tufty grass clearly marked where the walls of the township used to stand. There were four post-medieval farmsteads in this area comprising of thirty-two buildings, several enclosures, and six kilns - indicating a once thriving community. Gradually depopulated, only one of the farmsteads, 'Ruidh Moraig', hung on in existence until around 1867.

Spying a lone stone by the side of the trail, no doubt once part of a farmstead's wall, I used it as a mounting block to clamber back up onto Yogi. Gathered together, I took a moment to admire the scene down over Loch Moraig which from this angle was now again in view.

In the foreground the grass was speckled with yellow flowers, the midground was dappled with white sheep, and the slopes prior to the loch were dotted with the brown backs of cattle. The loch's flat surface reflected the shapes of the clouds and rising from its far shores were bright green hills. Darker tree-covered hills followed before the grand finale of the higher mountains hiding in haze behind.

Pulling away from this beauty, we continued up the trail and the sharp, triangular form of the Munro, Carn

Liath, powerfully filled our view. Flecks of bright-coloured walkers freckled the wide and obvious path to the peak. This path looked steep but was perfectly passable by horse and I knew Yogi would love its upness.

"We're not going up that thing now, are we?" said Swift, as she came to an abrupt standstill in protest.

"Not today, my love, but it is logged as a possible Munro for the future."

"Hmph! I'll sit that one out thanks," Swift stated, swishing her tail to underline her point.

Convincing her to move forward on the flatter trail of the glen, I could see yet another gate ahead and was dreading another predicted tangle of rope and wire. I could also see three people who were approaching this gate too, so I urged Team Swogi up a gear, to arrive there at the same time as them. The walkers were quite surprised by horses appearing so suddenly behind them, so we waited politely while they recovered and also unlatched the gate.

The usual questions arose: what was I doing? Where was I going? Was I doing this alone? What on earth were the horses wearing on their feet? As I answered all the questions, Yogi and Swift took full advantage of yet another snack break.

Explanations complete and curiosity contented, we mooched through the gate and the walkers closed it behind. Kindly letting us set off first, so as not to hinder our faster progress, I was a little embarrassed when Swift and Yogi both stopped for a long drink at the next ford only a short way from the gate. It appeared that the frequent stops due to difficult gates had created a rather relaxed attitude within the team today, so I invited the walkers to splash their way around us.

Yogi was enjoying the cool of the water on his toes and the warmth of the sun on his bum. The sky had settled on a mix of bright blue patches encircled by fluffy white clouds and as I raised my face to the warmth, I hoped it was here to stay. The brown peaty stream seemed to glow red in the light, and with Yogi's reflection a bright orange too, it looked like his coat had gone through a hot wash and was running its colours into the waters below. We both giggled as he lifted his white left fore and said, "I think you might be right!"

Hot Wash and Running Colours

Swift was savouring the sweet, fresh taste of her last big slurp of the stream. Her lips pursed to hold it in, and her eyes glazed in full appreciation. I love how she always holds this last intake in her mouth for what seems like an age before it disappears down in a huge swallow, the descending gulp visible for the full length of her long, slender neck.

Eventually moving on and after another two kilometres, we arrived at a bend in the track that signified the start of the descent to cross the river I'd been warned about. The falling track gradually grew a heathery centre, and reaching its end, the river crossing didn't appear as complex as I'd been led to believe. Finding the trail on the other side, however, was looking rather problematic. There were numerous tiny trails up through the heather, leading in a wide variety of directions, none apparently brave enough to strongly proclaim the principal role.

According to the map, after climbing this eastward slope, we were supposed to meet a wider track aligned in a north to south direction. In theory then, if we went up through the heather on any of the tiny trails, we should dissect the wider track, somewhere along its length.

"Up did you say?" said Yogi, gleefully, and set off not caring if there was a trail to follow or not.

Bashing through the heather was hard work, as the thin trail we'd started on soon ran out and the day was getting hotter with more blue sky than cloud. Thankfully, the higher we climbed the more of a cooling breeze was found and eventually our upward progression was dissected in the predicted direction by an obvious path crossing the slope. I found a patch of grass and jumped off to let the horses rest, while I grabbed a bite to eat and admired the view we were to have for the traverse along the side of the glen.

To our left now were the three prominent peaks of the Beinn A'Ghlo range (Mountain of Mist). Luckily, today the clouds had lifted and there was no mist in sight to hide the glorious summits of Braigh Coire Chruinn-bhalgain (Corrie of Round Blisters), Airgoid Bheinn (Silver Mountain), and Carn nan Gabhar (Cairn of the Goats). The range included Carn Liath (Grey Peak), which we'd passed earlier, making a full circuit of Munros for the fit and able.

The range covers twenty-four square kilometres, includes around eighteen corries, three Munros, and numerous secondary peaks. Designated a Special Area of

Conservation and a Site of Special Scientific Interest, its slopes and peaks foster a wide variety of rare alpine and marshland plants.

Viewing those slopes and peaks, the stony grey tops perched above the angled bases of vibrant purple heather made the mountains look like three wise (but bald) kings. They were dressed in velvet-robed splendour and appeared ready to hold council to the court in the glen below.

My imaginary kings weren't the only royal connection to this part of Scotland, as Mary Queen of Scots is reputed to have hunted here. On one occasion she famously caused the death of several beaters, by allegedly releasing her hunting hounds too early in the process and causing the deer to stampede over the men.

Queen Victoria was also a visitor, and viewing the mountain range from Glen Tilt in 1844 wrote, "We came upon a lovely view — Beinn a' Ghlò straight before us — and under these high hills the River Tilt gushing and winding over stones and slates ... and the air so pure and fine but no description can do it justice."

I agreed with the Queen's opinion, as my attempt to compare the scene to three majestic kings wasn't attributing enough credit to the magnificent panorama ahead. Nevertheless, I would undoubtedly enjoy the Monarch's company as we followed the ancient trail through to the next glen.

The track for a while was narrow and peaty with loose rocks, so I left Swift to follow us along at her own pace, leading Yogi up front. Undulating along the side of the hill, we were offered a spectacular perspective of the three bald kings on the other side of the glen. Yogi's usual up-hill enthusiasm was in full play, and our abrupt and clattering arrival at the top of a rise promptly disturbed a flock of recently shorn sheep.

Their newly exposed coats were dazzling in the sunshine, like the 'pure brilliant white' proclaimed on many tins. I've never seen a 'Shorn-Sheep White' advertised by paint manufacturers, but if based on the sight before me they could promise a blinding shade. Shocked by their recent salon visit (and our sudden appearance), the quivering flock looked a little chilly in the strong breeze despite the warmth of the sun. As they scattered off the track, waving curly white flags of surrender behind, I considered that at least the stampede we'd caused might warm them up.

Moving through the parting strands of wool, the trail zigzagged then straightened again at a sadly demised member of the flock. This poor sheep, reduced to an exposed skull and prominent ribs, had possibly achieved a greater significance in death than in life - just another number when roaming the hills, she now was an important trail marker for me. Found during my recce from this side of the glen, I knew that from here the path would widen and become easier under foot. Paying respects, I jumped back on, gathered up Swift, and continued under the watchful eyes of the king's court to descend to the ruin of Ruigh-Chuilein – the remains of one of the seven sheilings of Loch Loch.

Now, Loch Loch isn't the most imaginative of names, but since it dwells in Glen Loch, I guess it didn't stand much chance at being awarded a grander title. The loch has a constriction in the middle dividing it in two, so perhaps 'a loch there' and 'a loch over there' would have been shortened regardless of where it lived.

Aside from the most unimaginative title, in more recent times the loch has a much gloomier claim to fame. On 27th May 1993, an RAF Hercules on a training exercise is thought to have stalled its engines at a height too low for recovery and the plane crashed near its waters. Unfortunately, all nine servicemen were killed.

As though to emphasise the sadness of this spine-shivering thought, a singular dark cloud appeared overhead and began to release its rain. I hadn't realised that mournful thoughts could precisely change the weather, but all around the skies were merry and bright. Overshadowed, we followed the trail round to the right in a more southerly direction to arrive at Daldhu and a junction of trails. The doleful cloud followed too.

Here, as we entered Gleann Fearnach (Valley of the Alder Trees, now often shortened to Glenfernate), we joined an ancient drovers' route linking Kirkmichael in the south to Deeside in the north, connecting through Glen Tilt. The tryst (or market) at Kirkmichael was thought to be one of the biggest in Scotland in the mid, 18th century, with various drove roads converging at the village. The drove road from Glen Tilt was certainly in high use in the mid, 18th century as William Roy included the route on his Military Map following his survey of 1747-1755.

Roy, a respected draughtsman, was tasked with surveying the land by embarrassed Hanoverian commanders in Scotland, who regularly got lost due to a lack of detailed topography. Not only would the resulting map aid the movement of troops, but it would also be the basis for the continued construction of a connected road network linking forts and military strongholds.

Roy was a strong believer in accuracy and regularly promoted triangulation of the whole of Britain. Finally, his perseverance won through and when Jesse Ramsden designed a new three-foot theodolite, they together underpinned the Trigonometrical Survey of Great Britain in 1791 (completed a year after Roy's death). This later became the Ordnance Survey that we know and love today and something I strongly rely on for navigation in the hills.

Shortly after leaving Daldhu, the rough gravel road crossed the river and Swift signalled with a bob of her head and a point of her nose that she'd like to take a drink. I found a way down the banks at the side of the bridge for both horses to drink their fill for a second time today. The black cloud joined us and hovered above, continuing to contribute to the refreshing waters below. It waited patiently for its new friends to finish their slurps but the slurping soon moved on to munching, and Swift had her head buried in a tuft of grass.

"Look, I'm an Irish Cob," she giggled, lifting her head and modelling an Imperial Moustache made of sheep's wool. She flounced around with the wool stuck to her top lip, looking very pleased with herself indeed.

"Can you see it, Yogi, can you?" she said, bobbing her head near his face.

"Fool!" he replied, rolling his eyes, but I could feel his ribs chuckle a little underneath me.

I enjoyed a moment of reflection back to a time only three years ago, when the sight of sheep's wool lying on the ground would bring Swift to a juddering halt. Certainly not scared of it now, it was a sign of how much she had matured - well to a point I supposed, as she was still acting the clown.

With roughly another six kilometres still to go, I guided Team Swogi over the bridge and onwards down the glen. We tiptoed away from our new companion, leaving the cloud sadly snoozing over the bridge which was now shadowed by its presence. Away from the cloud the skies were blue, and it looked set to be a lovely evening. Already anticipating a scenic and serene camp by the side of Loch Crannach whatever the weather, the sunshine would certainly enrich the occasion.

The private glen road stayed close to the river, the Allt Fearnach, as we ambled along. Its waters glistened in the afternoon sun as their long journey to join the mighty River Tay began, via the Ardle, the Ericht, and then the Isla which joined the Tay near Coupar Angus. It's no surprise that with such a vast catchment area (approximately 5,200km2), the River Tay is the longest river in Scotland and it's the largest in the UK in terms of volume, too.

As we crossed the river to travel along its opposite bank, it was tempting to head straight up the grassy hill ahead. This would provide a short-cut to camp, but the threat of a fence that might block our way checked my venturesome inclination. Sensing some discontent below me, I reassured Yogi that he'd still have a climb to finish the day if we stuck to the trail instead. He wasn't disappointed, as turning left at Crannach House the trail increased its gradient all the way to the lochside, and Yogi enjoyed this finale of the trail, striding out with his usual uphill passion.

Unpacking the bags and untacking the horses (removing the hoof boots first this time), I was delighted to find remnants of a fence close to the loch that could be used to help construct a corral. It made for a sizeable area for the horses to enjoy, by just closing some gaps with lengths of my electric tape. If the breeze dropped, Team Swogi could be in for a midge-maddening night this close to still water and allowing them room to move would make them much more comfortable.

As always, I saw to the horse's needs first with a brush, a fly-rug, water, and a feed each, before making my own camp which I assembled down by the water's edge. The grass all around was lengthy despite evidence of recent sheep grazing, but here had the shortest I could find. I'd have to be more wary of ticks tonight, in my nightly tick-checking routine, as they are often more concentrated in numbers in the territory of sheep. Beside my pitch were two handy trees for hanging up my tarp and I tucked all equipment underneath it that wasn't required until morning.

Dinner cooked and appetite only partially satisfied, as often in the evening, I had itchy feet. Despite my aching calves and the serene view in front of me, I felt too restless to just sit. I grabbed my camera and set off towards a boathouse situated on the north-west side. Strolling along the water's edge, I took delight in the glistening sparkles formed by the sun's reflections and admired the artistic patterns - shaped by the breeze and highlighted by the sun - as the ripples approached the bank.

Sitting for a while on the boathouse veranda, I tried to settle myself here instead - but to no avail. My mind strongly argued that there was still discovering to be done, so I set off on a walk around the loch. With no path, I negotiated my own way slowly, through long grass, lumpy ground, and over a few fallen trees.

I rarely feel truly present when sitting still, as my mind tends to wander and worry away from the here and now. That's why I love long days on the trail and the rhythm of the horse's movement as it keeps me focussed. Movement and the physical effort that comes with it is my way to truly feel part of it all, to feel at one with nature and wilderness.

Motion fills me with a sense of purpose and a fluidity, like a burn flowing down a glen. The physical effort expended to reach somewhere, to the top of a hill or end of a pass, grounds me. If a location has been reached with ease, say by motorised means, I find myself looking in through a window; the view obscured by the mist of my breath on the glass. That sense of connection, belonging, and presence is not attained by such a brief encounter. In *my* heart and soul, the harmony and the oneness must be acquired by physical effort.

Feeling more at peace, and with curiosity a little more satisfied, I arrived back at camp and waved to a lone fisherman who'd set himself up off to my right. *Another person on a solo endeavour,* I thought to myself. Sitting by the loch, sipping from my hip flask, I watched the sun's reflections, gave into my wandering mind, and experienced a few reflections of my own.

Going solo can at first be intimidating, but it also evokes a sense of freedom, flexibility, and independence. When things go well, self-belief grows, as does the feeling of empowerment. Your success (or failure) is yours alone, it's down to you and your own physical and mental efforts to reach the top of a hill, progress through a tricky glen, or complete the intended distance. It's a lone responsibility, finding your individual capability and how you manage the challenges faced. As you undertake trials and errors, you do so alone without feedback or critique. Only you can unravel the puzzles to benefit from lessons learned. Solitary lessons are often harder to take, but as a result they tend to be more significant and memorable.

There is, however, only a small step between solitude and loneliness and going solo can be a lonely undertaking, not just when the chips are down (a problem shared is a problem halved after all) but when times are good, too. As Charlotte Bronte once wrote, "Happiness quite unshared can scarcely be called happiness; it has no taste."

Now, I'm not sure I totally agreed with this thought, as I was quite happy with the taste from my hip flask and it was nice not to have to share that. I did, however, understand what she meant, and it had taken me a long while to become comfortable with solo travel. Particularly to be content with only myself for company and with no opportunity to spontaneously share any discovered delights.

Before long-distance horse travel, I'd never have dreamed of heading up into the hills on my own on a backpacking excursion. There was perhaps a lack of self-confidence back then, but I also considered it a lonely, strange, and potentially uninspiring thing to do. Having equines as companions had taught me a different view. They are *the* best tutors for teaching self-awareness, patience, living in the moment, and development of an inner-calm. Through them I'd become more comfortable in my own skin, happy in my own thoughts, and perhaps a little more introvert than I used to be. I don't consider this to be a particularly bad thing and I don't feel the need to apologise for my enjoyment of solitude.

Solo travel is grounding, it's releasing, and there's a sense of freedom as you lose yourself in time. Time spent fascinated by bubbles in a pond, the tinkles and turns of a stream, or the sound of a bird's cry. I love that it's just me, on my own with nature as I peacefully fit in, and that there's no external intrusion. I also don't get overheard talking to my horses and putting voices in their heads...

A quote from Paulo Coelho's *Manuscript Found in Accra* sums it up nicely: "If you are never alone, you cannot know yourself." I was finding that my alone self (at least alone with Yogi and Swift) was generally more at peace than when in the company of society's stresses and strains. Also, sometimes more at peace (but not always) than when exploring wild places with those I love. I do enjoy travelling with others, there is more warmth to the experience, but when travelling by oneself

I find more mindfulness, more living in the moment, and a deeper connection with surroundings.

Don't get me wrong - on my own, I couldn't fully block out the future or the fear of the unknown for the days ahead, but those worries through the day are fleeting, they normally bother my brain more at night. That's possibly why I feel restless upon reaching camp and go off exploring the place, to take me back to the present with appreciation of the here and now. The bright flash of colour from a flower, the ripple of grass in the breeze, or the shadows and shapes formed by sunlight flickering through trees as I keep moving to see what I can find to pull me back into focus.

During the day, if my mind should wander to concerns ahead, I am brought back to the present more easily by the next step of the horses' feet. Negotiating my way through soft ground, rough rocks or through streams gives enough challenge to be fully immersed in the present and provides a release from future concerns or past reflections.

When solo, there's no need to check in with travel companions as there's no one to defer to, and no reason to be reminded of memories or future matters as there's no one to distract you. With a human fellow traveller, even moving in companionable, mutual silence, I tend to think ahead more or think towards them as I consider their needs and feelings. I obviously have that to a certain extent with my equine companions, but we have such a deep connection from living and breathing together 24/7 that they feel like an extension of me, so although 'us' it still feels like 'I'.

I know from experience that it's not just humans who think the grass is always greener on the other side, but horses do have less concern for the past and less ambition for the future (so long as they have a few basic needs met in the present). They often cope well without companionship too, whereas humans are encouraged to seek out others, almost as a primeval need. To be solitary is viewed as lonely, rather than valuable time spent connecting with self.

Horses are creatures who unquestionably live for the moment and who don't complicate life by searching for a better one. I am incredibly grateful that Yogi and Swift are showing me how to come along for the ride.

All Trussed Up

Day 5: Loch Crannach to Glenshee (Distance 31km, Ascent 696m)

I awoke early, knowing that today was a longer one on the trail. Breakfast was devoured on the shores of the loch, well away from Swift's prying eyes. With complete stillness and no whiff of a breeze, the waters were a dreamy blend of mirrored swirling clouds, rich rocky reflections, and infinite layers, depending on where you focused. It was hard not to get drawn into its depths. Pulling myself away, the usual tacking up and packing up routine flowed nicely and was bang on schedule with just the corral to take down. Least that shouldn't take too long this morning, aided as it was by the fence-line found last night.

Crack! "Aah! Barnacles!" I shouted, as I sprung back from the fence in surprise, or more accurately, shock!

While I shook the sizzle from my hand, both horses looked up and I looked down in complete puzzlement at the energiser sitting at my feet. There was a moment of stunned stupor as I checked and doubled checked the on/off switch. I'm not sure why that was my first reaction, as I'd already disconnected it from the fence several minutes ago. I can only put it down to the fact that I wasn't fully awake yet, despite the jolt I'd just received.

It's amazing how your mind plays tricks with you during the element of surprise. *That fence couldn't actually have shocked me, could it? The wire can't be live,* I thought.

"Ouch! Balderdash!" *Well, shut the front door, IT IS*! I discovered this as I tried a second attempt to remove my wire tape from the wooden post it was attached to.

Yogi by now was looking a little alarmed at my shouts and jumps, whilst Swift was looking on with interest ... sniggering.

“This could be fun viewing, Yogi, and worth a pause in breakfast,” she whispered, giving him a gentle dig in the ribs with her nose.

I was still extremely confused. Yesterday, I’d set the fence up with no shock in sight, so where was the source? My tape was attached to wood at both ends which shouldn’t conduct much anyway. This just didn’t make any sense. It also didn’t make it easy to release Team Swogi from their confines to continue with today’s travels.

With my hands safely behind my back, I explored the wooden posts to either side of my line of tape. These posts did have a thick wire attached which ran along the main part of the fence, but my tape was spaced well away from this. I assumed this wire was now live, but that didn’t provide explanation as to why mine was too. On closer inspection I discovered the posts were freckled with numerous metal staples and with the wood being a little damp, this could produce a current flow I supposed, so I set off to find its origin.

The strength of shocks received felt like a direct connection to the grid (being on the melodramatic side), but the nearest house was half a mile away and the fact I was still standing suggested otherwise. I searched for a field battery towards the Boat House, then again in the other direction to a small dam. The power of the shock, I assumed, was to deal with insulated woolly sheep. I also assumed that to generate such oomph, it wouldn’t be a particularly small source, but despite my desperate search, I completely drew a blank.

Swift followed my movements closely as I arrived back at the tape line. She was slowly chewing a long straw of grass sticking out from the side of her mouth, and with her front legs crossed, was casually leaning her shoulder on Yogi.

"Would you like some popcorn to enhance your entertainment experience?" I asked.

Searching around for a couple of sticks, I came up with a tentative plan. With a habit of always tying quick release knots anywhere around horses, I hoped I might be able to release my tape without using my hands. I could still feel the zap through the sticks, but nothing like before and managed to undo the first knot with success and only the odd flinch. I tried the same at the other end.

"Boo!" Swift shouted, with a cheeky grin on her face.

"Arrrh! Don't do that, that's mean," I exclaimed, with my hand on my already dicky ticker.

Shocking Entertainment

The second knot was more of a struggle, and I had to stick my tongue out to the side of my mouth to get it to release. I was feeling very pleased with myself as the knot gave way (Swift looked a little disappointed), until the tape dropped to become jammed between post and live wire. "Doh!" A poke with a stick wouldn't suffice, this was a *suck-it-up* kind of situation. Still ... least it gave Swift a satisfying start to her day.

Finally on our way, I couldn't believe how much time the tricky task had taken, and our schedule was now considerably behind. Not that this should matter when undertaking solo quests, but today we had a place to be by lunchtime to meet up with a friend (Leanne) who was going to walk with us for the afternoon. As we descended the glen, I knew I was going to have to face my nemesis to compensate for the delayed departure.

We would soon emerge on the A924 through Straloch, which linked Kirkmichael to Pitlochry. Not the busiest of roads, but still a risky undertaking as far as I was concerned as it was only just wide enough to have earned its 'A' status. I hated riding horses in today's impatient traffic, so had arranged a diversion through the grounds of Straloch House to avoid most of it. Whilst this was only one and a half kilometres more, it would add a lot of time with numerous gates to open, particularly at the shepherd's house, where I'd not been made overly welcome on my recce despite their landlord's decree.

I also knew that if I took this diversion, I'd not be able to refrain from visiting the Clach Mór (the Witch's Stone) which would delay even further. According to legend, the stone had been dropped at the bottom of Glenfernate by the Witch of Badenoch. For a large amount of gold, the witch had agreed to help the Lords of Badenoch (the Comyns) build a castle like no other, one which could never be breached nor destroyed by human hands

Transporting the huge boulder from where she'd sourced it on the Isle of Man, she surprised a hunter by flying high overhead with the boulder wrapped in her apron. He'd cried out with the holy name “Dhia gleidh sinn” (God bless us), breaking her witchy powers, which then broke her apron strings and the boulder crashed to the ground. Apparently, it weighs one thousand tonnes, is twenty feet high and seventy-four feet round, but I couldn’t see it off to the west of the track I was on due to a layer of trees.

The stone wasn’t going anywhere soon, so I made the decision to take the road and dismounted to lead Team Swogi along the tarmac. Keeping my pace up at a gentle jog, we arrived at our turn off in only twenty minutes and with only two car encounters. As I wiped my brow and prepared to remount, I counted my lucky stars - as six motorcycles, two motorhomes, and a rather large road-filling bus zoomed past.

The peace of the track along the River Alder felt more meaningful after facing my main fear and our near miss of the sudden surge in road use. We had woodland to our right and fields to our left that looked out across the river’s bright-green valley. As a dotted-line of trees joined us on the left, obscuring the view a little, we soon arrived at the Kindrogan Field Centre, a beautiful Victorian house now converted to an environmental training centre. Their course repertoire is quite astounding: wildlife observation, plant identification, outdoor adventure, willow basketry, and even, if you wish, tuition on the ancient skill of how to build a coracle.

One kilometre more and we merged with the waymarked Cateran Trail, a circuit one-hundred-and-four kilometres long (or thirty-five if you choose the Minitrail loop). The Catarans, lightly armed and numbered in bands of five to five hundred, terrorised the area around Glenshee in the middle-ages with their cattle thievery. Livestock were of high value in areas where it was hard to make ends meet on marginal farmland, and as the climate became wetter and colder from the early 1300's it made conditions even more tough. To survive, many either stole cattle or drove them to try and eke out a better living.

Kirkmichael, our lunchtime destination, was a crossroads of numerous drovers' roads and one of Scotland's principal cattle markets, so it's no surprise that the Caterans concentrated their efforts here. Records from the Scottish Government of the time list endless complaints about the Cateran Reivers. Old accounts state that they are "more to be dreaded than either wolves and other wild beasts!" and urges lairds "to follow and pursue thame with fire and sword." - suggesting that they should be 'killed on sight'.

Yogi, being the anxious sort, was now on high alert for any such hill bandits hiding in the trees. He picked up his pace through the next woodland and didn't start to slow until out in the open on the approach to Kirkmichael village. We entered the settlement along a narrow backstreet with a row of flower-fronted cottages, cosy-looking and quaint with their colourful floral displays, and arrived at the carpark on the south-east side of the river. Waiting for us there was Leanne with a hot cup of coffee and a large slice of cake, bought from the corner shop and placed invitingly on a picnic table.

I let Team Swogi free to mow the grass at the side of the carpark and went over to give my friend a big hug, reaching around her as I did for that tantalising slice of cake!

"Is it carrot flavour by any chance?" asked Yogi, snuffling my elbow with his nose.

"No, it's coffee and walnut actually," replied Leanne, pulling two apples from the depths of her pockets. "But you didn't think I'd forget you two, did you?"

Yogi and Swift soon had huge grins on their faces and apple juice all down their chins. Not only were they pleased with the treat, but they were delighted to find another human who could also hear them speak.

Before we set off, all refreshed, Leanne introduced me to her dog, Foxy, rescued from the streets of Romania. She was a large, red, hairy-but-wary lab-retriever type cross.

"Only wary of strangers," Leanne assured me, as I was carefully introduced.

Foxy was apparently loving, faithful, and cuddly once you got to know her. She was a stunning looking girl, a happy-go-lucky dog, and appeared excited for a good adventure. I don't think Foxy or Leanne realised quite how far we still had to go before completing our day, but thankfully they both seemed game.

Crossing the bridge over the dark waters of the River Ardle, we took a small track by the side of the hotel then squeezed past two inconsiderately parked cars almost blocking this ancient byway, and onwards into a sunken lane. Holloways (as sunken lanes are also known) are carved out by frequent footfall on an unsurfaced, well-travelled road. It's not certain when this old route linking Kirkmichael to Glenshee came into being, but since weekly markets here were reputed as far back as the early 1500's, it is likely that it was a busy lane back then.

Trees and shrubbery lined both high banks on either side, giving the route a tunnel-like feel. The light at the end emerged in a field and we tracked around its edge. Although this ancient route was well sign-posted from the village, its direction across the fields was vague. I'd fathomed it out on my recce after much toing and froing, but unfortunately had also found two locked gates.

The local estate had been contacted about this inconvenience (for those with four-hooves in particular) and the gamekeeper was due to meet us at the first of them, another reason why I was anxious about my late start this morning. Arriving only ten minutes later than the agreed time, at the first locked gate surrounded by trees in the corner of a field, there was no sign of the keeper. With the trees, there was no breeze, and the clegs were out in force. It was a tortuous and worrying wait while I considered what to do if this were to be a 'no go' due to a 'no show' on the estate's behalf.

Luckily, after only five clegg bites later, the keeper arrived in a noisy All-Terrain Vehicle (ATV), full to the brim with barking dogs. He skidded to a halt and all animals of our now bigger team scattered. Leanne had managed to keep hold of Foxy who was now cowering behind her legs, so while the keeper tended the lock I gathered up my flock as they hadn't scattered far, just to the next patch of tasty grass. I then held Team Swogi tight as we allowed the keeper to start his engine and get on his way back up the hill, before proceeding through the field ourselves. Thankfully, he disappeared over the brow with less speed and flare than he'd arrived with, so all team members remained composed.

It was a tricky ascent to the Craig Dally woods at the top of the hill as the lower slopes were wet, boggy, and severely rutted by cattle's feet. Trying my best to stick to small embankments seemingly scattered around, we zig-zagged our way up the slope and I managed to keep Yogi (with his bog phobia) calm.

I wasn't sure if these levees had been formed by design, like the runrig crofting systems found on the west, but as I progressed I became aware that they seemed to have a regular, almost squared pattern. Whether by accident or design, their existence and the dry route they offered was very much appreciated by all, at every ninety-degree turn.

There were six gates to get through across this series of fields, with only the first and last found locked on my recce, so I was quite surprised to find the keeper waiting at the next unlocked gate at the edge of the woods. He opened it ahead of us and closed it behind, then sped off in his ATV with a wave, leaving a mist of dog hair in his wake.

Negotiating the larger field on the other side of this gate, and the wide boggy ditch it contained, we arrived at the next gate to be treated to a repeat performance. I tried to protest that this level of service really wasn't required, but he'd hear none of it above his engine and the melody of barking from his boot. At the final gate, escorted off the premises (at least that's how it felt), we arrived at Ashintully Castle and paused for a short rest.

The castle dates back to 1583 when it was built as a fortified tower by the Spalding family. It's supposed to have been a scene of murder on many occasions and thus has a haunted reputation. The most prominent ghost in the mix is Green Jean, who was due to inherit the castle and lands. Her uncle, wanting this for himself, killed her (allegedly) and instructed her servant to stuff her up the chimney in the blood-stained green dress she was wearing.

Now I don't believe in ghosts, and I certainly don't believe that a chimney is a well-thought-out place to hide a body, but I do, however, believe another of the castle's claims to fame - that Rob Roy MacGregor was a frequent visitor here. The Wild MacGregors earned their living through cattle reiving and/or offering protection from thieves for a fee, certainly a profitable business in the land of their rivals (or possibly partners in crime) - the Catarans.

As we set off across the final field before the track would lead into the hills, Leanne asked if she could lead Swift. I didn't see why not as Swift was good with dogs and Leanne good with horses. She'd completed a long-distance walk of her own, not all that long ago, with her pony Candy, her Shetland Tinkerbelle, and of course Foxy the dog. Travelling from Speybay to The Royal (Dick) Equine Vets in Edinburgh, a distance of 525 kilometres, to raise money for the charity Equine Grass Sickness Fund.

Equine grass sickness is an illness that unfortunately strikes fast, paralysing the horse's intestines though damage of the nervous system. Despite being recognised and a subject of research since around 1907, the root cause remains unknown. Science points to some sort of toxin found in the ground or grass, but this isn't a certain or sole cause. It's a disease that strikes terror in all horse owners as you can't prevent against an unknown enemy, and with treatment facing the same challenge, even rapid diagnosis often doesn't help. Around 80% of cases prove fatal.

Leanne's pony, Candy is a rarity by being a grass sickness survivor; through a little luck no doubt, but also due to the twenty-four-hour care Leanne administered. The stimulation of human contact is still the mainstay of treatment and Leanne had given it her all, with her efforts mercifully conquering the very slim odds.

The team hadn't taken more than ten strides in their new formation when there was a shrill squeal and a loud thump from behind. I'd never known Swift to kick a dog, but I have to confess, as I turned, I did fear the worst. My heart jumped up to my throat as I peered behind me, but my immediate attention was drawn to the fact that Swift had her face towards Leanne and Foxy and her back feet nowhere near. *Phew!*

Swift, with her ears out to the sides, was looking somewhat confused. She was trying to back out of the situation, but her lead rope was taut around Leanne and Foxy who were trussed up together in an entwined heap on the ground. Adding to the tangle was Foxy's lead providing a constricting wrap of its own, right around Leanne's legs.

Leanne hadn't banged her head but was rather vague about what just happened. We concluded that whatever it was, it had been fast, and exceptionally effective. I left Yogi to graze (often an appropriate anchor), aided the untangle, then helped Leanne to her feet. Swift, usually amused by a human blunder, was too shocked to snigger, but I was having to stifle a giggle or two as I checked all three for any injuries. I was relieved to find that apart from a bruised bum (Leanne's) all emerged unscathed.

Back in an orderly procession we progressed up the pass without further upheaval. Soon the path would fork and rather than follow the (badly) waymarked trail, we'd branch off for a more northly route.

When checking this section out on the recce I'd found the public byway boggy and blocked (for those with hooves) by several stone-dyke walls. Standing disappointed at the time with slightly soggy feet and a shivering Jack Russell – my dog, Tully - I'd scanned the area for an alternative route and had spotted a large group of people with vans and tents on a far hillside. I'd estimated a kilometre and half between us and had set off on a straight-line trajectory towards them.

I knew from having looked at my map that there was an unmarked section between the track that these people were on, to another I could possibly use, but the gap was less than a kilometre in length. I was, therefore, hopeful that the trails might link up on land, as sometimes tiny hill tracks aren't picked up by Ordnance Survey. Assuming the hillside folk were estate workers, they seemed a likely source of local information.

When I'd arrived amongst them, I'd had a hard job in capturing their attention, focussed as they were on excavating several large holes in the ground. It didn't take long to work out that I'd happened upon an archaeological dig of a Pictish theme, and I'd soon forgotten my personal quest, becoming fascinated with what they'd found.

The dig was part of a five-year project to examine the remains of turf, timber, and thatch longhouses, discovered so rarely in Scotland outside of the Western Isles. This sizeable township suggested a permanent settlement, with evidence of rye, barley, and oat production alongside cattle and sheep ownership, and even textile making. Well-preserved on a rough hillside, this site hadn't suffered damage by industrial scale farming so was intact, interesting, and important.

The Picts were a fierce, proud warrior people of the Dark Ages (476 AD – 1000 AD) who defended their land from Roman, Angle, and Viking invasions. Known as Picti (the Painted Ones), here along the banks of the Allt Corra-lairige they'd constructed a dispersed settlement of longhouses on the site of an earlier prehistoric settlement of probable Bronze or Iron Age. No wonder these holes were so deep, with the many layers of history to unravel and record.

Eventually remembering why I was there, I was pointed to someone who knew the area well. He confirmed that although the two tracks I'd detected didn't meet, there was a route through a hill pass between them. He suggested it was well-used by drovers in the past, possibly more than the dyke-strewn southernly route with the byway label. I thanked him as I set off on a new course to explore this hidden alternative through the hills.

Initially, I was disappointed as the end of the first track on the map disappeared into a boggy bowl. Struggling through this was worthwhile though, as on the other side was an amazing wee gully which felt like a special place. It was a tiny cleft through the hill with a rocky base and sides. A vision flooded my mind of a scattered herd of cattle, squeezing together to filter through the gap before spreading out again on the other side, as they were driven to market in days gone by. There was an unlocked gate at the top and I explored downhill to make sure I could meet the proper track on the other side, which actually reached further upslope than the map suggested.

About to return triumphant in recce, I was surprised to see a gamekeeper driving up towards me in an ATV. He appeared just as surprised to meet me. Initial exchanges were guarded as he was questioning my reason for being there "up here remote on your own" - but once the conversation focused on my intended journey in a few weeks' time, he softened a little.

Content that I wasn't up to mischief he offered myself and Tully a ride back to the gate at the top. I have to say that despite his now amicable mood, I questioned my vulnerability for a moment as between us, next to the gear stick, sat a large (no doubt loaded) rifle. I was thankful to have a fierce Jack Russell between us too.

Once back at the gate I'd waved goodbye, then spent a good hour marking a safe route around the boggy bowl. Marking as best I could with a stone pile, a deer antler I'd found, and a fence post buried in heather that I forced into the ground in a more upright fashion. Oh, and like near Loch Loch, there was another dead sheep to suggest our way. Despite this tricky bowl to negotiate, I couldn't wait to bring Team Swogi here – to this secret, special feeling route through the hills.

Our menagerie ascended this northerly route, and we puffed our way up the hill to the gate at the top.

"I like ups," said Yogi, between pants, as even he was finding the climb a little steep for his lungs.

The narrow pass between Lamh Dearg and Meall Easganan consisted of a grassy strip of around four metres wide from which rose lumpy, heather-strewn slopes on both sides. The grass was speckled with the white of cottongrass, indicating a damp core, but the left-hand edge was solid enough for hooves.

Yogi and I waited just after the old metal gate, admiring the view through the rocky cleft down into Glenshee, and in my mind I ran through the route that would take us across the boggy bowl to follow. Leanne arrived a short while later, still a little out of puff, but easily accepted the complex set of instructions.

"Through this stony valley, heather bash to the edge of the burn, drop down into its bed and walk along it for two-hundred metres. Left at the pile of stones, up the (very) steep slope, left again at the antlers, then contour around the hill side until you arrive at the dead sheep. Turn right there towards the fence post (that I'm still hoping is upright), sharp left at that, and that's you on an old hill track hidden in long grass..."

"I'll just follow you, shall I?" she replied, a little perplexed.

Thankfully Leanne appeared to be as happy-go-lucky as her dog Foxy, and not once had she complained about the distance travelled or the height reached.

Neither did she question my maze through the bog, or the strange variety of signposts used.

Eventually, with the complexity conquered, we emerged from the long grass at the edge of an old settlement – Corra-lairig. The word Corra here didn't mean 'a hollow on the side of a mountain', but 'occasional or sometimes' (according to the archaeologist at the dig). Likely this had been a hillside summer sheiling for those living down the valley at Lair. We paused again as the rough ground had been tough going, and I noticed that Swift was looking rather pleased with herself. This always arouses my suspicion...

"Look, I'm a proper deer pony now," she stated, smugly.

Taking a closer inspection of the load she was carrying, I smiled as I realised Leanne had collected the deer antler marker on her travels and had attached them to Swift's saddlebags as a souvenir. She did look the part I agreed, apart from her height, as at 16.2hh she'd not be the choice of most keepers trying to lift a heavy deer carcass to that kind of elevation.

"Carcass, did you say?" asked Swift, less sure of herself now. She shook herself from nose to tail as she considered the deer ponies' true undertaking.

Descending the hillside on short, sheep-pruned grass was a welcomed relief from the boggy maze navigation and, in another kilometre, we were passing the Pictish longhouses. All filled in now and covered up for protection, I was glad I'd had the opportunity to see them a few weeks before. If not for the recce I'd have ambled on by not realising the magnitude of what lay under our feet. To an untrained eye, they just looked like the natural undulations of rough hill-ground.

It was a strange feeling to be passing by a place of such past significance. Now rewilded it was no longer remarkable, although I was still enjoying its ambience;

but I couldn't help wondering, in times to come, would it ever again become a place of importance? The probability was slim, but then you never know where a UFO may choose to land...

Reaching Lair, we met the A93 - the now tarmacked route of an old military road (constructed by Major Caulfeild in the 1750's) - linking Blairgowrie to Braemar through the Spittal of Glenshee. The new road roughly follows the old route and has covered most of it over, although parts of the more twisty original can be seen in loops and lay-bys as you drive by.

Around 1800 kilometres of roads were constructed between 1725 and 1767, and while General Wade is more commonly associated with these, it was Major Caulfield who was responsible for 1300 kilometres in length.

So far, since joining forces with Leanne, I'd walked while leading Yogi to be more sociable. It was nice to give Yogi a well-earned break and be more sociable with him, too. There is something satisfying about being at the same height as your horse, matching their stride, facing the same obstacles at the same level, and communicating eye-to-eye. It enhances the oneness and deepens the bond and I often spend many hours on my own two feet during long journeys for this reason, but also to give their back and my bottom a bit of a break.

It was my bruised calves that were screaming for respite now though, as the descent from the pass had caused them to tighten up. From Lair we'd be finishing the day on five kilometres of tarmac, and I asked Leanne if she'd mind me concluding this from up top, to give my calves a less punishing end to the day.

Leanne, amicable as she is, didn't seem to mind any change to procedure or arrangements made, so on reaching the minor road at Cray I scrambled aboard. This road segregated the rough lower slopes of Mount Blair to our left, from the green farmland stretching down to the Black Water river on our right. With only a handful of houses along its length, it wasn't a busy throughfare and we didn't meet any traffic at all.

As I relaxed into Yogi's cadence, it felt a long time since my electrifying experience this morning and these last five kilometres were seeming to stretch on forever. The longer length of day was taking its toll and underlined that I was sensible to keep most other days short while I still wasn't in the best of health. Yogi, on the other hand, didn't seem to be up nor down which was pleasing news indeed as far as his health concerns were concerned.

Eventually we reached the T-Junction at Blacklunans and turned left towards our stop for the night at the Glenshee Ecocamp. No wild camping tonight, I'd booked into a place with hot showers as tomorrow would be our first rest day.

"Rest day did you say?" shouted Swift, from the back. "Yippee, hurry up, up front!" she exclaimed, bumping Leanne along with her nose.

"Oh, my goodness, *what ... are ... those?"* said Yogi in alarm as he slammed to a standstill (not for the first time this trip).

We'd reached the end of a field that Team Swogi were to stay in for the night (although we'd have to walk right round it to gain entry) and Yogi was referring to their temporary new neighbours who were standing by a wall, poking their heads over the top. It was a tall wall, but their heads were well above it, attached as they were to the long lengths of llama's necks.

"*Those* are Jet, Atticus, and Bradford, three llamas, and I hope some new pals," I replied, optimistically.

"What on earth are *llamas?*" asked Swift, with suspicion - looking at them over Leanne's shoulder and using her as a protective shield.

"They are animals from the Andes, a bit like camels I suppose ... they are very cute and fluffy," I continued in a positive tone.

"Well, I don't like them whatever they are," stated Yogi nervously as he spun around, and I quickly jumped off.

"Silly old bear," I said reassuringly, running my hand down his neck. "Let's go and introduce ourselves."

Team Swogi switched from nervous jogging to standstill assessments as we worked our way along the llama's field. The llamas merrily matched these procedures along their side of the fence too, as we walked towards the campsite's driveway.

Introductions made to the campsite owners and with human and equine instructions received, I took Yogi and Swift down to the field, dumping the tack, boots, and bags in the spot I'd pitch my tent. Wrapped up in their stripy fly-rugs, I let them free in the field and observed the amusing sight of two zebras, meeting three llamas (and two donkeys) over a wall. There was a lot of cavorting, spitting, and hee-hawing in amongst the mix, but I knew they'd soon settle down.

I pitched my tent and stashed away my gear, then went back up to the campsite's bothy where I'd left Leanne and Foxy recovering from their long walk. Both were cuddled up by the fire and it was hard to see where one ended and the other started, so intertwined as they were (without Swift's help this time). We made a cup of coffee and waited for Yvonne to arrive with my half-way supplies. There is nothing more delightful than clean clothes and a good feed in the midst of an adventure, and the large box that Yvonne arrived with contained both.

I grabbed a brief hug and a quick but wonderfully warm shower, while Leanne helped Yvonne pitch her tent. Leanne would be heading home but Yvonne was going to stay for the night and, despite my solo ruminations beside Loch Crannach, I'd be grateful for the camaraderie.

Yvonne and I dropped Leanne at her car, giving her a hug and Foxy a cuddle (no longer wary now) and set off to a local hotel for a meal. Not wanting to linger as the horses still needed to be fed, we ate fast (I inhaled mine) then made a brief stop at a shop to find new contents for my now empty hip flask.

I was amazed to find that this shop in the Highlands (the only one in the village) didn't stock a single bottle of single malt. The closest I could find was a bottle of ginger mead. I'd have preferred a drop of whisky, but this strange, sweet honey-taste for my onward journey fitted well with my fascination for all historic affairs. Possibly the ancestor of all alcoholic beverages and enjoyed worldwide for thousands of years, its golden hue was often referred to as a 'nectar of the gods.'

Back at camp, as Yvonne stoked the fire in the bothy, I nipped down to give Team Swogi their well-earned feed. They too enjoyed the advantages of a half-way restock with extra tasty rations. Differences explored and hierarchy no doubt established, both equines and camelids appeared content.

"I'm still keeping a close eye on them though," said Yogi, raising his wary eyes from his bucket only briefly.

My tent was pitched right next to the field and, rolling *my* eyes, I reassured him that I wouldn't be far away should he have any trouble from his neighbours through the night.

The fire was spreading its glow widely when I returned to the bothy and it welcomed me into the warm embrace. Yvonne gave me a hug too before inviting me to become Professor Plum, in the ballroom, with the candlestick. We engaged in a few board games and a few rounds of cards, but I left Yvonne *'whistfully'* to it, with other guests round the fire. I needed to restock, reorganise, and recharge for my next round of play.

Rather Boggy and Sad

Day 6: Rest Day Glen Shee
(Distance 0 km, Ascent 3m – I stood up!)

I awoke to heavy rain on the tent and was grateful I didn't have any miles to manage today. Yogi and Swift were standing side-by-side for warmth with their butts up against the wall. At least the llamas behind them no longer seemed a subject of concern.

"It's wet," said Swift with a sniff as I approached to say hello.

"Have you brought food?" enquired Yogi hopefully, as I ran my hands under his rug and gave him a good-morning hug.

To his delight I also produced a couple of treats for them each, acquired from my half-way supplies. Running my hand under Swift's rug too (much to her displeasure) I found their backs warm enough, but not particularly dry.

Selecting the right rug for a journey in June is always a debate. Weight is an issue and so are flies but the weather can be wintery too, even in the depths of summer. My compromise had been to find fly-rugs that offered a protective mesh underneath but with a waterproof strip that ran along their backs to keep main muscles warm and dry. I wasn't sure that the latter claim on these rugs' labels had ever been tested in Scottish weather though, and if the rain's deluge continued, I'd be keeping a close eye.

"Morning!" I shouted, as I heard rustlings from Yvonne back up at the tents.

"Be out soon, see you up at the bothy," was the muffled response from within.

The fire wasn't lit and in the absence of logs to facilitate this, I hovered by the warmth of the stove. As best I could at least, between other holidaymakers with the same kind of objective. It appeared I wasn't the only camper finding conditions a little chilly for June. The bothy was bustling with the morning routine of bacon rolls and hot beverages, and as Yvonne arrived we joined the queue to brew and boil our own breakfast.

Stomachs satisfied in a leisurely manner, and my tastebuds appreciating fresh milk in tea and an alternative to oats, we sat down at a table with a map spread between us. The plan had been to meander this morning, for a mooch up Mount Blair, but with the heavy rain this didn't look to be the most pleasant option. The map wasn't providing any localised indoors activities to entertain either and I decided the best course of action in these circumstances was to pop the kettle back on for another brew.

"Would you mind, if I just went home?" asked Yvonne tentatively as my back was turned.

"Not at all, I don't blame you," I replied, resisting the temptation to ask if I could come too.

Yvonne was intending to leave this afternoon anyway, so another few hours solo wouldn't make much difference in the scheme of things, especially considering I had another seven days on the trail to go. However, despite promoting the virtues of solo undertakings, the step away from good company always seems tough. As a result, a familiar heavy feeling settled in the pit of my stomach as I helped Yvonne pack up her tent.

Down at the carpark I left Yvonne with my box, half-way supplies now exchanged for smelly and dirty clothes. As I gave her a big thank you hug, I apologised for any odour she might encountered on her journey home and warned her to leave the lid firmly closed until I was back to retrieve it. Wishing me well on my onward journey,

Yvonne reiterated that she was available for an unplanned extraction if required, and as I watched her drive away, stood in the soaking rain, it was a good reminder that I was under no obligation (apart from my own) to complete this undertaking.

Starting to shiver a little, my concern as always returned to Team Swogi. I fetched some hay from the barn to aid with keeping them warm (Yvonne had brought some at my request) and walked back up to the field. Walking up the hill warmed me up at least, but the horses are never that sensible, accustomed as they are to extremely cosy home-comforts. They were still stood with their backs to the wall, heads lowered and rain dripping off the end of their noses.

Rather Boggy and Sad

"I've brought hay to warm you up!" I exclaimed, as cheerfully as I could.

"It's soggy," sighed Swift, miserably.

"Everything is, my dear." I replied, rolling my eyes at her diva-like lack of gratitude as I wiped rain drops from her face.

"It's all mine anyway," declared Yogi, as he claimed both piles as his own.

Standing for a while between them to establish leadership of the team, I ensured Swift could get a feed and settled Yogi's momentary food-obsessed inconsiderations. I left them nosing through the piles for the tastiest portions as I walked back to the bothy with a view to keeping myself warm too.

I settled by the fire with my book, a cup of tea, and the drip of my waterproofs hung as close to the flames as I dared. A long day of inactivity stretched before me, something I always find a struggle, but at least I wasn't on the next section of our journey in this weather, as it was a high and exposed route along a ridge.

I passed a few hours in this way, with an optimistic glance at the window from time to time – each expectant hope dashed by the steady stream flowing down the glass. With so many hours to kill (and preferring to execute that indoors), I was glad that I'd finally upgraded paperback books to a Kindle in recent years as I was soon onto book two. All I could do was keep my head down and keep all fingers crossed that this rain would pass before tomorrow.

Taking advantage of electricity, I charged my torch, phone, GPS, Kindle, and the power packs I carry to do this on the trail. With seven days unsupported ahead and only wild camps planned, I'd need maximum potential of power.

I was surprised to find the bothy quiet after the initial breakfast rush and wondered where the other unhappy campers were finding their entertainment on this rather soggy day. A few popped in from time to time for a quick brew, but by lunchtime the flow had dwindled, and I attacked the spare food from my cache all on my own.

Mid-afternoon, I again checked in on Team Swogi who were back to their spot by the wall. It didn't look like they'd eaten much of the hay at all. I had a sudden flash back to 'Eeyores' Gloomy Place: Rather Boggy and Sad' marked on the map of the Hundred Acre Wood in A.A Milne's Winnie-the-Pooh stories. I expected Swift to solemnly say "It's all for naught" and Yogi to gloomily proclaim "Could be worse. Not sure how, but it could be." I knew Yogi for sure would appreciate even the simplicity of a house made of sticks right now, but like Eeyore he was expecting his friends to help make it happen. They certainly weren't helping themselves as down at the other end of the field they'd find more shelter under some trees, and they hadn't eaten much of the belly warming hay only a few steps away.

I didn't have a pot for honey (to keep things in) nor a red balloon to help cheer them up, but I did have a few more treats to hand out that had a short-lived effect. I completed another rug check and found two wet, cold backs and could see that Swift was starting to shiver. This was not looking good with another fifteen hours of rain forecast.

I took them for two laps round the field to get them moving and stopped under the trees to show them the more sheltered gloomy place. As soon as I removed their headcollars though, they set off back to the exposed spot by the wall. I guess they'd bonded with the llamas next door more than I'd appreciated. *Oh Bother!* I thought - in a Pooh kind of way.

The llamas appeared to be fine in the wet, and with their thick and lofty fleeces I'm not sure they'd even noticed it was raining. If Yvonne's ponies had been here they'd have been the same, with their thick native manes and coats to offer ample protection. Team Swogi have many plus sides but weatherability was not one of them.

I love that both Swift and Yogi are quick moving, sensitive to requests, decisive, brave, have a large amount of endurance, and are always willing to 'work'. I obviously love their characters dearly too and can't imagine life without them. However, in bad weather I would consider them more high maintenance than ideal in the Scottish hills.

Yogi's coat inclines towards his Thoroughbred half and, unlike his Highland belly part, remains thin even in winter. Appaloosas, like Swift, generally aren't known to grow much of a mane, and her coat, evolved on American plains, doesn't provide much warmth. I reminded myself that there's no such thing as a perfect horse so if I was going to have well and working horses by morning (despite their flaws) I'd need to find a solution. I set off on an *Expotition* – not for the North Pole, but to see if I could find them more shelter.

Negotiations with the campsite owner (and his llamas) went well, and Team Swogi were soon ensconced in a narrow but tall shelter, designed obviously for those with slim bodies and long lengths of neck. This suited Swift just fine, but Yogi and his Highland belly were finding it a bit of a squeeze. I removed their drenched fly-rugs and hung them in the barn to dry as much as they could by morning.

With no rain battering the horses' backs, and by standing close together, they'd be much warmer without them. They were also now sensibly getting stuck into the hay nets I'd provided. The llamas, still oblivious to the rain, were watching from over the fence. There seemed to be a renewed fascination now their neighbours had moved house to the other side of the field – and who now also had food.

Happy that Team Swogi were in a better place, on the way back to the bothy I checked my saggy-and-sorry-for-itself tent and adjusted the tautness of the guy lines by moving the pegs out a little. It was now a lonely sight in a field absent of any companions. I guess the rain had been a bit too much for the other campers who had either gone home or had found drier options of accommodation. This restored my self-image a little, for at least it explained the absence of company up at the bothy, and back there by the fire, with no one to distract, my thoughts turned to the road ahead.

Tomorrow was a day of unknowns, as I'd only had chance to recce the camp spot. Approaching it from the opposite direction, I'd tried to find a route through from there to this side of the valley but had arrived against an impassable obstacle on the marked path – a huge deer-fence stile at the head of Glen Finlet. Not that a smaller stile would have been any more helpful as far as hoof negotiations were concerned.

With a lack of time and a lack of regular heart beats to explore further, I'd had to take to the internet and trust suggestions from fellow travellers. Therefore, I had a route proposed on paper that hadn't been assessed for suitability against our capabilities – which is always an individual and fluid appraisal. It had a steep section of pathlessness to navigate, and I just had to trust that Team Swogi were up to it and that my navigation skills were too.

My adventures always have two goals: a destination and a completion date, and this obviously dictates the approach. Under these circumstances, it is sensible to recce more than I would if my objective was only destination driven, as the commitment of work-shifts unfortunately lurk at the end of my journeys. Any delay due to obstacles that require a work-around or lengthy detour may mean a failure to complete as I have to return to work on a set date. Whatever the aims of your adventurous undertaking, there is always a balancing act between the fear of the unknown versus the excitement of discovery.

As you get out on the trail more, gather experience, and increase competence and confidence, the need for prior route inspection reduces. Omitting it is always a risk though, not only for being able to stick to schedule (if you have one) but also in terms of avoiding trouble that even your enhanced capabilities can't cope with. It's always exciting to head off into the uncharted as it adds a sense of adventure and an amplified thrill, but with that comes an acceptance of increased risk and the probable need to step outside your comfort zone from time to time.

Comfort zones don't really have defined edges. They are a little on the malleable side, and as you try to expand them, the position of the edge can depend on something as minor as your mood on the day (and that of your horses). That's before you consider numerous other external influencing factors (e.g., weather). So, as you try to push the boundary, you don't always get it right. However, it's okay to make mistakes as this is where the learning happens – where you try, fail, succeed, grow, count your blessings, celebrate exploits, and truly feel alive.

There's only so far you can stretch this zone though - it requires a rational amount of challenge. The last thing you want to do is snap the elastic, as it will probably hit you painfully in the eye and you're unlikely to be able to see your way back to whatever it was you were trying to do.

However, if you can manage the balance well, the rewards are vast. Not only are you likely to become more confident and proficient at your task, but in exploration of the flexible edge, you will probably discover that you are more capable than you ever thought. With an understanding and an appreciation of your own capabilities (and transferring these to other aspects of life), comes purpose, assurance, more opportunities, and usually, a heightened happiness.

I've experienced this process many times in life, but the biggest battles against the balance have been in white-water kayaking, paramedicine, and of course dobbineering. Reaching the highest level of coaching in white water kayaking and surviving trips down the Brahmaputra and the Grand Canyon involved many years of stretching the elastic, but I rarely choose to push the zone in a boat these days.

Comfort zones continue to be stretched in my day job of dealing with the unknowns of 999 calls, but to a much lesser degree than in the past due to years of experience now under my belt. I am, however, still very much in the learning zone with dobbineering, and am excited to see where that leads next.

The more you carefully stretch, the more you accomplish, and the more you feel you can achieve in the future. It's worthwhile noting that my original aims in all three areas mentioned were much lower than the eventual achievements, and as I didn't do this alone, this makes me feel humble. Freedom to explore is of core importance to me, to explore self, others, and the environment that I'm in, and I have a huge recognition that I've been fortunate in life. Conditions and circumstances have allowed a continuation of my childlike curiosity to try new things and see what's around the next corner.

Facing risks and possible failures is often considered a harder path to follow than staying within the comfort zone. However, the initial contentment that comfort provides rapidly descends to apathy, routine, and monotony. A dreariness that certainly gets me down, and which I consider to be a tougher task to deal with. By facing a fear, you become the one in control; by avoidance, it controls you. As John Wayne famously said, “Courage is being scared to death and saddling up anyway.” But what if you’ve never had the initial support to be able to get your foot in the stirrup?

I am incredibly grateful for the opportunities that have crossed my path, and extremely thankful for the right amount of nurture that allows me to take them on. Taking that first step, giving the edge that first push, often requires assistance - as do many of the larger strides along the way. I am indebted to those who’ve supported me on my learning journeys. The fear of the unknown often shouldn’t be, and doesn’t have to be, faced entirely alone.

I would, however, be facing the unknown on my own tomorrow and as I accepted that risk, I tried to remain focused on the excitement and thrill side of things - but a few concerns surfaced. The next three days held a large amount of uncharted territory ahead and it still didn’t look like the nicest weather to see it in. There was the worry of going into more remote territory in unsettled weather, with horses that don’t weather the storm too well, but there was also the unease of wondering whether my heart would stand up to the excursions required when the going got tough.

Like the weather, my heart hadn’t been particularly settled today but perhaps, I considered optimistically, the irregularities were more noticeable when still and not distracted. My own fragility was a new comfort zone to stretch, and I was still exploring those particular boundaries.

I turned my attention to dinner and to devouring the last delights of non-camp food cuisine before repacking the bags ready for tomorrow. Donning my waterproofs once again, I did a final feed and check of Team Swogi, who were still sensibly tucked up in the shelter. I left them eating more hay with warm dry backs and I turned in for the night. Tempting as it was to return to the warmth of the fire, the bothy only had hard wooden seats, and a stone floor. I knew I'd be more comfortable, and cosy enough in my sleeping bag back in my tent and trusted its resilience to keep me dry 'til morn.

The Spirit of Ecstasy

Day 7: Glenshee to Glenprosen Lodge (Distance 27km, Ascent 946m)

I listened intently in the morning but couldn't hear a drop of rain on the flysheet. I couldn't quite believe it. Three hours ago, I'd been disturbed from my sleep by the noise of the heavy rain. I couldn't hear it now, and I sincerely hoped it had worn itself out. The air was still very damp, so there didn't seem much point in leaving my tent standing to dry for a while. Carefully keeping the wet outer separate from the dry inner, I packed it up and set off down to the horses, enjoying the ease of facilities in the bothy for breakfast on my way.

Swift was standing by the fence of the small enclosure, with her head stretched over it chatting to Jet, Atticus, and Bradford. She seemed to be relating well to these comparable creatures, as with lanky legs and long necks they had a similar outlook on life.

"I can't understand a word they say," grumbled Yogi, from the mouth of the shelter (he'd kept his butt just inside the doorway in case there was a further drop of rain).

Despite his grumblings, both horses appeared much happier than the shivering position I'd found them in yesterday afternoon and had dry backs upon which to put the saddles (which Swift still moaned about obviously). Their rugs were still quite damp but had at least dried a little in the barn overnight.

I was just putting the finishing touches to boots, bags, and bridles, when Leanne and Foxy appeared. Knowing my fear of roads and with today starting out on one, Leanne had kindly offered to walk the first stretch with me. It appeared that the long steep trails of the other day hadn't put her (or Foxy) off, and secretly, I think she'd fallen in love with Swift just a little.

"Well obviously," said Swift with a smirk and a toss of her sticky-up mane.

Poor Swift, it was hard for a girl to have a 'Loreal moment' without long locks to flick. I took a moment of reflection to wonder if this is why it had taken her so long in life to find her inner poise. Ever since I'd known Swift (from two years of age), she'd been somewhat insecure about life. Not that she was prepared to let you know that, accomplished as she was at hiding the fact with a tough and grumpy front.

Many times, struggling with her behaviour, I'd be asked "Well what did you expect from an Appaloosa mare?" as both the breed and the gender are renowned for their complexities. To be honest, I had no expectations, but I wanted her to be happy and most of the time it appeared that she was not, so my mission became written in stone.

In equestrian circles, it's folklore that your "heart horse will find you once in your lifetime." Not a sentiment, you'll notice, that involves detail of *you* finding *your perfect horse*. It's very much based on a horse finding you, but it's the horse you *need* and not the one you necessarily desire who turns out to be important in your life. Initially I thought I'd found this in Yogi, as although he wasn't straight-forward in the beginning, I did feel a 'love at first sight' moment the first time we met.

However, on getting him home, there were a lot of issues to work through before we found harmony and sync. Once through the worst, I discovered that we were very much alike. Often stressing over unnecessary things, melodramatic at times, and keen to attack challenges head on, but with a desire to relax when we could and fiercely loyal to companions. We shared the same sense of humour, and our relationship was trusting, easy, and uncomplicated. I felt fulfilled, so why would I need more?

Well apparently I did, because along came Swift. She was scruffy, complicated, difficult, quirky, and at times downright dangerous, and in the beginning I'd definitely bitten off more than I could chew. She was certainly not easy and our relationship was volatile, but I still fell in love. Over some very hard times, she taught me the things I needed to know. Things far from equine-specific skills, like emotional control, gentleness, tolerance, an adjustment of expectations, and most importantly, an inner peace.

Another equine folklore is that horses mirror your soul, so if Swift was insecure, complex, and quirky, so must I be. She taught me to know myself better and how to embrace my eccentricity. Her teachings were never easy, and they continue to test, but she is just as much a heart horse as Yogi is, despite the turbulent times. Not everyone sees through her quirks, and her apparent surface 'failings', but she opens things within me and I'm opening things within her, so that must mean that we are meant to be.

I feel extremely lucky indeed to have been found by two heart horses in one lifetime. Both involve comfort: one wraps a blanket around me, and the other pushes the zone.

Back in our familiar procession, we left the campsite behind and enjoyed the view over Drumore Loch to our right. Tall, leafy ferns rose from the dry-stone wall at the side of the road. A lumpy mass of grass extended down to the loch on which two white swans were dabbling in amongst the reeds on the far side. Up ended, they looked like tiny sail boats drifting in the wind. Beyond, the tree-lined slopes gradually disappeared into the mist, distant features concealed by its white breath.

On the near shore stood a lonely, neglected, but substantial two-storey boathouse - a listed building dating back to 1864. Now in disrepair but often admired, and the focus of keen photographers due to its striking pose and aesthetic setting.

The Drumore estate of old belonged to the Spaldings of Ashintully, the castle we'd passed during our previous day on the trail. Travelling by horse at a steady pace provides a different perspective of distance and the sizeable reach of boundaries that the lairds lorded over in times gone by, long before motorised transport. Contemplating the distance on foot from here to Ashintully Castle, and despite the modern material of tarmac under hoof, I enjoyed a brief historical moment with the DeLorean's counter set to the early 1800's.

I must have made a mistake with the setting though, as I suddenly jumped *Back to the Future* by one hundred years with the appearance of a traditionally-coloured black 'Tin Lizzie'. Team Swogi also jumped at the rumbling engine and the prominent mudguards and headlights of the Model T Ford car. There was a moment of minor panic and much scuffling as Leanne and I organised our circus to let it squeeze by on the narrow road.

Swift and Yogi weren't as impressed by this strange-sounding, and abnormal-looking vehicle as I was. They couldn't find a similar profile (within their comfort zone filing system) regarding machines they'd met before.

"What *was* that noisy and smelly contraption?" asked Yogi, keeping a close watch as it slowly disappeared into the distance.

"I'd say it was rude, loud, and brash," exclaimed Swift, still recovering from the experience.

"It was an unusual sight, I have to agree, on a tiny backroad in the middle of nowhere," I said, turning to Leanne.

"Lovely to see though," she replied, with her usual relaxed attitude to the eccentricities of life.

With the road now restored to a quieter state, we enjoyed the company of a curious herd of cows who huffed and puffed their way alongside us. They were knee-deep in lush green grass in a field on the southerly slopes of Mount Blair and Team Swogi very much wanted to join them. There was, however, plenty of fodder to keep stomachs satisfied (yes, even Yogi's) along the verges and both horses merrily munched their way by.

Up high over Mount Blair's peak was a spiralling circle of birds-of-prey, no doubt enjoying uplift from mountainside thermals, although it was still chilly and hard to believe there was any warm air to be found.

Our peace was soon shattered by the approach from behind of another shiny, vintage vehicle. Behind that, spaced out in a parade towards us, came a long line of strange shapes, curves, high tops and low - with shimmering sticky-out mirrors and badges. At each meeting, the drivers slowed to allow Team Swogi to prance past them (all grass forgotten for now). The only way for the horses to cope with the unfamiliar sounds, sights, and sparkles was to about-face them to confront each curious-looking car.

They weren't keen on the huge noisy bonnets, large lights, and shiny wing mirrors at the front, but were fascinated with the back end of each vehicle. Many had hampers within easy reach, perched on their derrières and each one was assessed for their openability (Swift's department), and likely treats held within (Yogi's division). Swift bumped each lid with her nose to see if it might pop open, while Yogi gave the base a huge, assessing sniff with nostrils spread out wide. Their mutual appreciation of each other's strengths and the synergy of co-operation towards a shared goal was teamwork worthy of admiration.

There was a short break until one remaining vehicle, which I hoped would be the last of the procession, approached. I don't know much about cars, but the figure on the front gave the manufacturer away, flying proudly as she was.

"Excuse me," shouted Swift, as she pushed past me in panic, doing a flying lady impression of her own.

The roof was down and as the driver stopped for a chat, he turned off the thunderous engine much to our relief. We exchanged a brief explanation of reasons, aims, well wishes, and historical appreciations. Every day is a school day and I learnt that I was admiring the curvy form of a Phantom from the 1920's on a local vintage rally, while the driver discovered that he was regarding the sleekness and spots of an Appaloosa on a long-distance adventure.

Yogi, studying these strange contraptions, learned that the bonnets weren't that scary when silent and still. He was also studying his own reflection in the polished wing. As he moved closer to confirm his good looks and to decide which side was his most handsome, I did something I don't normally do and pulled him back sharply. I didn't think the owner would appreciate the addition of horse nose-art on their otherwise immaculate presentation, and my bank balance wouldn't welcome the expense of any repair.

"Keep Swift's teeth well away too," I warned Leanne.

Swift looked a little offended by this, but we both know that she likes to have exploratory nibbles of anything unfamiliar.

The Flying Lady (Spirit of Ecstasy)

No sooner had we waved goodbye to the last car in the rally (confirmed by the Phantom's driver), when we were faced with another event that kept Team Swogi dancing on their toes. These profiles were much more familiar, but no less exciting as two grey horses thundered across a field towards us. In an elevated position above the road, they looked down on us with much perky poise, and proceeded to prance along the fence with high knees, pricked ears, and arched necks.

Swift launched into her full Arabian horse impression. With her tail raised high above her back, she provided a display of her own by trotting up and down with an effortless, smooth glide to the full extent of her lead rope. It's rare she expends this sort of additional energy, but once applied, her elegance is a joy to behold. At least it would be if it weren't for her flared nostrils, also held high, that were emitting regular dinosaur-like snorts.

Yogi had a temporary prance too but nothing as dramatic as the other three continued to do, and he soon returned his attention to mowing the verge as we finished the last stretch of the road. We'd reached a T-Junction and the new bridge over the River Isla which was constructed in 1970.

The older Brewlands bridge (also called the Claypots) still proudly spans the waters too but is now closed off to the public. It was constructed in 1836 in an early example of a community investment collaboration, and the cost (£280) was covered by public subscription split between fifty or so households thought to benefit from the easier crossing. Prior to this they had to risk the precarious stepping-stones positioned downstream.

At a turning on the other side, we paused on a patch of grass for a moment as from here I'd continue alone. Leanne and Foxy had a five-kilometre return and I only had one-and-a-half kilometres on road left to do, before heading for the hills. Leanne and I shared simple hugs and well-wishes (with added thanks from me), but dished out ear rubs, butt scratches, and soft-nosed smooches to each other's animals before heading our separate ways.

The view from the trail tracking uphill from the road was still dominated by Mount Blair to the west. Before long, at some trees, we'd re-join the Cateran Trail for a short section, but just before this the trail began to get terribly muddy. Machinery off to the right revealed the reason, as extensive forestry was taking place in the woodland ahead.

The driver of a delimber machine seemed indifferent as we rode on by, giving us the merest of glances. Not used to this lack of interest in their presence, Team

Swogi appeared a little offended. I, however, was grateful for the horses offering their own disregard in response, as they were more familiar with forestry machines than vintage cars, I didn't have to worry.

Through the gate, the ground of the route through the trees was even worse and progress became heavy going. The thick clay clogged up the horse's hoof boots with every step, and I pointlessly wished for a forestry worker to be there to clean them at the end of the day. The recent fall of thirty-six hours of heavy rain hadn't helped, but at least neither horse appeared to be struggling too much with traction.

Emerging from the remains of the forest onto heathered lowlands, and thankfully onto a better grassy track, we were offered a beautiful view over Auchintaple Loch to Mount Blair's smaller neighbour, Carn an Fhidhleir (Rock of the Fiddler). Bright-violet foxgloves by the side of the trail provided a vivid splash of colour in an otherwise green-grey terrain. The view might be beautiful, but the clouds hadn't relinquished their damp dreariness yet.

Between us and the loch lay the remains of an old chapel, reduced to a pile of stones now, but near it were the waters of the Lady Well, very much still providing a clean and clear flow. Reputed to have miraculous healing properties, the best time to take a sip (apparently) was before sunrise on the first Sabbath in May.

Too late in month or time of day for this restorative redeemer, I turned Yogi to his happy place, uphill, towards the recommended diversion from my original plan (avoiding the stile over the deer-fence). I thanked my lucky stars that I'd not planned to complete the Cateran circuit unseen, now or at any point in the past, as it too (heading off to the north-west) was blocked by a smaller stile over the stone wall. There didn't appear to be any gate alternative in this stony barrier for as far as I could see.

Obstructions to hoof travel like these are a frustration, especially given the joint time and distance aims of my regular excursions, but they are also understandable. Unfortunately for reasons I can't comprehend, my passion for dobbineering in present times is only shared by a handful of others. Therefore, those constructing or maintaining passage often don't consider the modest demand worth the effort of supply. Indeed, many don't even contemplate the need in the first place, as they haven't seen a horse in the hills for many years.

Our diversion, although one mile less in length, had an ascent of three-hundred metres more. Not a huge climb in the scheme of things, but it involved an exposed ridge instead of a sheltered forest and apparently culminated in a steep descent through heather where no path existed. With the unsettled weather and the unmarked trail section ahead, it felt like an enforced acceptance of risk that was, to a degree, imposed by someone else.

We left the Caterans behind and set off into the unknowns of the high hills ahead. The trail was wide, solid, and surrounded by the heathered patchwork pattern of managed burning. Stretching for miles it looked like a half-finished jigsaw puzzle with pieces missing, which my mind creatively tried to fill in. Suddenly, there was a terrifying eruption from its stalky-brown midst. Like a sibling pillow fight taken too far, the outburst was accompanied by a shrill cry of "Mum, Mum, Mum!" and immediately followed by a startling explosion of feathers.

"It's a pheasant," said Yogi, barely raising his head and certainly not missing a stride.

"I heard it ages ago," sighed Swift, rolling her eyes. "Don't be so dramatic."

To be fair, it is the pheasants that are the dramatic ones, as they always respond in this way when startled. It's not their fault that their natural defence is an imitation of Rocky from *Chicken Run* being fired from the circus canon, and after all, *he'd* found that to be quite alarming. I gathered my thoughts, and hoped my heart would slow down soon...

We were now traversing along the mid slopes of Badandun Hill and below us to the right was the dark-green belt of trees that filled Glen Finlet, the sheltered forest we should have been riding through today. From my position up high, I could clearly see the regimented lines of trees within the forestry plantation, arranged with precision like a troop on parade. Planted no doubt with efficiency in mind, each tree was only granted the exact amount of light and nutrients needed for growth to a size deemed suitable for timber. This forest looked mature and tightly packed, with no room for each trunk to stretch out a branch to 'open order dress right' for the march.

Its dark depths would be cool and quiet, with scarce shafts of dusty light. The heaviness of woven branches putting a dampener on any sound and footfall silenced by a thick sponge of needles. I loved the thrill of forests like these and the sheer weight of the atmosphere as you attempt to silently pass through, acutely aware that one small stumble or snapped twig may cause reverberations for miles through intertwined roots. Your breath becomes shallow and every intake perceived, sympathy felt for the trees squeezed together 'without interval' and no room to fill their lungs. Even in strong winds like today, the forest centre would be still, earthy, and extremely close.

Far from that today though, it was windy on this ridge, and we were still a fair distance from the highest point. The weather thankfully hadn't turned out as bad as forecast, there hadn't been any rain yet and the clouds had lifted a little. As a result, I was admiring a long-stretching view to the north of numerous peaks – the most prominent of which (Mayar and Driesh) are Munros. Their distant summits were a stark reminder of scale as we'd stay at the base of Driesh in a few nights time.

As I flicked between scales on my Ordnance Survey maps, plotting the route ahead in my mind, I noticed a typo. On the 1:50k scale, the hill beside us was named 'Badandua' but on the 1:25k it was 'Badandun.' The latter I think is correct, and as I vocally explored both names, I was reminded of a pony from the past – who was both bad and dun.

Not many cared to ride Jasper at the pony club, but in the invincibility of youth, I found him thrilling. I think he was part racehorse (due to his speed and attitude) and part Fjord horse, having the distinctive dun colour and the sticky-up mane so characteristic of the breed.

"The best sort of horse then," interrupted Swift, smugly.

I remember his mane specifically, as it didn't give you much to hang onto when he got you into trouble, which was often. I loved his spring, his speed, and his zeal, but not so much the deposits in mud when I couldn't keep up with his sharp mind.

They say: "You're not a good rider unless you've fallen off seven times"; "Fall seven times, get up eight";

and "Always get back on the horse." Advice I'd taken regularly during my relationship with high-spirited Jasper.

"You've fallen off me three ... so does that mean there's four to go?" counted Swift, with a glint in her eye.

"No! Don't get any ideas, I don't bounce so well these days."

Yogi had paused to explore some tasty morsels in the heather, not bothering to count that I'd never fallen off him - despite his best bucking efforts in our early relationship. Swift was scratching an ear with her hind leg, transporting me back to the first time I'd mustered the courage to sit on her (an occasion I'd thought might be one of the seven).

Backing a horse is always a tense event; for the horse if you've misjudged their readiness, and for the rider even if you've been correct in calculations. Swift's height, athleticism, insecurities, and past demonstrations of panic when stretching her comfort zone, had all combined to make me particularly nervous when sitting on her for the first time.

We'd not completed more than five steps forward under saddle with me sitting upright for the first time, a major achievement in itself, when she'd stopped dead. I'd sat ... quietly ... waiting ... not knowing whether even a minor encouragement might push her over the edge into a panicked and rodeo response.

I'd tried to force some air into my lungs as I felt her twist underneath me, but the twist was slow and considered, not the action of an about-to-bronc horse. So, prising open one eye (not realising until that point that I'd tightly closed them), I watched her right hind leg stretching tentatively around mine towards her ear for a scratch.

This display of flexibility, strength, and independence didn't help my nerves much and instantly realised, what a different experience this was going to be compared to riding Yogi. He never wants to have anything to do with independence and enjoys having his personal groom at beck and call. After all, "Why bother to have a human as a pet, then scratch your ear yourself?"

At least Swift had felt relaxed enough about the backing process to pause to address her itchy lug issue right there and then. You never can be totally sure with Swift though, it could have been an elaborate ruse to lull me into a false sense of security!

Not sure if she was kidding me now, she had suddenly switched to high-alert mode, pointing intensely to the slopes to our right. I checked first with Yogi to see if he had sensed some danger too and noted his more trusted response was the same. With my eyes and ears now attentive, I also turned to observe the hillside. It appeared to be alive, with a brown, rippling movement like an avalanche of mud.

It took a moment to comprehend that we were all watching an enormous herd of deer, streaming in a tight-packed mass of fear, fur, and antlers. Like a murmuration of starlings, they moved as one, running and leaping startled by our presence. Their lone leader, stopping a few steps to the side every so often to check our progress (and possibly our intention).

They melted away across the valley and, still climbing, we moved on to Craig Lair and Mid Hill. The ·ws to Caenlochan Glen and the Glenshee hills to the re splendid, and Yogi enjoyed posing his perky f plentiful photographs. Twisting in the nat the panorama behind Swift was as the valley we'd ascended dropped down to more rolling hills which trundled all the way to the distant horizon. The patchwork patterns were a full-coloured palette of greens, yellows, and browns.

Between us and the last top of the day was Tarmach Cairn (referring to the tarmachan, or ptarmigan) and I kept a close eye out for these birds too, in case they were also prone to pillow fights in the rough. At a T-junction in the trail, I decided to head to the left, although our onward route lay to the right. It was a forty-metre climb in the wrong direction, to the peak of Bawhelps, but I felt this would be a more significant grand finale for the ridge than the unremarkable junction.

It was a curious name for a hill, one I think which relates to cow or heifers, but whatever the origins, its highpoint certainly presented an enhanced outlook over the magnificent surroundings. I paused for a moment to enjoy the full three-hundred-and-sixty-degree view.

Bawhelps summit itself was featureless, just a rise in the heather with a gradual descent on the other side, but its eastern perimeter dropped away sharply over a ledge into the head of Glen Prosen. The ledge was too steep to negotiate down to the glen here, so we'd use the edge of the ridge as a handrail to follow it back the way we'd arrived, then onwards to a gap in the rocky profile which offered, hopefully, an easier way down.

The track was covered in loose stones so I jumped off for the descent. Anticipating that the ground ahead would become tricky where the path was supposed to run out, I planned to walk right down to the heart of Glen Prosen. It would be safer to tackle this section on my own two feet. The wind was fierce now and biting through my clothes, so I hoped the walk would warm me up a bit too.

Back at the T-junction, we continued our descent to Broom Hill to hopefully find a safe passage through the Glack of Balquhader (Hollow of Hut) to the river and glen below. It wasn't long before the wide, firm track dwindled to a sheep-track through the heather with frequent branching options. On either side, the blocky, black forms of exposed peat hags hissed their threat of a sinking downfall should I fail to navigate well. Keeping Team Swogi in line behind me, I advanced to the edge of the cleft and peered into its depths.

To the right lay a small track descending steeply towards the deep, dark forest of Glen Finlet – the direction we could have arrived by if not for the deer-fence stile. To the left was a tiny trail, hanging onto the steep slope of Broom hill, which appeared to contour around, above the gravities of the Glack. Another option was a vague track which disappeared into the cleft.

I decided that the higher route looked the better of the two, as the depths of the hollow looked boggy and water-logged. The trail was tiny, but it thankfully persisted, and I took care (reminding Team Swogi to do the same) traversing the incline around the hill. The track eventually vanished into the heather, and I turned the team directly downhill, dissecting contours at ninety degrees to descend at a rapid rate.

As heather gave way to sodden grass beneath us, the horses feet gave way too, and we slithered and slipped our way downwards. It was so steep; the horse's backsides were high above them, and I wondered at one point whether Swift's saddle bags might slide over her head to tumble away in front.

"That's what I'm hoping for," she sighed.

"I don't like downs," said Yogi, slipping his comment into the conversation as he slid to a slithering halt.

I tried my best to zig-zag a route down, but unlike the fabled skills of haggis (with two legs shorter on one side to traverse the slopes in an anti-clockwise direction), horses aren't keen on facing across slope when there's no flat trail to stand on. Their legs are all the same length and can't facilitate the tilt too well. We were all relieved, therefore, to reach the more gradual gradient of lower ground - only to a point though, as there was a boggy three-hundred metres to negotiate before reaching the river's ford.

Warm now, perspiring a little, and with my lower reaches covered in mud, I gave my boots and chaps a quick wash in the river then ambled on to Kilbo Bothy for our rest for the night. To our left, the wide Kilbo path to Glendoll pointed directly up the hill. It's an old path, existing on original Ordnance Survey maps, but it's not known if it was once most significant as an important drovers' route or as a stalkers' trail. Whichever, it is a more direct approach to Glendoll than the one I was planning (through Glen Prosen first) but very steep with a treacherous descent down the Shank of Drumfollow. A path that required a prior recce for horses, as far as I was concerned, but not one I'd had time to check.

Arriving at Kilbo Bothy, I was dismayed to find that it was now surrounded by scaffolding. Dismayed for me and Team Swogi but not for the bothy itself, as it seemed mightily pleased to finally be given the attention it thought it deserved.

Earlier in the day, up high on the ridge, I'd managed to get an up-to-date weather forecast which was unfortunately warning about the approach of a sizeable storm. My plan had been to construct a corral in the lee of the bothy, up close to the walls, to offer a wind break for my tent and abutted protection for Yogi and Swift.

Knowing that both horses enjoyed regular butt scratching sessions on any surface after a hard day on the trail, my concern now was that they'd use the metal poles. Fending off a storm was one thing, but shielding from falling planks and poles wasn't an item listed on my tent's protective properties. Looking around, I assessed that this would be an exposed position, particularly away from the bothy walls and with the forecasted wind direction.

The storm was due to hit hard overnight and predicted to linger for twenty-four hours. I knew it had been a long day already (given the amount of ups and downs), but the further we could travel today while the weather was still passable seemed a sensible decision. Apologising, I pulled the horses heads up from the grass and their butts away from the poles and continued to walk them down the glen.

Twenty minutes later, I found a patch of ground next to some trees and a burn, and stopped to give it consideration; but it offered little to no protection from the predicted prevailing wind. It was five kilometres to the end of this track where the tarmac road of the glen began, and in my mind that appeared to be a good place to aim for anyway. The track was easy going and the weather still dry, so the extra distance was a stress-free stroll to arrive at Glenprosen Lodge.

Swift and Yogi followed me tentatively into the gamekeeper's yard and after a few knocks on doors and a few shouts of "Whooo hooo, anyone there?" I manage to attract some attention. The head keeper was fetched, and he led us round to appraise a potential field for the night.

"It has grass," stated Team Swogi, in unified satisfaction.

Blissfully unaware of the forecast, it met their immediate requirements, but I cleared some debris and old wire away from where I'd corral them – in the corner with the most protection. There was no offer of blether or beverage from this keeper this evening, but I was grateful to be accommodated without any prior arrangement and thanked him profusely.

"There's a big storm coming in, hope your night's not too rough," he said, on his departure.

The corralled corner was bordered to the east and north by tall pines, although the road was between the fence and the trees to the north. With wind due to be from the north-north-east, I hoped the trees would lift all the weather over our heads. Rugs on, feeds fed, and water poured, I pitched my tent on a triangle of grass on the other side of the road. Here there was a bonus of a picnic-bench to sit on whilst eating my dinner and enough space between me and Swift for the better prospect of a peaceful breakfast. I was pleased to find such an unexpected luxury, but not so happy to find a network of tiny holes and tunnels in the ground surrounding my tent. Carefully packing my food away, I contemplated that I could be in for a rustle of a night and not just from the storm.

Rein Check

Day 8: Glenprosen Lodge to Glenprosen Hostel (Distance 6km, Ascent 106m)

The tent had been flapped by the wind a few times through the night, but not as bad as expected and I'd slept soundly with no rodent interruptions. Prior to poking my head out of the door, I was optimistic about the day's weather - but only then did I fully appreciate how much the trees were providing protection. For me and my tent at least, but with the width of road to the field, Team Swogi were more in the thick of things. Huddled in the corral's corner, they looked thoroughly miserable and my heart sank.

I packed up as fast I as could, not even lighting the stove this morning, and gathered them from the field to the embrace of the branches beside me.

"It's c-c-c-cold," said Yogi, trembling.

"F-f-f-freezing more like," Swift replied, quivering as well.

They were both soaked, shivering, and stiff-backed, and the guilt I felt about my night in a cosy tent was overwhelming. I threw my poncho over Swift, the tarp over Yogi, and my arms around his neck. None of which would have any long-term warming effect, as anyone on the brink of hypothermia really needed to be out of wet clothes and ensconced somewhere warm with food to generate heat from within. I felt sick to my stomach about having left them so exposed.

Pulling myself together, I couldn't undo the done, and just needed to get on with making things better as soon as I possibly could. Considering options, there was no food for Team Swogi in the shelter of these trees, the field didn't have any alternative protection and the keeper had no suitable barn. Swift and Yogi needed to walk to warm up too, so I felt there was no choice but to move on.

Looking around though, the storm was still very much in force, with heavy rain being driven in a horizontal direction over the tops of the trees. I couldn't imagine how bad it would be when we reached the other side of the forest to face it full on (or at least to be hit from the side), but we couldn't stay here.

Preparing Swift and Yogi for departure was harrowing. Neither wanted to accept their saddles for a start, as their large back muscles felt like hard blocks of ice. Forcing this upon them felt disrespectful, insulting, and against every listen-to-your-horse training method I believed in. They were reluctant to lift their feet too as their legs, stiff with cold, were disinclined to bend in the middle for hoof boot application. As I struggled, I also became chilled, and my hands became numb and clumsy. Frustration, guilt, and concern filled the saddle bags faster than the equipment.

Finally ready, I hoped that the layer of saddlebags positioned on Swift's back would help to insulate and warm her a little. I covered Yogi as much as I could with my poncho and set off down the road. Tree branches on both sides of the road waved us on our way, creaking and groaning as they were thrashed from side to side in the wind. Yogi and Swift, usually sensible in this situation, were uneasy and skittish. The chill of their bodies added a new layer of vulnerability, making them hypersensitive to the movement and noise.

After only a couple of scampering minutes, we left the animated trees behind and, as anticipated, felt the full force of the wind slam into our sides. There was a long straight of road ahead with zero protection against the prevailing wind. The best approach, I shouted to the team, would be heads down and keep moving, but progress was slow.

Every few minutes or so, an invisible force slammed into us before retreating as fast as it arrived. When this happened, Team Swogi spun to turn their backs to the wind-driven rain. Kit would flap, the poncho would lift, and I'd have to spend time battening down hatches before convincing them to proceed forward again.

Eventually, we were joined by a line of trees to our left, which offered a slither of shelter and I paused to look at the map. Yogi spun his butt to the wind and dropped his head down between his front feet with his nose only an inch off the tarmac. Swift also stood, head down in despair, with the rain dripping down her face (from long ears to long nose). She wasn't even feeling inclined to take a nibble or two from the verge under her feet. This was a BAD sign, for a half-Highland boy with a full grass obsession and a gal who usually approaches a grass-eating opportunity like a velociraptor snatching a kill. We were in trouble...

One kilometre more on the map, there were a collection of buildings and judging by their size, one of them should be a barn. Distant or near, there was no sign that the weather would change anytime soon, and these buildings offered a possibility of respite. I solemnly promised Swift and Yogi that I'd find them some shelter soon, then persuaded them to continue our spinning battle along the lane. Pitched at a slant against the onslaught of wind, little by little, we were making progress. I wasn't sure if the horses were heating up any with the movement and spins, but I certainly wasn't.

Reaching the collection of buildings, I'd been correct in my assumption as there were big barns to the left of the road. Heading instead to the right, I walked up to the farmhouse and banged on the door as loudly as my frozen hands would allow - but to no response.

"Knock harder," said Yogi, in desperation.

"Would you like me to kick it?" asked Swift, deadly serious with her request.

"I don't think that would be the best introduction if I'm honest, but it's kind of you to offer."

"Desperate times call for desperate measures," I heard her mutter from behind as I led them across to the barns to try there instead.

The barns looked substantial, but all were closed, locked, and quiet within. With no vehicles in sight, I realised we weren't likely to be successful in our search. Hunkered down by the wall of a barn, I again checked my map and with dread, realised that the next buildings were three kilometres more.

"At least it looks like a more substantial farm than this one, and it's closer to the village where we might find someone to help us," I said, as cheerfully as I could between chattering teeth.

My statement didn't provoke a response from either companion, standing as they were with ears drooped in a combination of disappointment and sheer ear-heaviness due to the weight of the water soaked into them. In the lee of the barn, the rain was free to drip as gravity intended, from the horses' eyelashes, manes, tails, and noses, all the way to their toes(es).

I wasn't fairing much better with droplets falling from the brim of my hat and the knowledge that the rain had already seeped through my clothes. I could feel cold wet patches between my shoulder blades, on my chest, down my sleeves, and up my legs to my waist. Despite my trusty chaps, the insides of my boots were soggy too and if I did have any dry patches anywhere, they were scarce enough to be unidentified at present.

In anguish, I dragged Team Swogi back to the road. Three kilometres was less than an hour and surely we could do that despite conditions, couldn't we? The doubt weighed more heavily on my shoulders than my sodden clothing and I pleaded for the storm to simmer down and for shelter to be found. We were now on another long and exposed straight, and as a gust of wind slammed into us hard, both Swift and Yogi spun abruptly again. The doubt gained a few extra pounds as I untangled, tied down, realigned the team, and held back the tears.

In my struggle I hadn't noticed the arrival of a vehicle in front of us which was now approaching with caution towards our commotion. It was a small red van driven with determination for its daily delivery by a postman in a matching uniform. I stopped short of throwing myself in front of the bonnet but did stop its progress with a desperate wave of my arms. *If anyone would know the area well, the local postman is sure to,* I thought.

The driver opened his window, just a crack, trying no doubt to preserve the warmth held within.

"It's no day to be outside," he declared, with an incorrect level on his 'cheerometer' as far as I was concerned.

"Exactly!" I replied. "Do you know of a farm with a barn so I could get my horses inside?" I didn't give him long to consider my request. "They're freezing, I'm desperate, and I need to get them out of this storm." I added this detail in case my dank demeanour and frantic arm waving hadn't been evidence enough.

Yogi and Swift were looking on with their first bit of interest in proceedings thus far today. The postie was oblivious, but I could clearly see they were considering if there might be enough room for two horses to fit in the back of his van.

"We could throw out a few parcels and sit on the rest," offered Yogi helpfully.

"Head for the hostel, they have horses and a shelter, they are sure to help," said the Postie through the window's slit.

"Where is it?" I asked, the words catching in my throat.

"Down to the bridge, you'll find the owner at the first yellow house, you can't miss it."

Incorrect Cheerometer Level

I thanked him profusely and hoped the rain had hidden the relieved tears, no longer controlled, streaming down my cheeks. Bleary-eyed but with renewed resolved, I encouraged Team Swogi onwards with a picture-perfect vision of a warm shelter and two happy, furry faces poking out of it at the end of this ordeal.

We struggled on for another kilometre or so with the same butt-to-wind rotations interrupting progress on regular basis. I noted with a dismayed glance at the flapping map that the next (and last) kilometre-and-a-half along the road would again have next-to-no tree cover and next-to-no protection from the storm. As we left the shelter of the last tree and continued onto exposed ground, the horses again spun around. *Funny,* I thought, *I didn't feel a wind gust just then.*

If it hadn't been for the spin, followed by Swift pointing vigorously behind her, I'd not have noticed the car at her rear, the noise of the engine drowned as it was by the wind's bluster. The lady behind the wheel gave me a wave and a smile as I manoeuvred the team to the side to let her pass by but as she drew level, she lowered her window all the way down - braver than the postie.

"I've phoned Robbie at the hostel; they are expecting you," she said.

Word flowed fast in the glen it seemed, as did renewed tears from my eyes. The confirmation that the hostel would help was such a relief. Women are generally more astute than men and there was no disguising my tears as rain drops this time.

"Bless you," she said. "Not far to go now, you'll be alright, the hostel is lovely and warm."

As her car disappeared down the road, I realised I hadn't given *my* warmth and comfort one single thought. I was cold and soaked through too, but I'd have been happy to bed down in the corner of the horse shelter if that was all that was on offer, just so long as Team Swogi could get cosy and dry.

The confirmation of the hostel's help didn't provide any bodily warmth, but it did restore a flicker of fortitude and we were soon crossing the bridge to the village. Right in front of us was a huge yellow house, and the postie was correct – "You couldn't miss it!"

Well, I couldn't miss it, but I also couldn't get to the front door, not with horses in tow anyway as there was a cattle grid across the driveway, blocking progress for those with hooves. I also couldn't leave the horses free this close to the road. I considered tying them to the fence, but all it would take was a vehicle to splash in one of the numerous puddles and mayhem might ensue.

I opened the gate to the field next to the house and 'parked' the horses under the shelter of a huge tree on some long grass. Leaving them huddled and munching, I climbed the fence and went to knock on the door. The house was silent, and my knocks remained unanswered. It was most definitely yellow, huge, and incredibly obvious when crossing the bridge, and I felt I'd followed the postie's instructions to the letter, but no owner of house or hostel was to be found here.

If it hadn't been for meeting the two vehicles on the road, I'd have thought there'd been an apocalypse of Armageddon proportions in the glen. *Where was everyone*? And why weren't they indoors sheltering from this storm like I wanted to be?

Back under the shelter of the tree, and with cold, numb fingers, I fetched out my phone to see if I could find a number for the hostel online but there was no reception. The GPS satellite device I carried was good for many things, but Google searches wasn't one of them. My only option was to continue to the village towards the hostel to see if I could find anyone there.

At least down here there was more shelter from the storm, but Team Swogi were still reluctant to leave the lush grass and tree shelter for more tarmac drudgery in the rain. With my mind fixed on finding the correct yellow house, I ignored a couple of cottages and the pretty kirk (church) as they were all painted white, then came to a pause at a sign for the hostel and a rare sight these days, a traditional red telephone box.

As I turned back on myself up a small side road (following the sign) I could see another big yellow house. Not as huge as the last one, and certainly easier to miss from my initial direction of travel, but with a car in the driveway and it being closer to the hostel, it looked more promising.

For the first time today, my knock on a door was answered and thankfully I was the only one looking like I'd risen from the dead. The woman who answered the door wasn't the hostel owner either, but she knew Robbie the manager and so tried, unsuccessfully, to give him a call. As housekeeper, Sharon also knew that the hostel was empty as she'd just been up there, so couldn't say where he might be.

I'm not sure whether it was the forlorn expression on my face or the triply-unified shivers from all of us that caught her attention, but half-way through giving me directions on how to find the manager's house (back down past the kirk), she suddenly stopped and said, "Just wait here, I'll jump in my car and go find him and if I can't, I'll try to find Hector instead - he's the owner." For this I was enormously grateful, as were Team Swogi who made a start at mowing her lawn as an offering of thanks whilst waiting for her return.

Sharon didn't take long to come back but it was a cold and shivering wait. It always amazes me how fast you chill when standing still. Her excursion had been unproductive; Robbie was still missing in action, and Hector was unfound, but unperturbed she instructed me to follow her up to the hostel anyway as she was sure it would all be fine. I wasn't going to argue, and arriving a moment after her car, I could see that all indeed would be fine as there was a strong shelter to the right of the hostel, currently empty of equines. It might have been my imagination, but I'm sure it had 'Team Swogi' written all over it.

Sharon patiently waited for me to drop my saddle bags and tack near the door of the hostel, then led the way to the shelter. She helped me to close gates to keep the horses contained, find a tap for water, and showed me where I could find hay.

Understanding that I needed to see to the horses first, she gave me the code to the hostel door, explained where the drying room was, and told me to help myself. I thought there wasn't much more that could be done to top this level of helpfulness but I was wrong, as she stated that she'd be back soon with a pickup full of straw so that the horses could lay down to sleep overnight.

Speechless at this thoughtfulness, I turned my attention to Team Swogi who were now tucked up in the back of the shelter. Shielded from the wind and rain, they'd soon dry out, but they also needed some food. Yogi was tucked up in more ways than one, as his flanks were beginning to look sunken and drawn up, a sign of cold and/or stress. This used to be a common occurrence with stress-head Yogi in the early days of dobbineering when everything was unfamiliar and disturbing, but was something I'd not seen now for many years.

Thankfully a fix was usually simple and was one that he was more than happy to help with. I plonked two generous piles of hay at the opening of the shelter and Yogi began to address his taut tummy issues with huge mouthfuls of it. Another reason horses can become 'tucked up' is through lack of water. Considering the amount of rain we'd had over the last few days and the puddles we'd splashed through this morning, I doubted this would be the cause - but just in case, I found a bucket to fill and left it inside the shelter too.

It was an immense relief to have Team Swogi cosy and safe. The storm was still in full force, and I was so grateful to have been offered a place to get them out of its reaches. I didn't appear to be having the best run of weather for this trek and I hoped that tomorrow would bring some fairer change.

With Swift and Yogi content in the shelter, drying out and stuffing their faces, I turned attentions to myself and the mountain of drenched kit I needed to contend with. The kit was heaped on the ground under a lean-to next to the hostel door. It was soaked through and heavy, and I didn't know quite where to start. I opened the bag containing human food, pulled out the (no-longer) dry bag holding the teabags and decided to take my soggy offering inside - to start the unpacking and drying process by firstly making a quick cup of tea.

I'd striped my drenched outer layers off under the lean-to before making a dash for the door, but when walking to the kettle it was apparent that the layers underneath were soggy too as I'd left a trail of small puddles across the floor. So, as the kettle boiled, I removed my socks and rolled up my jodhpurs in an effort to prevent more drips, then searched the hostel for a mop.

The accommodation was bigger than it looked from the outside. The kitchen was spacious, with a large dining table to one side and at the back of this open plan room was a mezzanine lounge. Its edges were lined with comfy sofas, all facing a wood-burning stove, and I so looked forward to soaking up its warmth once I'd got out of these soaking clothes.

A corridor led down to a number of bathrooms and bedrooms equipped with bunkbeds. All the rooms were empty of personal possessions, so it looked like I could take my pick of a bed for the night. Behind one of the doors in the corridor, I found a mop waiting eagerly in a cupboard.

Walking backwards, I mopped my way over to the kettle and with the mop in one hand and a cuppa in the other, I retreated out to the porch, clearing the puddles as I went. There was no point in getting changed yet as I still had horse care and kit care to attend to and the rain was still falling hard. In the porch doorway, I stared out at the rain and wrapped my hands around the steaming mug for warmth. Despite the weather ruining our plans for the day, and the worry it had caused with the horses getting so cold, it was very impressive.

Big weather is always an exhilarating experience. A thunderous lightning display, a cascade of torrential rain, a terrifying gale, or a period of relentless heavy snowfall that smothers the familiar in mere moments, does a fantastic job of making you feel small and insignificant in the world. It also leaves you feeling mightily awed by the power of the natural world.

Sometimes it can invigorate, like the glee felt by a welly-clad toddler jumping up and down in puddles, but at other times it can scare the wellies and socks right off your feet. It all depends, I guess, on the situation as now that I was safely at the hostel with the horses tucked up warm, this storm didn't seem half as bad as it was earlier. The wind was still gusting at 70mph according to reliable sources on the internet though.

I gulped down the remains of my warming tea, slipped my cold feet into my disgustingly wet boots and dashed to the lean-to to start triaging the gear. Horse rugs of course were given top priority, followed by tent, tarp, and poncho. If I could get these all dry whilst here, we'd last a while longer if the bad weather did the same.

The saddle pads and saddle bags become heavy when wet, so they'd be next on the list. The rest of my stuff (food, clothes, etc.) were all in dry bags and although contents might be a little damp, they'd soon dry out by the fire.

Grabbing the two rugs and the tent, I ran for the drying room in the nearby outbuilding and opened the door to a more-than-welcomed wave of heat. This was in fact the boiler room, but in and around the tanks and pipes were plenty of hooks and beams on which to hang my gear. I seriously hoped nobody else turned up damp and dishevelled, wanting to use this space too as the air was about to become decidedly pungent!

Rugs and tent hung and dripping, I returned to the lean-to. I bent down to process the next items on the list and immediately felt my heart go into arrhythmia, the one where it beats far faster than it's supposed to, a rhythm called Super Ventricular Tachycardia or SVT.

I tried not to panic as this had happened numerous times over the last year, often after exertion or a positional change such as lying down or bending over as I'd just done. I also tried not to think that this could be slightly problematic happening out here at the end of a remote glen, as sometimes my heart reverted to a normal rhythm itself and sometimes it didn't. When it didn't, I usually needed a trip to the nearest Accident and Emergency Department (AED) for a shot of a heart-slowing medication (adenosine).

I did have a few tricks up my sleeve though to give my heart a helping hand to revert to a more sensible pace. With shaking hands, and feeling a little breathless, I searched for my first aid kit in amongst the pile. Finding the 10ml syringe packed solely for this purpose, I cleared my bags away from the back wall and sat down, close to it but facing it. I was attempting to carry out a modified valsalva manoeuvre, the recognised first-line management for SVT, and I tried to block out the thought that I'd only been successful once before when trying this on my own.

The idea was to blow into the syringe as hard as I could for fifteen seconds, attempting to move the plunger with my breath (apparently generating 40mmHg of intrathoracic pressure), followed rapidly by a postural change which involved me lying down on my back with my feet up high against the wall. Keeping my feet there was the challenge when solo, as the process, when done correctly causes you to almost pass out for a moment.

Studies have shown that this technique, which stimulates the vagal nerve (leading to a slowing of the heart), is successful in more than 40% of cases of SVT, and as I blew hard into the syringe, I sincerely hoped that I was one of this percentage today.

I'm not sure whether it was my increased motivation to move the plunger, given my remote situation, or whether it was help from the little mouse that ran over my chest as I lay on my back, but I could no longer feel my heart pounding. The mouse had been a surreal addition to the procedure and I'm not sure whether this enhancement is one applied in any AED, but it seemed to have done the trick.

Confirming a return to normal sinus rhythm by feeling my radial pulse, I felt a profound relief but a reluctance to move. I didn't want a repeat performance by changing position, as I wasn't sure where the mouse had gone to aid with a second attempt. Hearing a car arrive in the carpark got me slowly to my feet though; well, that and the cold. I was shivering again, although I suspected some of the tremors were likely shakes due to the scare I'd just endured.

Sharon had arrived with the straw as promised and either she was extremely polite, or years of dealing with the eccentricities of the general public had taught her that it's just best not to ask, but she didn't mention the position she'd found me in, nor the dust all over my back. Together we carried piles of straw over to the shelter, much to the delight of the horses, and as we bedded them down I was delighted too - to find four warm ears and a much less tucked up Yogi. I left two new piles of hay though just to be sure.

Thanking Sharon profusely for her thoughtfulness and kindness, I returned to the lean-to to hang up the rest of the gear – being careful this time to move a little slower. With the boiler room now fully decorated, it had taken on a new ambiance that wasn't all that pleasant but at least I could see that things were starting to dry. Thinking back to the random rodent from earlier, I made sure to carry all remanence of food into the safety of the hostel. I also made sure to take some extra heart medication.

I was suddenly feeling exhausted, but there was one more job to do before heading for a hot shower, which was to light the stove to warm the lounge. A huge basket of logs had been provided, and I estimated there'd be enough there to keep me cosy for the rest of the day. I ensured the flames had taken hold and that they had enough available fuel to keep them fed until my return, then went for a shower.

The restorative properties of hot water refreshed a little and back in the kitchen, I formed a plan of action which was to eat, re-plan the route, restock hay, eat, repack, and sleep – most within the reaches of the wood-burner's glow.

Over lunch, I connected to the hostel's wifi to check the storm's status and was relieved to find that it should blow itself out sometime through the night. If that were the case, I'd still be able to complete my circuit as per the original time and distance objectives, but only if I rejigged the plan a little. I had two very short days ahead, designed to cater for health, but also to provide options for circumstances such as these. If I combined the two shorts into one long, I could get back on track, and still finish before being due back to work. I just hoped my heart would behave better than it had today, particularly during the long day which involved a steep climb and a remote plateau.

Stopping here wasn't what I'd planned, but I certainly felt that I'd landed on my feet. The hostel was absolutely lovely, very well equipped, and I was surprised to have such luxuries all to myself even though it was midweek. I also felt glad that my contingency plan allowed for continuation (despite the weather) unlike another expedition planned in Glen Prosen, which unfortunately came to an ill-fated conclusion.

In 1910, the Atlantic explorers Caption Robert Scott and his scientific officer Dr Edward Wilson planned their epic Terra Nova expedition to the South Pole here in Glen Prosen. They spent six months at Burnside Lodge, a property owned by Wilson, planning and using the Angus Glens for endurance training.

They set off with sixteen men, twenty-three dogs, and ten ponies, reaching the pole a few months later on the 17th January 1912. The out and return journey should have been a total of 2,465 kilometres but unfortunately Scott died together with Wilson at the end of March on the Ross Ice Shelf - only eighteen kilometres from a much-needed supply depot. Unable to progress their return in a timely manner due to frostbitten feet and continued storms, all five members of the South Pole party succumbed, the last three to a combination of hypothermia, dehydration, and starvation as they ran out of food and fuel, stormbound and unable to move.

A huge granite monument was constructed further down the Angus Glen, and at thirty tonnes it was the largest granite sculpture created in Scotland since the 1920's. It commemorates Scott, Wilson, their men, the ponies, dogs, and even penguins – the subject of their scientific research. I thought it best not to mention to Team Swogi that only a small number of the ponies survived. Many were unfortunately shot for food, once their job of kit hauling was complete.

Glad that I'd found a safer place to sit out a storm than the middle of a snowy ice shelf, I threw another log onto the fire and refilled my cup with tea. There would be no hypothermia, starvation, or dehydration here - although hypothermia had felt like a possibility earlier on today. I again marvelled at just how harsh Scottish weather can be, even in our so-called summer.

I whiled away the afternoon in front of the fire, dipping into books on the hostel's shelf, drinking tea, and occasionally drifting off to sleep. Every so often I popped out to check Team Swogi and offered more hay when required. On my way back each time, I turned and rotated the kit in the drying room and repacked as much as I could.

The storm was still very much in force, and I was so grateful that all of us could stay well out of it. Thank goodness we hadn't stopped higher up the glen at the Kilbo Bothy last night, as it would have been a rough night in the wind and rain, and we'd still be out there now.

Still undisturbed and with the hostel to myself, I made a heartier dinner than I usually experienced on the trail thanks to the contents of a cupboard marked 'food to share'. A lowly tin of baked beans and a packet of Smash gave a gourmet grade to tonight's grub, and while the storm still raged outside, it felt like a meal fit for kings. With my stomach satisfied, I stepped outside one last time for a replenishment of hay and gave the snug duo a goodnight hug. I then retired to a cosy bed and settled in for a good night's sleep.

Yogi on the Trail *Swift on the Trail*

Through the Ears at Glen Feshie

The Toll Tree, Glen Feshie

Quarzite Cairns on the Minigaig Pass

Dropping Down into Glen Bruar

Flora the Friendly Highland Cow

Convincing Yogi to Pause at the Allt Sheicheachan Bothy

The Three Bald Kings

An Imperial Moustache and a Cob Impression

Swift, Leanne, and Foxy near the Spittal of Glenshee

Meeting Jet, Atticus, and Bradford

The View from Bawhelps

Hiding from the Storm at Glenprosen Hostel

All Around the Bloomin Heather – The Minister's Path

Glen Clova Hotel – Luxury on the Trail

Climbing the Capel Mounth, Glendoll

The Beautiful View and the Descent to Loch Muick

The Full Team at Glen Muick

The Prehistoric Creature of Lochnagar

Between Gelder Shiel and Mar Lodge

The Peaceful Camp at Mar Lodge

Yogi – Rest Day Snoozes and almost in REM Sleep

Swift, Showing How REM Sleep is Done

Leaving Bob Scott's Bothy Along the Green River

Helicopter Watching in Glen Derry

Approaching The Pass of the Calves

The Handsome Bear, Lairig an Loigh

Spotty Bum in the Lairig an Loigh

Crossing the Fords of Avon

The Vast Expanse of the Bynack Moor

Looking Back Down the Bynack Moor

Yogi and Swift Keen to Go

The Righteous Path

Day 9: Glenprosen Hostel to Glendoll (Distance 18km, Ascent 496m)

The brightness of the day from behind the curtains woke me gently five minutes before my alarm. I lingered, enjoying the fresh sheets and plump pillow for a while longer as I read a chapter of my book. I was mostly repacked, and with no camp or corral to deconstruct this morning there was no need to rush. I applied the same leisurely approach to breakfast and lingered over my maps too with a third cup of tea.

Opening the door of the hostel, I could see that the weather was much improved. It was still overcast and looked like it might rain at some point today, but the wind had died down considerably. I rounded the corner of the outbuilding and was immediately greeted by loud whinnies from Yogi and Swift. They were outside of the shelter, nibbling the grass at the edges of the enclosure, but both lifted their heads for a moment to shout their morning cheer.

The good night's sleep with soft and cosy beds had been beneficial for us all, but particularly Swift it seemed. It's such a rarity to get any sort of morning acknowledgement from her, more than a mere glance or mare-glare. Her deeply layered and rich-sounding voice is enchanting and it always fills my heart, but I'm not honoured to hear it all that often. A hearty vocal welcome suggested she'd had a comfortable night, was feeling cheerful, and would probably be on top form today.

"Scratch here, please, that bit I can't reach," she politely requested on my arrival.

Wow, I thought, *an ask rather than a diva-demand. Well that makes a change.*

"This bit here, my love?" I checked, as the directional point with her nose had been a little vague.

I scratched around until her head dropped, her eyes glazed over, and her happy nose twitches told me I'd found just the right spot. I smiled as she let out a long, contented sigh followed by a huge, sleepy yawn.

"Can I have a bit of that too?" asked Yogi, plonking his butt between Swift and myself – destroying the rare moment of companionable connection I'd been enjoying with my mare.

"Yes of course you can," I replied, rolling my eyes, but laughing inside at his accurate reverse parking skills which had manoeuvred the favourite part of his anatomy into prime scratching position.

I tried to continue to pamper Swift too (with my other hand), but she was most upset by Yogi jumping the queue and stormed off to the other side of the enclosure, angrily swishing her tail. Our moment of serenity lost; I hoped the rude interruption hadn't totally destroyed her good mood. I gathered her back into the herd, popped headcollars on, and led them both over to the lean-to to tack up. Luckily there was a square of tasty green grass to keep them both amused (and reasonably contained) while I carried out the usual daily pre-trail preparations.

Half-way through the procedure, the owner of the hostel arrived. Hector appeared to be a true gent, concerned as he was with our recovery from the storm, if we'd been comfortable overnight, whether the horse's needs had fully been met; and he apologised profusely for missing our arrival yesterday.

"The shelter and straw made for a cosy sleep, thank you," said Swift, unprompted, still seemingly in a happy and appreciative place.

"If I might suggest a small enhancement?" asked Yogi, as politely as he could. "An all you can eat carrot buffet by the shelter would increase ratings by at least two stars."

As politely as he'd tried, this was a little rude considering how well we'd been looked after, but a hungry pre-breakfast Bear sometimes just can't help himself. I was glad that Hector hadn't overheard as he was busy telling me not to worry about payment for our stay.

"Just get in touch when you get back home, and we'll sort it out then," he stated, with obvious trust.

Feeling optimistic and bolstered by our comfy stay, we set out for the day ignoring the clouds which were still threatening rain. Our route would take us from Glen Prosen, the second of the Angus Glens, up and over into Glen Clova, the third of the five. From west to east, the main glens of Angus: Isla, Prosen, Clova, Lethnot, and Esk are said to resemble the thumb and fingers of a giant's hand, with the palm resting over the lowlands and towns of Strathmore.

These valleys that run in a north-westwards direction between the Grampian Mountains and the Strathmore Vale were formed in glacial times, but I prefer the giant's explanation to their origins. I don't find a giant slamming down his right hand to create five glens all that far-fetched, particularly given that a flying boy and a fairy also had their beginnings in Kirriemuir (a Strathmore town) as the birthplace of JM Barrie, the creator of *Peter Pan*.

Like the digits on a hand, each glen is said to have different traits. The thumb of Isla is green, the index of Prosen peaceful, the middle Clova is craggy, the ring of Lethnot is wild, and the pinky Esk is remote. Their individual beauty captivates all who explore, beckoning you on between steep sides, to discover the fullness of their depths; and deep they are, over sixteen kilometres in length. Rising up to the mountains at their head and each following their own river or water, adding sparkle to their splendour.

With the Prosen Water to our right, we crossed a bridge over its tributary and turned left towards the little white kirk. The church was built in 1802, paid for by the local community, and is modest in its oblong shape and white-washed walls. Nothing of note, except for the unique feature of a cross on the porch gable created by embedding slates into the wall. A fairly insignificant structure, but I paused to acknowledge this humble place of worship before continuing up the hill for good reason.

Today's travels would take us over high moorland to link the peaceful Prosen with craggy Clova, following a very special trail called The Minister's Path. At least, I'd given it the 'special' label as I loved the story of its foundation. The path takes its name from the fact that the minister of the parish officiated over both Glenprosen Kirk and that of Glen Clova. He rode his pony between the two, using this path with ecclesiastical purpose, to give service in each glen on the sabbath.

In the 18th century, with scattered and remote populations, it wasn't unusual for ministers to have large parishes, presiding over more than one place of worship. Indeed, it was often a requirement of contract to secure a Royal Bounty, a subsidy of wages by government and charity keen to improve education and religious practice within the Highlands. The drive was to encourage Gaels to be loyal Presbyterians away from the perceived dangers of Catholicism, as "Catholicism and jacobitism were interchangeable in the eyes of the presbyterian church" – according to *Records of the Scottish Church History Society, 33 (2003)*. Often granted an annual amount of one thousand pounds, ministers were "appointed to preach so many services at one place and so many at another."

This shortcut over the moors was a practical solution to one minister serving two parishes, but the rough terrain and inclement weather (such as yesterday's example) would have meant for arduous travel, and a test of his faith, on many Sundays of the year. As the minister aged, accounts suggest he was no longer able to ride his pony, and the parishioners joined forces to widen the track to allow for a trap to be pulled. By either method, it is thought that his pony so used to the regular excursion, could make the journey without any guidance or assistance.

"Well, I'm going to need assistance," said Yogi, bumping his nose against the gate we'd arrived at. "As I can't undo this gate."

I couldn't undo it either. It wasn't locked but the clasp that held the links of the chain together wouldn't open far enough to unhook. Whichever way I twisted and turned, it just wouldn't budge. Yogi soon turned his attention to the grass at the side of the fence and Swift followed suit, leaving me to bear this cross all on my own. As I wrestled with the gate, I couldn't ignore the metaphor of a failure to unlock my spiritual side throughout life, but I didn't think the minister's memory would pull any divine rites of passage here.

It seemed sacrilege to apply my hacksaw to the chain as doing so would leave the route insecure. An alternative technique, lifting the gate off its hinges, to open (and close) it from the other side was thwarted too, as the hinges were capped at the top. With nothing else for it, I picked up a stone and went for a brute force and ignorance approach, which soon scared the clasp into giving up its hold.

Through the gate, I jumped up on Yogi and we set off along a stony track beside a woodland that climbed the eastern side of Glen Tairie. The stones didn't seem to hinder the horse's progress at all, as both had a spring in their steps after a good night's rest and a fill of hay. We soon reached another gate and the trail ahead stretched out across the moor in a wide and grassy manner.

Through the gate (easily opened this time), on either side of the trail, the heather's purple bells were tolling out their bloom and I couldn't help but launch into a tune myself of "Will Ye Go Lassie Go." Following in the minister's footsteps, I wondered how much the view had changed in the last two hundred years. I also wondered if he sang hymns or rehearsed his sermon on his journeys - with only the wild mountain thyme, the flowers of the mountain, and his pony's ears to appraise his holy words.

My attempts weren't overly appreciated by my small congregation. Yogi's ears were flicking back and forth and Swift was rolling her eyes. I had a sudden pang for companionship, of my trail partner Yvonne who often sang on our travels, but with a more melodious tune than I could ever muster.

The trail remained grassy as it contoured the edge of the glen, before turning more easterly to climb fifty metres (or so) in height to a small gate at the top. The gate was a tight squeeze for those of us with a Highland belly and those carrying bags, but somehow, we managed to negotiate our way through without me having to dismount.

"My belly hardly touched it," said Yogi, looking round at his midriff. "I'm fading away. More hay AND carrots are required tonight."

"That gate's spring was fierce! It closed so fast behind my spotty bum. Just as well I'm swift," said Swift.

The next section of trail had strangely been upgraded. The new portion of raised, hard-packed gravel was in the middle of nowhere and only lasted for one-hundred metres. It didn't look wide enough for the minister's trap here, but I was grateful for the improvements, as the trail was flanked on either side by deep, dark waters. Yogi's head was turning from side to side looking out for kelpies, a shape-shifting spirit reputed to live in Scottish waters.

Although a fellow equine, and described as a powerful black horse, a kelpie's character differed greatly from my amiable companions. The kelpie preyed on victims (particularly children) by carrying them off into the pools to devour them, and when satisfied, would throw their remaining entrails to the water's edge. Their hooves are reversed compared to those of a normal horse, their manes made of serpents, and their backs able to extend to carry extra victims.

The kelpie tales were likely just a legend to keep children away from hazardous areas of water, but Yogi wasn't taking any chances and broke into a trot, which only increased in speed once back on the grass at the end of the gravel. I was amused to see that Swift, generally disbelieving of mythical creatures, was hot on his tail and even overtook to challenge him for the lead. I guess she'd found the magical trail through dark waters a little eery too.

The heather to either side of the trail was brown and not yet in bloom, and I noted how such a small difference in height can so drastically change vegetation's habits. The weather had changed too, the wind was a little stronger and with more chill to its bite. I focussed on a small patch of blue sky ahead and blocked out the dark band of cloud which was amassing to my left. Unfortunately, even with Team Swogi's spurt of speed, we didn't outrun the cloud's reaches and a heavy shower commenced. By the time we reached the top of the rise on the Hill of Drumwhern's flanks, we were all drenched again.

Fording a stream to arrive at a crossroads, the shower passed overhead and I pulled out my map. The original Minister's Path took a left turn here, but the route straight ahead was a shorter way down to Glen Clova. I slid my finger down the older winding trail on the map and savoured its twists and turns, confirming yet again why I like to find my route the old-fashioned way. A map allows you to look ahead, to anticipate the whole journey and consider options, rather than simply follow a flashing arrow on a screen.

The new route to the east looked wide and sure, but the original trail to the north caught my attention, as through the trees it narrowed, meandered, and exuded excitement. Turning Team Swogi northwards, we stepped around a fallen wooden gate and climbed up to Elf Hillock in the lee of the dark clouds that had thankfully ceased their cascade.

When the descendants of present-day Scots took over the land from Picts in the 9th century, they found peculiar entities they could not always rationalise. The Picts supposed that many mysterious happenings were of supernatural cause and elves and fairies were believed to hide their homes within hillocks such as this one. There are numerous elf howes, caves, barrows, and hills in Britain, and in folklore these would periodically rise or open to reveal feasting and music within.

Considering that Angus was inhabited since the Neolithic period, it's not surprising that ancient stories abound from every stone or bump in its land. Indeed, the county of Angus takes its name from an 8th century Pictish king (Óengus mac Fergusa) reigning from 820 until 834. According to legend, Saint Andrew appeared before the king on the eve of battle to advise him to watch for the “sign of the Cross of Christ in the air” for which the Picts agreed to venerate the Saint.

It was a confusing time back then, with Picts holding onto pagan beliefs amongst the introduction of Christian practice, but “where the Roman Empire failed to conquer the Picts, the Christian church succeeded” – according to Stuart McHardy in his *A New History of the Picts*. This hillock, however, had held onto its Pictish roots (at least by name), despite the regular visits of the Christian minister passing by in later centuries.

Stories of elves and other faerie folk also hold on in a significant number of ballads, often describing rapture of their beauty, their magical powers, and fear of their temper-driven retaliations. One of their curses known as ‘elf-shot’ was an illness mainly associated with horses and cattle but could be imposed on humans too. With a shot from their arrow, the elves could inflict sudden shooting pains focussed in one area of the body. References to ‘elf-shot’ as a reason for strange maladies and unexplained deaths persisted into the 20th century, and many believe our more modern term ‘stroke’ originates from ‘elf-stroke’.

A cure could be found by touching the area of pain with an elves’ arrow or by drinking water that an arrow had been soaked in. Archaeological finds of neolithic arrowheads within pre-historical burial mounds were often believed to be elf arrows kept as amulets and protective charms. Feverfew, red nettles, and waybread, with their spear-shaped leaves, were said to ease the pains too.

Paths that fairies and elves travel along are usual stated as being best avoided, and perhaps that’s why The Minister’s Path took a sharp turn here. It was also considered bad luck to let livestock graze on any place where elf-folk have been.

"Quatt-pttui!" said Yogi, as he rapidly spat out the mouthful of grass he'd just grabbed.

The single-track route was living up to expectations and was weaving its way through undulating hillocks. We wound our way over fallen branches, tufts of heather, rocks, and clumps of blueberries not yet in bloom. I couldn't deny a magical and mystical feel to the place that made me want to dwell longer, and I gave the enchanted setting once last glance as we dropped into the cool depths of the trees.

Out of the wind, the track twisted back and forth as it descended sharply. This forest had plenty of room to breathe with a light and airy feel, and a rich carpet of green grass. The path snaked its way amongst the trees, and I had to duck underneath the outstretched branches. I could imagine the minister getting a little hot under his collar as his gown snagged and his hat was knocked off his head – even on a pony of shorter stature than mine. With one final steep switch-back of the trail, we emerged at the edge of a clearing and the track ahead was stony. It was raised up through soft ground on either side and intersected by drainage channels every few hundred yards.

The channels were lined on each side by huge boulders, the spacing of which influenced whether Team Swogi tackled these with a large stride or a neat leap. The leaping (although careful and precise) began to attract the attention of the field's inhabitants, and we were soon accompanied on our hurdling traverse by a herd of fascinated cows, sloshing through deep mud to our left. Yogi and Swift, focussed as they were on the regular rocky channels, didn't seem to mind the noisy and splattering presence of our new companions. I didn't mind either and enjoyed the fine view to the hills of Clova to our right, periodically interrupted by a bounce or two.

At the end of this rocky trail, we entered a section of forest. It was dark, leafy, filled with fern, and smelt fresh and earthy at the same time. The scent was no doubt enhanced by the recent rain. Dark as it was, the numerous shades of green were still discernible in the gloomy depths, before emerging into the open glen, with its opposing brightness, on the road that ran along the length of the River South Esk.

Both Glen Prosen and Glen Clova have minor roads serving their length, one on each side of their valley. The locals have an unwritten one-way system, often disrupted by tourists not-in-the-know. I set off towards the bridge that crossed the river, unsure if I was going against the flow, but didn't meet any traffic to attest any such arrangements. After crossing the bridge, we paused for a while to admire the Clova Kirk, a pretty terminal for the minister each Sunday after his traverse across the hills.

Made from granite stone, the church was built in 1855 on the site of a previous one dating back to the early 18th century. Pink blocks defined its corners and surrounded each white, latticed window in precise contrast to the grey stone walls. There was a finial cross on one gable head and a bellcote elegantly positioned on the other.

No longer a parish church, it was still used for weddings and ecumenical services by the local community, but I felt sad for the minister's memory - that his efforts to uphold tradition didn't last the test of time. My sadness continued as I bade farewell to his company, but I was soon cheered by our arrival at the Glen Clova Hotel.

There had been an inn here since the 1850's, serving drovers back in the day and a sizeable number of local people. In 1755 Glen Clova had around 1200 inhabitants, but numbers had dwindled to around 400 now. The hotel was still frequented by many though, popular with climbers and all else who travel to admire the glen's mountainous beauty and abundant wildlife. I fancied frequenting it today too, as it's rare to be able to stop at a pub on my travels and besides, it's only right when following drovers' trails to mimic their actions as closely as one could.

I drove Team Swogi across the hotel's carpark to look for a suitable park for horses. There was a large expanse of grass, but since the large sign on its edge clearly stated 'No Dogs', I didn't feel equines would be welcome either. Disappointed, I turned back towards the road and spotted a small enclosure behind the gateway to a field. With one short strip of electric tape, it created the perfect corral, and I hoped nobody would mind my temporary placement of ponies.

I was just closing the gate behind me when a man pulled up in his pickup on the opposite side of the road. Dressed as he was in wellies and a cheque-shirt, I presumed he was the farmer, so went over to check that I wouldn't be in his way. The response to my equable enquiry was a blunt and gruff reply.

"Well, you're there already, aren't you!"

"I can easily move if it's any sort of problem," I responded, although not really wanting to with a pint of beer so temptingly within reach.

He didn't respond to my offer, just shrugged his shoulders, jumped back in his truck, and drove off. I had been about to offer him the choice of his favourite tipple, to be placed on tab behind the bar for his troubles and the end of his long day. His loss, I suppose. Shrugging my shoulders too and with Yogi and Swift happily munching, I set off to the bar to find my own refreshments and nibbles.

It was rather classy inside. I felt completely out of place in my grubby clothes from over a week on the trail, and it didn't feel right to sit on the posh furnishings. Instead, I wondered around the walls, exploring previous decades as I waited for my pint to be poured, as the walls of the bar were decorated with black and white photos and memorabilia of times gone by. Carrying my pint and a packet of crips, I went back outside to where I'd feel more at ease and could keep an eye on Yogi and Swift.

I was like a kid in a sweetshop, blissfully happy and excited to savour my first and probably only beer on this trail. I'd obviously managed a short pub stop back in Glen Shee with Yvonne, but there, the horses had been left in their rest-stop field.

In my humble opinion, there is nothing that beats the luxury of a beer on the trail, especially when enhanced by the sounds of munching and contented sighs from my companions. The velvety malt taste of Guinness certainly felt luxurious, alongside the added delights of tangy salt-and-vinegar crips. These combined with the warm sunshine that had finally pushed through the clouds gave a true holiday feel to this moment on the trail.

The savouring didn't last too long though, as the thick and creamy delight disappeared at an alarming rate and I could only surmise that it suffered evaporation from the heat of the sun. Every day is a school day and I discovered that there *is* one thing that beats the luxury of a beer on the trail ... which is *two* beers on the trail! With the excuse of topping up my iron content to keep my heart behaving, I checked with Team Swogi to see if they might mind me pausing a while longer.

Luxury on the Trail

"Hmmm... chomp... yum," said Yogi, between mouthfuls of grass.

"No problem," said Swift. "Fill your boots, we're quite happy here."

I didn't think the farmer could be any more displeased, so a second pint wouldn't make things worse. As far as I was concerned, it would improve things immeasurably.

Eagerly anticipated, round two was as good as the first (with a similar rate of evaporation), and in a contented haze I turned my attention to the rest of the day's ride. We only had about five kilometres to go to the head of the glen at Glendoll. I hadn't pre-recced a camp spot there but was sure we'd find something suitable somewhere. Resisting the temptation of 'one for the road', I untied the electrical tape, moved any poo to the field's edges, mounted Yogi - a little unsteadily - and moseyed on up the road.

Our exodus felt funnelled by the sky, as to either side were bands of dark clouds hovering over the mountaintops, but the central passage was bright with a clear V of blue that was guiding us up the glen. I wondered if our minister friend had provided a farewell sermon (*'...all baptized into Moses in the cloud and in the sea.'* Corinthians 10:1-2), stretching out his hands for the clouds to be divided like the Red Sea during an altogether different exodus in a different time.

As we made our way up the road, to our right was the remains of Clova Castle, built in the 1500's. The only surviving feature is part of the castle's circular tower on its south-east side, still standing to a height of around three metres. The rest of the structure is unfortunately no more than a rectangular grassy mound. Any significance in battle has been lost through time, but it certainly had a strategic position at the narrowest part of the glen. The impenetrable steep sides of the mountains on either side would force all to follow the glen's floor, under the scrutinising stare of the sentry on watch.

The wind was picking up, and was 'under the horse's tails', so both broke into a fast trot which wasn't all that comfortable after two pints of Ireland's finest. They wouldn't heed any requests to slow down though, and I accepted that each vice in life requires a disagreeable consequence to balance up the scales. As the road wound up the glen, we met infrequent cars, quadbikes, and vans. The road was narrow, only single track, so I was relieved to find that all drivers were patient and courteous as I did my best to quickly move the team out of their way.

Team Swogi were most obliging to trot up when required, but *their* patience was distinctly lacking when it came to standing still to allow the postman to pass for a second time.

"The wind is behind us, it gives me the scurries," said, Yogi, fidgeting his feet as the red van squeezed by.

"When he gets the scurries, I get the hurries," explained Swift, to justify her dotty domino-effect deeds.

Like in many places, delivery of post in Glen Clova wasn't always done by van. In the 1940's, despite the long routes and difficult terrain, it was mostly carried out on foot or by bike, particularly during the war with fuel rations in force. During World War II, many jobs traditionally done by men were left to the women, and the postie role of Glen Clova was filled by a daring nineteen-year-old called Jean Cameron.

Struggling through snow, crossing burns, climbing stone stiles, walking rocky paths, and negotiating muddy bogs, Jean soon became annoyed with the skirted dress-code for women. In 1941, she persuaded management to change uniform regulations to offer more gender equality by allowing them to wear trousers (or 'Camerons' as they then became known). She revolutionised female fashion in the workplace, had a huge impact on women's rights, and her story is told in a 1944 film *The Coming of the Camerons*.

"I consider myself to be a fashion trend-setter too and all for the merits of mares," said Swift, as she pushed in front and waggled her spotty butt to make sure we'd got her point.

Almost at the end of the road, where the mountains surround to create the beautiful bowl of Glendoll (shrouded in cloud today), another car patiently passed by. I smiled as the occupants looked up in marvel at our convoy with beaming faces and frantic, friendly waves. A short way ahead, they turned left down a tree-lined driveway to a building hidden from view. We also turned left but a little further along, into the visitor's carpark next to the Ranger Centre.

I hadn't planned any further than to find a patch of grass at the top of this glen. There was plenty around the carpark but it was in a pristine condition, scattered with picnic benches, and the carpark was busy with campervans that looked to be staying the night. Therefore, it didn't feel like an appropriate place to park two horses who would deposit dunghills through the night. I did a U-turn and instead followed a track up the east side of South Esk river towards the route we'd take tomorrow.

There I found a patch of grass to the left of the trail and jumped off to scope it out. Like Goldilocks, this didn't satisfy standards either. The grass was lumpy, the ground incredibly rough, and it wouldn't make for a comfortable night for any of us. It was also very close to the track and the last thing I wanted were two excited horses, cavorting and snorting on uneven terrain as a tractor came past, putting ligaments and tendons at risk. Dissatisfied, I continued my search for ground 'that was just right.'

I returned the way I'd arrived, following a gut feeling, and following the route that the friendly car passengers had taken, I went down the tree-lined driveway. Meeting one of the friendly faces in the carpark of the building, I tentatively asked if they knew of anywhere suitable for two hungry horses overnight.

A bit surprised but seemingly delighted, Inez informed me that I'd arrived at the Carn Dearg Mountaineering Club hut and although I was welcome, she'd have to double check with one of the committee members, who happened to be her husband. Phil was duly found and after another welcome, a short discussion of adventures, and a review of potential grass requirements, he led me round to the back of the hut. Yogi and Swift followed, not wanting to be left out of the suitability and grass-quality estimations.

Phil and I soon formed a symbiotic agreement. I'd have a flat surface and a secure space on which to park my friends for the night, and by morning, he'd have short grass to save time spent mowing, and fertiliser for the flowers. Yogi and Swift happily agreed to play their part in this arrangement.

As I untacked and set up the corral, Phil explained that he couldn't wait for his daughter to arrive. Zoe loved horses and would be in for a big surprise to find Team Swogi at the hut. During conversation, I soon realised I was in fact gate-crashing an annual family gathering. Arriving shortly would be Phil's sister Emma, her husband Tomo, and their three kids, Kayley, Jake, and Dale.

Hearing that the building was a mountain club hut, I'd expected a weekend of random people formed together over a shared interest in the outdoors. I hadn't realised I was interrupting some quality family time. I was, however, banned from feeling uncomfortable and was told to "treat the place and the family as your own."

Their hospitality knew no bounds and offers of a hot shower and a bed followed, if I didn't mind sharing the bunkroom for the night with my new kin that was. Sharing space with strangers is the norm for true outdoor folk, and it was lovely to be invited into the warmth of their midst.

When I emerged from the shower, the rest of the clan had arrived and introductions and explanations commenced. I was both amused and impressed that my unexpected presence was so easily accepted by all – particularly the kids who didn't bat an eye. I took Zoe outside to be introduced to Yogi and Swift and soon struck up a rapport, discussing virtues of types of horse and the variety of equine sports. Our activities were very different but mutual respect was quickly found. I was full of admiration for her bravery over cross-country courses and Zoe marvelled at my mountainous adventures.

In no time at all, I was fully embraced in the family tradition of a campfire on the edge of the river's bed, accompanied - I might add - by a fine spread of food. Kayley, Jack, and Dale enjoyed the additional freedom that an outdoor life provides. They played football, threw stones, poked the fire, and splashed their wellies in the river's edges.

It was an evening full of fun, laughter, and cheer, finishing with the obligatory toasting of marshmallows which not only the young kids adored. I retired to bed easily in amongst newfound friends and marvelled once again at the way life on the trail can take such unexpected turns. I'd merely enquired for a camp and corral spot but had been gifted so much more.

All the White Horses

Day 10: Glendoll to Gelder Shiel (Distance 23km, Ascent 967m)

The morning's schedule within the club hut was an equally social and sharing affair, but I politely declined the offer of a full-cooked breakfast. Our day would start with a very steep climb, something I didn't fancy attempting with a stuffed stomach, so I stuck to my usual portion of porridge.

There were four ways out of the natural glacial amphitheatre of Glendoll. One way was back down the glen on the road we'd arrived by yesterday, and the other three involved climbing the steep sides of the bowl, directly over the mountains. These three high passes were equally sheer, similarly dramatic, and all had important heritage, particularly for droving.

The droving trade between Scotland and England came into being at the start of the 1600's when free trade was agreed with the union of the crowns under King James VI, and it was ongoing until the agricultural revolution changed farming practice in the middle of the 19th century. At the time, the highland areas of rough grasslands were best placed for cattle and sheep grazing whereas the lowland's rich soils were best preserved for crops.

Cattle were driven from the far reaches of Scotland to markets or trysts in the Borders and onwards down into England. The drovers moved herds of several hundred at a time over vast distances and through great hardships, often on foot themselves or by pony. Not only did they have the risks of mountain weather and mountain terrain to deal with but warring clans and cattle thieves or reivers were plenty, and it was a highly dangerous occupation. Also, on some routes like from the Isle of Skye to the mainland, they even had to swim themselves and their cattle across wide, watery divides.

It was a tough life and one I'm a little fascinated with. I feel a small kinship with them as I travel their ways in a similar manner, albeit without reivers and warring clans to contend with (thankfully).

The first of the three high passes leaves Glendoll in a south-westerly direction. It links Glendoll with Glen Prosen over the sharp Shank of Drumfollow - between the Munros Mayar and Driesh. This follows the Kilbo Path to arrive at the scaffolded bothy that would have failed to shelter us from the storm three nights ago. Not considered to be such an important route for those undertaking long-distance travel in times gone by, it was more likely used by locals (people living in either glen) to travel back and forth for work or supplies.

The cliffs of the Shank of Drumfollow made for a dangerous passing for drovers and their flocks, but they did still use it at times. Some preferred the road less travelled for more abundant grazing to fatten their sheep prior to market. It was reportedly a perfect place for the reivers to hide, too.

The second high pass, the Tolmounth, exits abruptly in a north-easterly direction, via Jock's Road and Glen Callater, in almost a direct line to Braemar. The Mounth is a name with Pictish origins, and it was used to describe the broad upland in north-east Scotland which formed a considerable barrier to trade and culture, isolating north-east Scotland from the Scottish Lowlands.

Numerous roadways were established to cross the Mounth, all challenging routes, and many with fierce reputations. The Tolmounth (and Jock's Road) is the most thrilling of the three ascending from Glendoll, not only in its exciting way through the hills, but its importance in terms of droving and access rights.

It is probably the most dangerous of all the Mounth passes being narrow, steep, and rough - and the site of tragedy for those who dared to traverse it as recently as the mid-1900's. Two incidents within four years (1956 and 1959) resulted in the deaths of seven walkers, and prompted a local hill man - Davie Glen - to construct Davie's Bourach, a small shelter high in the pass that was obviously much required.

In times before then, the Tolmounth saw regular droving 'traffic', with sheep taken from Braemar over its heights down to a tryst at Cullow at the Strathmore end of Glen Clova. The Cullow Market Stance (held in April and October) became an important market in the north of Scotland, usually held a few days after one at Braemar to allow the drovers time to get themselves and their flocks across the hills.

The Tolmounth's existence for movement of livestock is recorded well into the late 19th century, despite droving being on the decline by then, so it's surprising that there was ever any dispute over the path being a public right of way. In around 1883, the ownership of Glendoll and its splendid shooting lodge fell to a Duncan Macpherson from Inverness-shire. He very much kept it as a shooting estate, with a large population of deer for his clients to hunt. Macpherson complained that pedestrians passing through unsettled the herd and so began to disrupt the passage of drovers and travellers, directing them on a longer route that avoided 'his private land.'

The Scottish Rights of Way and Access Society took up the fight only thirty-five years after a similar and successful case in Glen Tilt. They erected new signposts and explained their position to Macpherson; however, obstruction of the route continued. The society were left with no option but to head to the courts, concluding in victory with over fifty witnessed accounts for the judge to hear. Macpherson fought hard and appealed when he lost (which was also rejected), creating thousands of pounds of legal fees, nearly bankrupting both himself and the society in the process.

As far as I'm aware the third and final high pass out of Glendoll has never been subject to dispute. The Mounth Capell is marked on maps dating as far back as the 1300's, and links this Angus glen with Ballater in Aberdeenshire, passing through the beautiful Glen Muick of the Royal Deeside estate.

Now more commonly known as the Capel Mounth, its name is believed to originate from the placement of a hospice/hospital for wayfarers at the Spittal of Glenmuick. Established by the bishop of Aberdeen, the hospice would have had its own chapel and both buildings were perfectly positioned at the foot of the hardest part of the pass – where travellers would need to eat, rest, and possibly pray for a safe passage for the route ahead.

After my modest breakfast (compared to the industrial scale one I'd been offered) I readied to leave, making sure to check and double check I'd left nothing behind. It's funny how my tightly packed dry bags could suddenly explode when given just a small amount of space more in which to do so. Here, amongst the organised chaos of a large family, it would be easy to mistakenly leave an essential item tucked under someone else's kit. Eventually, I was sure I had all my possessions, and it was time to head out to continue our journey over the Capel Mounth.

Saying goodbye to my new-found family outside, it was clear that Team Swogi had taken their role seriously in fulfilling the clause of our contract to stay. They'd certainly mown the grass right down overnight and had provided plenty of fertiliser, which I'd scattered around the flowers, bushes, and heather. Phil seemed pleased with our end of the bargain but I felt that I'd received more than expected, and that the balance of arrangements had predominantly been in my favour. I voiced my appreciation as much as I could during our departure, and Zoe and I swapped contact details so we could remain in touch.

Waving goodbye I set off up the gravel track, walking beside Yogi and Swift towards the start of the Capel Mounth. The day had dawned hot and sunny but with a cooling, gentle breeze, and it finally appeared that all signs of the unsettled weather we'd been subjected to over the last four days had gone. The sky was blue, our spirits were high, and I was looking forward to fantastic views from the heights of the Mounth's plateau. I was only slightly dreading the near five-hundred metre climb we'd have to complete first though.

"I like climbs," said Yogi, with pricked ears and an energetic stride.

"You'll need to pace yourself though my friend, it's reputed to be a tough one."

"We'll definitely need to take it slow then, with frequent snack breaks too," said Swift, flustered.

She was having to trot to keep up as it was, and not managing to grab her usual trail-side munchies. Yogi chose to ignore us both and continued with a high rate of cadence and much keenness.

I had thought to stay walking until I could gauge the gradient of the climb, trying to be fair to my companions. If it was as 'heartily steep' as suggested online, then I could share the load of bags between the two and carry myself up the hill, rather than subject Yogi to the extra weight of me in the saddle. However, I could quickly see that this plan was destined to fail right from the start, as

I couldn't keep up with Yogi's enthusiasm this morning – even on the flat.

In no time at all, we were at the junction in the trail, where a signpost clearly guided us to the right with the words 'Public Footpath to Ballater by Capel Mounth.' The track here was still showing no inclination to rise, as it meandered through the trees and lush green grass, so I decided to jump on for a while. I used a handy tree stump to help me mount and Swift used the pause in proceedings to happily catch up with her morning munches.

The trail emerged from the trees and followed the forest's edge, offering stunning views across to the Moulnie Craig, Dog Hillock, and The Strone. I couldn't quite see Juanjorge yet, the name of a rocky outcrop to the west of Moulnie, but this didn't stop me wondering who Juan Jorge was and why someone with a possible Spanish or Mexican heritage might end up with a cliff-face named after them.

There are some theories that the name may have evolved from the Gaelic 'Dionn Deorid' (hill or fortress of melancholy creature), but the word evolution seemed too far a transition to me. I like to think that Juan was a climber who put up a difficult route on the cliffs, or a geologist exploring the nature of its diorite igneous pluton. This intrusion into the surrounding sediments occurred during the late Caledonian period and was the beginning of the creation of Glendoll's splendid corries.

It might have been my distraction that was to blame, but in my defence, I don't think Yogi was paying upmost attention either as we reached the small but fast-flowing Capel Burn. There was a sharp drop down to the water and an even steeper rocky exit on the other side and the last moment, only one hoofprint away from the water's edge, Yogi refused to cross and spun around sharply. This took both me and Swift by surprise, as both of us were quite relaxed about this complication in the trail.

"Well, I'm not. That stream looks cold, fast, and is making a terrific din. I'm not sure it's safe."

By the time Yogi had fully expressed his concerns, he and I were pointing back the way we'd arrived while Swift was still pointing in the original direction of travel. There wasn't much room on the trail to sort this circle out and as I steered him back along the trail a little way to find a place to turn, poor Swift ended up doing a full three-sixty to get us back in the correct running order and facing the correct direction.

"Look Yogi, there's an up on the other side and you like ups," I said, to give encouragement.

On the second approach, with both our minds fully engaged, he rushed through the water, sorted his feet out, and made a frantic leap up the bank. Swift, with unflappable composure, followed steadily through, placing each hoof with considered thought and joined us calmly on top of the rise.

"Good girl Swifty, and silly old Bear," I said, as I contemplated yet again how I'd ended up with two completely different characters as my companions.

A short way from the burn, the trail took a right turn and started its bold ascent of the south-west slope of Ferrowie. The trail here was strewn with boulders and stones of various sizes, but as we wove our way over and in-between, Yogi hardly seemed to notice their presence. His sure-footedness always amazes and delights, almost as much as his focus, which was solely concentrated on reaching the top of the hill in the shortest possible time.

Despite this day being longer than originally planned (due to the enforced rest from the storm), we still had time to take this ascent slowly. I'd made sure of an early departure from the club hut to minimise any time-pressures in reaching the top of the plateau. However, I was struggling to share this concept with Yogi, who seemed to have set a time-trial target of his own. As we climbed steeply, I initiated plenty of stops, none of which lasted long as Swift seemed uncharacteristically keen for the climb too. If Yogi didn't impatiently break the pause then she would, by bumping him with her nose from behind.

I was just beginning to wonder why I'd even contemplated having to walk this section myself, when Yogi instigated his own break for the first time. Both horses were puffing hard and as we traversed the edge of the Capel Burn in a zig-zag fashion, the frequency of these breaks increased. By my altimeter estimations we'd climbed over two hundred metres in height with another two-hundred-and-fifty to go, and it was clear that Yogi's initial enthusiasm was beginning to wane.

I couldn't complain about the weather, not after wishing for a change, but it was extremely hot and even with the breeze, the horses were soaked in sweat. The next time Yogi stopped to catch his breath of his own accord, I jumped off to make his climb less strenuous. Given Swift's atypical enthusiasm today, and to make *my* climb easier, I put her in the lead. No matter what the terrain or gradient, Swift seems to glide along at the same rate, whereas Yogi tends to stop and start in an 'all or nothing' kind of way. Swift by far would be the better lead for setting a more comfortable and steadier pace.

To keep the team amused during our continued exertions, I imparted stories of the numerous footsteps we were following. This high route is depicted on the Gough Map, the oldest road map of Britain created in the 1300's, but some historians suggest that Iron Age travellers would have crossed the Mounth by this route before then. Heavily wooded back then, the preference would have been to stay on high ground to avoid the boggy lands below.

In the 1300's, Robert the Bruce and his army certainly travelled this way to Tullich, just east of Ballater, during the Wars of Independence. Reverting to guerrilla warfare tactics, Robert used remote ways through the hills to attack and conquer individual strongholds by small-scale raids. In 1308 he concentrated his efforts on the north-east of Scotland, expelling most of the English from the burghs lying north of the Mounth.

Jacobites also marched across here after their victory at Killiecrankie in 1689, and to their famous crushing defeat at Culloden in 1745. After this battle, the remnants of the Angus regiment returned across the Mounth to disband in Glen Clova and to go their separate ways. The plateau was once packed with pilgrims too (almost a century later) on their way to the Pannanich Wells, east of Ballater. Here waters could be found with healing properties, discovered after a local woman was cured of scrofula (lymph node tuberculosis) through regular bathing in the cold spring.

With visits and endorsement from famous historical figures such as Lord Byron, Sir Walter Scott, and Queen Victoria (who visited the springs on more than one occasion), the small settlement of Tullich became overwhelmed with pilgrims suffering from a wide variety of ailments. The local town of Ballater soon developed into a spa town to accommodate the influx from near and far, many arriving over the Mounth.

Dr John Ogilvie, a local minister of the time, sums up the experience well in his 1795 poem:

"I've seen the sick to health return,
I've seen the sad forget to mourn,
I've seen the lame their crutches burn,
And loup and fling at Pannanich.

I've seen the auld seem young and frisky,
Without the aid of ale or whisky,
I've seen the dullest hearts grow brisky
At blithesome, helpful Pannanich."

My distraction of chatter and prose seemed to have worked and in no time at all we'd reached the edge of the plateau, which stretched ahead of us for several kilometres. We wouldn't be following the pilgrim's path as far as the Pannanich waters at the end of Glen Muick; instead, after our descent, we'd turn west, aiming for an overnight stop near Easter Balmoral.

I let Team Swogi pause for a while in the cooling breeze now that the hardest work of the day was done. They soon got stuck into the grass on the slopes of Gallow Hillock, but with less enthusiasm than normal, their bites and chews having to fit between deep breaths as they recovered from the climb.

"That was tough, especially the first part," gasped Yogi.

"It's all about pacing yourself," said Swift. "You need to learn to relax about ups."

"She has a point you know, Yogi. If you'd taken your time at the start, you wouldn't be so tired now."

"I just can't help myself," he replied, a little dismayed.

"Never mind my silly Bear, the rest of the day is easier and mostly all downhill."

"I like downs," he said, with a complete change of tune.

The sun was still warm despite the stronger breeze that often accompanies height; however, I couldn't help but shiver a little at the name of the hill beside us. I associate the word 'Gallow' with a site of execution, but this location seemed rather remote to have been the scene of such events. Unless the steep climb to get here was considered an apt additional punishment – especially if those condemned were forced to walk at Yogi's kind of pace!

Likely the name evolved from the Gaelic words gall or gael - meaning bog myrtle (sweet gale) or white, respectively - but I couldn't deny feeling a peculiar energy to the place. I've often wondered whether landscapes - and particular sites within them - hold onto sensations born from significant events that happened there, or perhaps retain the emotions of those who passed through.

Was I feeling an unrecorded but noteworthy happening from the past, or the relief of pilgrims and Jacobites having survived their ordeals and their traverse of the Capel's heights? If not, then perhaps it was my own sense of relief following the climb, my elation due to the better weather, or the power of this remote setting with magnificent views that all who pause here feel.

At the start, the path across the plateau was far from the edge with a wide expanse of green vegetation between us and the steep drop to the glen below. Even carried high on Yogi's back (who had now fully recovered), I could only see the very tips of the mountains that were lining the opposite valleyside. As we continued our traverse, we crept closer to the edge and began to see the full depth of the cleft. The dark blue waters of Loch Muick in its base gave scale to the heights we'd reached on our climb.

The trail started to descend, and an incredible view opened up to our left. We were aiming for the northern reaches of the loch with the trail approaching this at an angle, so its two-and-a-half-mile length stretched out over my left shoulder. The vast waters looked intensely dark in comparison to the bright and light blue of the sky. The deep-blue shade, at first glance, could be attributed to shadows cast by the steep hills surrounding the loch which rise abruptly from the water's edge on both sides. However, the loch - said to be more than forty fathoms in places - gains its intensity of colour from the water's profound depths, which apparently have never been fully explored.

The loch looked calm and motionless from up here, but I knew the wind would be whipping up waves and ripples on its surface, causing turbulence only visible when on a similar plain. The seemingly flat expanse, held with care in the cupped palms of the mountain's hands, also looked like a fantastic backdrop for a team portrait - something difficult to obtain during solo travel. Luckily, I could see a group of three walkers heading up the trail towards us and after a short conversation, I asked if they might oblige.

All three took a large step backwards, but one less so than the others, and he was pushed forward by the two behind to approach. I guess not everyone is comfortable around the sizable bulk of horses, and despite Swift's relaxed attitude today and absence of scary mare-glares, the guy was still incredibly nervous. I stretched out my hand as far as I dared without falling off and handed him my camera. I rounded the horses into position with the beautiful view behind but noted the walker had retreated to a position far away and at completely the wrong angle.

Retrieving my camera in a similarly outstretched manner, I thanked them profusely and left them to continue their walk. The photo taken had nothing of the view on show and I was a little disappointed, but then beggars can't be choosers. I could always try again, as

Lock Muick is a popular place, and there might be a less equinophobic person (with a better angle of perspective) further down the trail.

Glancing back one last time before focusing on the descent, I could see the clump of trees on the north-west end of the loch that surrounds Glas-Allt Shiel, a house originally built for Queen Victoria in 1868 as a hunting lodge. Also known as the 'Widow's House', she retreated here following the death of her beloved Prince Albert. Sad and lonely she mourned, "thinking of the blessed happy past with dearest Albert, who always had wished to build here in this favourite spot."

Behind the main house is a storeroom converted into an open bothy for walkers and climbers, which is managed by the MBA. The lodge is now owned by the Balmoral Estate, and backpackers are still allowed to stay in the bothy even when royal parties visit, merely being asked to keep discreetly out of the way. We'd be staying at a bothy tonight also owned by the Balmoral Estate but at a different location, one I'd not been to visit since our cross-Scotland adventure three years ago. I was looking forward to a familiar and comfortable stop tonight.

The magnificent view accompanied us all the way down to the lochside, and as suspected, there were plenty of walkers enjoying the location too. Many stopped to chat, asking the usual questions about what on earth I was doing roaming the hills on my own with two horses in tow.

Just before crossing the River Muick, I managed to achieve the desired team portrait with help from one of the walkers, who this time captured the loch in the frame as a beautiful backdrop. Swift and Yogi both stood to pose, and on showing them the photo, they were satisfied that the guy had captured their 'best sides.'

I waved farewell and followed the water's edge to where the River Muick departed the loch to start its meandering flow down the glen. As I'd anticipated up on the Mounth, the waters were not flat and calm when viewed from down here. The wind had whipped up a frenzy of waves that were being pushed down the river and under the bridge.

The bridge was wooden and narrow, and with five steep steps at each end to negotiate it was not suitable for hooves. We'd have to ford instead, but at least it didn't look too deep. I steered Team Swogi to the loch side of the bridge where I could see an obvious crossing with a sandy beach for an easy exit on the other side. Despite the strong wind, a family with young children were playing on this beach, splashing in the water.

Yogi, for the second time today (and quite uncharacteristically for him), came to an abrupt stop, refusing to enter the water.

"It's full of white horses," he said. "They won't like us going in there too!"

"Don't be silly, it's perfectly fine, solid under foot and shallower than many crossings you've done."

"No, no, no, they might be kelpies," he responded, as he twisted around and went back the way we'd arrived.

Well, this new spin on things was a turn of events I hadn't expected. Usually brave when it came to water, the Bear seemed to have his head in a muddle today. Although, that said, he had never liked waves on the beach; and to be fair, the sun *was* making the ripples between the white horses sparkle.

The noise of the wind rushing across the loch, the white waves it was kicking up, and the sun's dazzling effect were an intense combination. Perhaps the kids playing at the river's edge was the straw that broke the camel's back. One or other of this cumulative effect had sent Yogi's brain into meltdown anyway, and knowing that negotiations under these conditions were futile, I turned to try below the bridge instead.

"It's rippled down here too," he said, before we'd even got close to the alternative crossing suggestion.

"Sigh! This is going to take a while isn't it," I replied, as I rubbed his neck to try and calm his stuck-in-a-rut thoughts.

We were now on a small grassy area next to the river below the bridge, and yes, the sun was still making the river's ripples glisten; but there was a nice sandy lead-in to the water, if I could only persuade Yogi to step off the grass onto it. But first I needed to convince him to pause and to stop backing up or spinning around, as this is the standard output of Yogi's overload setting.

We'd completed at least six circles already and although I now had him facing the river, he was backing up slowly away from it.

"Will you stand still!" hissed Swift in frustration. "This grass is sweet, and I could take my fill, if you'd just stop moving your feet. Besides," she continued, "I'm getting affa dizzy!"

"You really should listen to Swift you know, Yogi. There is nothing of concern here."

Like Swift, I wasn't asking much of him now, other than to stand still on the patch of grass - but when a Bear brain gets in a muddle, the overflow tends to fill his ears with sawdust, so he wasn't listening to either of us. *If I couldn't convince his feet to still, then maybe the best option would be to deploy them in another direction,* I thought.

Next to the grass was a small channel of water that joined the river further down. The water here was sheltered and shadowed from the sun's glare. *Perhaps he would enter the water there, then once in, I could steer him to the main ford...*

They Might be Kelpies

"Not on your nelly, no chance, no way! There could be kelpies in there too."

One of the reasons I love owning horses is that they can be a silent sounding board for the troubles and strifes of life, as you can tell them anything and they don't judge or critique over much. However, there are moments when you regret telling them certain details, such as the vivid description of kelpies I'd shared on the Minister's Path.

"I really don't want to get my feet wet, Yogi."

"Well, me neither," he stated, initiating yet another spin.

Swift was still trying to grab mouthfuls of the tasty grass while my battle with the Bear continued, but other than a little annoyance at the inconvenience of food on the go, she didn't seem overly scared so I initiated a new tactic and asked her to go into the river first. Swift, in general, has a more considered approach to life and putting her ahead for obstacles, even when packhorse, has been a successful strategy on more than one occasion.

Not today though! Either she was trying to manufacture a longer time on the sweet grass, or she was enjoying my struggles and didn't feel inclined to end her entertainment - but she pretended to be spooked by the kelpies too.

"Oh, for goodness' sake!" I shouted.

I then took a deep breath and let the air out slowly. As John Lyons once said (an American Natural Horsemanship Trainer), "There are only two emotions that belong in the saddle; one is a sense of humour and the other is patience." *My* humour was unquestionably wearing thin.

Still breathing deeply and thinking calm thoughts I resorted to something I only usually rely on in emergency situations – I slapped the end of my split reins repeatedly on the saddle bags on both sides of saddle. I hoped the sharp cracking noises might penetrate through Yogi's sawdust-filled ears to encourage him into forward motion. I also applied strong squeezes of leg and a few stronger words (that can't be listed here) and we finally advanced onto the sand at the side of the river.

Knowing I wouldn't have long before a spin or retreat would occur, I continued my systematic sensory surprise until one hoof was in the water. We then splashed our way below the bridge, through water that was no more than (horse) knee-deep without any further objections. Swift followed, calm and content behind.

"I don't know what all the fuss was about," said Yogi as he clambered up the grassy bank on the far side.

"Well, that's ten minutes of my life I'll never get back," I replied, as a tiny amount of humour returned.

I'm not a fan of whips and spurs as there are many more positive ways to come to a mutual understanding with your equine companion, but I do appreciate that on occasion something more than soft reasoning may be required. Yogi had got his brain in a right tizz. There was no danger ahead, of that I was certain, as I do listen when he has a valid reason to refuse. He'd just needed something to make him snap out of it.

However, I wasn't proud that I'd resorted to the rein slaps, especially since this had been witnessed by a gathering audience up on the bridge. This audience had accepted my methods, nobody called me out for it, and indeed had cheered when we eventually entered the water - but how were they to know whether I was slapping the bags or the horse?

The bad example I felt I'd set, that hitting a horse was an okay thing to do, had been so readily absorbed. *I* knew I didn't hit Yogi's behind, but *they* didn't. It astounds me that across the world, these beautifully gentle creatures who have helped to shape the success of man and continue to give so much in terms of sport and leisure, can be subjected to such cruelty.

Whips, spurs, harsh bits, endless hours 'trapped' in a stable, worked too young, too heavy loads, and tack that clamps their mouths closed – are all accepted. If such methods were used on dogs, at least in most countries, there would be uproar! I think Amber Senti sums this up in their famous quote: "The horse with beauty unsurpassed, strength immeasurable and grace unlike any other, still remains humble enough to carry a man upon his back." To this I'd add: "No matter what humans put them through."

Feeling humbled myself, I gave Yogi an appreciative rub of his neck as we passed the end of the bridge and the family playing on the sandy beach. They'd been oblivious to our struggles to cross the river with the bridge hiding a direct view, and the kids came running up from the waters edge in a noisy procession that caused a jig from both horse's hooves. Team Swogi hadn't quite settled from the previous excitement, and I barely managed a wave, hanging on tight as I was, as we scuttled on by.

The jigging continued as we made our way along the edge of the loch, as the noise of the crashing waves on the shore was loud to our left. In this bouncing fashion, we arrived at a little stone boathouse with double wooden doors that were receiving a rhythmic wash from the churned-up waters. I jumped off to take a look and left Team Swogi tucking into the grass beside it. The mouth-watering delights at their feet seemed to dispel any other watery concerns.

As I watched the waves lapping over the stone slip built to protect the boathouse, I also glanced at my watch. It was now nearing two o'clock and we still had eleven kilometres to do. We were effectively half-way through the distance of the day. My original plan had been to camp not far from here, at the unofficial campsite managed by the estate, but due to the Glen Prosen storm I was combining two days into one. Instead, we would go onwards towards Balmoral and the Gelder Shiel Bothy.

Remembering back to three years ago on our cross-Scotland adventure, when we'd also stayed at this bothy, this section (which we'd join in a kilometre or so) had felt like a long afternoon. That was without having climbed the Mounth first. The trail ahead had some rough, rocky sections, but at least we'd already ticked off two-thirds of the day's climb.

Feeling a little worn around the edges, I decided I'd best munch lunch on the move to avoid too late an arrival at the end of the day. I gathered up the devouring duo, used a rock to jump up onto Yogi's back, and turned right at the T-junction in the trail towards the Allt-na-Grubhsaich Lodge. This lodge, extended and developed in Queen Victoria's time (for her and Prince Albert to enjoy), had been abandoned after his death as she could no longer bear to stay there without him. Instead, she built and used the 'Widow's House' at the other end of the loch.

Turning left just before the lodge we entered the woods, meeting the trail from the north that we'd arrived on three years ago. Suddenly, the horses' ears pricked, their strides lengthened, and the spring in their steps exuded an energetic poise. It's amazing how a familiar trail can bolster confidence – even if it has been three years since you've travelled it. This confidence continued over the wooden bridge at the edge of the woods and onwards through a sizeable ford. All thoughts of hydrophobia were dismissed now, as the acquainted surroundings put Yogi's mind at ease.

The track I knew would start out sandy in nature, but as it began to rise in three-hundred metres of ascent, it would change to loose, rocky boulders. Secure in mind, both horses attacked this sandy climb with delight, breaking into canter when my encouragement to slow was not persuasive enough. We rounded the corner into the rocky section with much keenness, and to my surprise, progress seemed to continue at a similar rate.

There was the occasional side-line, up over the heather to the side of the track to avoid the worst of the rocks, and Yogi chose to make good use of these. However, where there were no such alternatives, he stormed up through the rock-strewn ground regardless, picking his way decisively through with Swift happily trotting up behind.

Thinking back to the last time here, it was hard to grasp the contrast. Yogi had still been keen as it was uphill, but he'd struggled with the rocks, and I'd jumped off to long-rein him through. Swift had delicately followed at a dainty and deliberate rate. Not now though; their feet harder and much better developed from the track system at home, were not feeling any discomfort at all. With their decision-making and route-finding improved too, they were making short work of this tricky trail.

Picking his route with ease, Yogi was humming away to himself, and Swift joined in - not quite managing harmony, but does she ever in life? The tunes soon carried us through the worst of the rocks, where we reached the top of the rise and a softer trail with a magnificent view across to the rocky slopes of Lochnagar to our left.

"It's thirsty work this," said Yogi, as he abruptly stopped from a trot for a drink from the ditch at the side of the track.

"Whoa there boy! You nearly had me off over your head. A little more warning would be appreciated next time."

"Oops, sorry, it just smelt particularly good."

"You're right," said Swift, as she plunged her nose into the moss-covered water. "I do enjoy a bit of added gloop."

Swift often is the first to demand a slurp stop and she seems to favour water with added flavour – stopping at the darkest puddles, no doubt full of extra minerals and bacteria abundant in peaty soil. She was wanting to linger here, savouring the mossy-taste, but Yogi, after a quick fill of his own, was keen to continue and wouldn't stand still.

Giving into his 'let's go' pleas, we arrived at a split in the trail where the walker's track up Lochnagar branched off to the left. Keeping to the main track to the right ourselves, the view opened up across Deeside and to the mountains beyond.

"Look guys!" I exclaimed. "Only one more set of mountains for us to get over before reaching home."

"One day at a time. Let's just get to the end of this one, shall we," Yogi replied, as he set off on the gradual descent with no let-up in his pace.

This had certainly been one of the most scenic days on the trip so far. The views down to Loch Muick from the Mounth were unsurpassed, but this longer view down across Deeside was giving it a run for its money. The centre of the wide track was a raised mixture of sand, stones, and grass. To the right, the bright green of the mossy-ditch formed a defined end to the heathered inclines of Caisteal na Caillach.

To our left, the track was bounded by a heather-covered and boulder-strewn mound which fell away on the far side to a wide area of dark green, tarnished in numerous places by peat bog browns. About a kilometre away, the darkened ground rose sharply where it met the lower slopes of the Lochnagar range. These slopes stretched up to its grey, craggy tops in amongst the clouds.

Following the dark-green reaches downhill, they splayed out into the valley below and I could see the small gathering of trees in which the bothy stood concealed. Ahead and behind this rose the next layer of mountains. Hazy and distant, they were a mix of browns, greens, blues, and greys, each peak and tier choosing a unique shade for the day. A few patches of lighter tones were scattered here and there, highlighted by the sun.

With Yogi's determination to get to the bothy as soon as we could, we rapidly descended through this scene and were rounding the final corner to the clump of trees by half past four. I tapped my watch twice. *Could that really be true*? That was a good average of four-and-a-half kilometres an hour over rough terrain.

As I untacked, unpacked, and built the corral in roughly the same place as three years before, I thanked Swift and Yogi for their hard work today - particularly for the speed that had supplied such an early arrival. Feeling pretty weary, as always, I saw to the horses first; making sure they had water, feed, rugs, and shelter.

By the time I stumbled into the bothy I felt ready to just retire to bed, but the delight in finding a new feature sitting in one corner bolstered me somewhat. Sometime in the three years since my last visit, the MBA had been to work. Not only were there additional windows in the door and roof to brighten the gloomy depths, the walls and floor were now clad in timber, and there was a new log burning stove in the corner to provide some cheer.

It was dry outside, but the wind was chilly now the sun had turned in, so I was delighted with this upgrade in facilities. It didn't take long to collect some wood to get the fire crackling and some warmth in the room. I cooked some food and settled down by the fire's glow to enjoy a cosy night in, immersed in a good book with my hip flask by my side.

The Best of Both Worlds

Day 11: Gelder Shiel to Mar Lodge (Distance 24km, Ascent 487m)

I'd slept well but awoke with extremely achy joints. Lyme disease is *not* a condition for those who don't like surprises. Still, at least my bruised calves had settled, and my heart appeared to be behaving for now. Feeling sore and stiff, I didn't rush to get out on the trail. There was no need for haste as I knew today's route was one we'd done before. If yesterday was anything to go by, the confidence from the familiar would flip Yogi into his turbo-boost mode and the twenty-four kilometres of relatively flat ground would be covered in no time at all.

Still in my pyjamas, I poked my head out of the bothy to check on Team Swogi.

"Good morning!" shouted Yogi at the top of his voice in a peace-shattering whinny.

"Hmph!" said Swift, not even bothering to turn towards me.

Satisfied that all was well, I retreated inside to pull clothes over sore bones. I might yet linger over breakfast, but there was an urgent call of nature to attend to first. Luckily this bothy had a composting toilet situated round the back, so I didn't have far to walk. I opened the door, admired the colourful hoof boots that I'd cleaned last night, lined up neatly along the base of the bothy wall, then rounded the corner to come face to tail (thankfully) with the biggest adder I'd ever seen. *Whhhaaaa!*

She was *HUGE!* I'd say at least seventy centimetres in length and a healthy girth too. My assumption of gender was due to the bigger size, and the reddish-brown base underneath the characteristic black zigzags down her back (males are usually smaller and light grey). Her eyes, facing away from me, weren't having the legendary hypnotic effect; but I was mesmerised by her beauty, nonetheless. Not only was she a healthy weight and length, but she had a shine to her skin any French polisher would have been proud of.

As I followed her slithers along the bothy wall (at a safe distance), I wondered if she'd recently shed her skin to achieve such shine, and my fascination mingled with much respect and a little bit of fear. Adders are Britain's only venomous snake, and although they only bite when under threat and their venom generally isn't strong enough to be fatal, it can be a painful and nasty experience for human *or horse!*

There's only been around fourteen cases of human fatality following an adder bite in the last one hundred years, but for small dogs it's a different matter altogether, as mortality rates are around five percent. Horses generally suffer mild symptoms, localized swelling and/or mild systemic signs, but more severe symptoms such as tissue necrosis, heart problems, paralysis of muscles that control swallowing, *and death*, are not unheard of.

As usual, my fears focussed on the thought of what a bite from an adder (particularly one this size) might do to Yogi or Swift. I wasn't considering what it might do to me, but then I probably had more sense and awareness not to tread on one. We hadn't met many adders on our travels through the years – surprising, maybe, as we favoured the same woodland and heathland. They are a protected species and a conservation priority due to dwindling numbers, so this may explain our lack of encounters, but there was one I clearly remembered that nearly resulted in a bite.

We'd just emerged from a spot of heather-bashing to arrive on a solid trail. I was walking at the time and leading both horses, with Yogi in front of Swift - both to my right-hand side. Knowing the ground was even underfoot, I was consulting the map as we continued to make progress on the day's miles. I'd looked up just in time before my next step would have landed on a coiled-up spring of a young adder, basking in the sun.

It was smaller than today's meeting, but face to face, and still a surprise. Not least for the snake which was hissing, displeased, and preparing to strike.

"Get back quick," I yelled at Yogi, throwing my right arm across his chest to halt any forward step.

"I can't," he replied. "Swift is right behind me, and anyway why?"

He hadn't seen the curled-up hazard at my feet, and neither had Swift who was impatiently bumping Yogi's butt with her nose. There was a pause that seemed to slow down time as the snake looked at me, I looked at it, and both horses bobbed their heads up and down with impatience. Thankfully, they kept their feet rooted to the ground. With one final hiss and a last alarming and threatening reach forward, the young adder uncoiled and slithered off into the heather at the side of the track.

"Phew! That was close," I said.

"What was?" asked Yogi.

"Can we go now?" enquired Swift, bumping her nose in my back, since her efforts with Yogi's butt had proved futile.

"I thought horses were supposed to have a heightened sense of danger. You guys would never survive alone in the wild."

"That's why we have a human slave," sniggered Swift.

The adder today hadn't been poised to strike; indeed, she hadn't even acknowledged my presence, but it was a sharp reminder of vulnerability out on the trail and how things may go wrong in the blink of an eye. As the snake slid off to the woods to the right, I quietly slunk to the left – keeping a close eye on the ground as I opened the toilet door.

Back in the bothy, still shocked from the early morning wildlife experience, I lit my stove and wandered round the room while the water came to the boil. I noted a commemorative plaque on the wall which answered my question as to when the bothy improvements took place. Seemingly, just a short while after I was here before.

"Gelder Shiel (Ernie's Bothy) Refurbishment
In Memory of the late
Ernie Rattray
Funded by the Ballater Charitable Chiels
With the Support of HRH the Duke of Rothesay
Balmoral Estate and the MBA
'Am Awa Tae the hill'
May 2015"

The Ballater Chiel's Facebook group describes "a group of local lads who raise funds for worthy causes and events on Deeside and beyond." Ernie had been their former president and a member of the Braemar Mountain Rescue team for many years and was obviously highly thought of, and fondly remembered. Following refurbishment at the re-opening ceremony, Ian 'Piper' Shand played a tune composed in his memory – "Ernie's Awa Tae the Hills" - and Prince Charles (the Duke of Rothesay) attended too.

Flicking through the pages of the bothy book, I didn't find the prince's signature (perhaps removed for safe keeping), but I was delighted to find my entry from May 2014, written during my cross-Scotland adventure. It was a strong reminder of how far we'd come in terms of experience on the trail, but also a return to health.

The previous night at this bothy was one of worry and anguish, as here Yogi had displayed his strange symptoms for the first time - signs that had eventually led to his Cushing's diagnosis. I was glad that his treatment appeared to be effective, as we were approaching the end of our trial-run back to the norm, and he was not only managing fine – but excelling at the task.

The water now boiled, I made porridge, a cup of tea, and a flask of coffee for later. Over breakfast, I added a new entry to the bothy book, thanking those involved in the refurb, and leaving a cartoon of Team Swogi for a bit of amusement. I'd soon swept the bothy floor, made sure of a pile of dry-kindling for the next visitor, and gathered all belongings, then made my way outside to begin the packing and tacking routine.

The day was at least dry, but the sky was overcast and there was a strong wind. I was glad of the trees and the bothy walls for shelter while I readied Team Swogi for the off. The wind was cold and it was biting through my clothes, not making my achy joints pleased, but we were soon booted and suited and warming up as we set off down the track - leaving the bothy's comforts behind.

As anticipated, Yogi was striding out with much enthusiasm on familiar turf, and I was struggling to walk alongside. Crossing the Gelder Burn at a turn in the trail, I found a rock to mount and from the additional height, savoured the full view of Lochnagar's ridge. Its prominent outline looked like the spine of a prehistoric creature, with two triangular peaks (one higher than the other) marking the head and tail of the beast as it rose from slumber from a soft heather bed.

Cac Carn Beag, the head of my imagined creature, is the 20th highest Munro in Scotland at 1153 metres. The tail (Meikle Pap) doesn't fall much short at 980 metres, but at least it has a better name (meikle meaning much or great). Cac Carn Beag translates as 'small cairn of faeces,' and I began to wonder if I'd attributed the head and tail to the wrong end of the ridge. Either way, the loch in the middle, Lochan na Gaire (or the little loch of the noisy sound), was placed just right in the rumbling tum of the beast's midriff.

The ridge is considered a periphery of the Cairngorms, as its rocks of red granite belong to the same igneous intrusion (through older schists) which form the main Cairngorm range further east. An outlier it may be, but a much celebrated one with royal connections (located as it is near Balmoral) and an ample bust. The old name, 'Two-breasted Mountain' (or Beinn-Cichean), was used in various forms until the late 17th century but has now fallen from use.

Queen Victoria climbed to the top in 1848, and the mountain features in the film *Mrs. Brown,* but it was Lord Byron's poem 'Lachin na Garr' written in 1807 that first brought the mountain into the limelight. "Oh for the crags that are wild and majestic! The steep frowning glories of the dark Loch na Garr." Looking at the crescent of rugged cliffs that cradled the dark loch below, I could easily imagine my prehistoric creature awakening and frowning in a pre-coffee state.

Prince Charles (now King Charles III) wrote in a lighter fashion about these cliffs. His 1980 children's book, *The Old Man of Lochnagar*, is a tale of bathtubs, pixies, magic flowers, and consequence. Later portrayed as an animated short film, a musical stage play, and even a ballet, I'm sure it inspires many a young person to view its slopes. Particularly given that the proceeds are donated to The Prince's Trust.

While I'd been lost in mythical muse and historical times, Yogi's fast pace had carried the team a few kilometres further on and we were now approaching a forest of ancient pines. The dark-green band filled the valley before us and spread out over a few low hills, but the taller peaks were bare due to the harshness found at height.

Scotland has an abnormally low treeline compared to other countries; a combination of forceful biting winds, a blanket growth of peat, and grazing pressures (both in the past and now), keeps their expanse under check. Considering it was July, but I was wrapped in maximum clothes to handle the effects of bitter winds and the icy rain that had just began to fall, I didn't blame the trees for huddling together as far downslope as they could.

The descent to their boundary offered a stark contrast of landscapes. Up here the bleak blanket of heather, patterned in places by bright splashes of purple, was exposed and bare. It appeared devoid of life with only a few protruding rocks to break the profile and the wind's unforgiving squall. At the trees, we descended into dusky depths, dark shadows, and a protective embrace of green limbs swaying in the breeze. The twitter and tweets of birdsong, no longer drowned by the wind's roar, denoted a more cordial abode.

The track hadn't improved any in the last three years and like before was rough with loose stones. The difference now was that Yogi no longer searched for the grass at the sides, but happily strode out straight down the centre. I glanced back to find Swift doing the same, but also noticed that her load had slipped alarmingly to the left.

"I tried to tell you, but you couldn't hear me over the wind," she said, shaking her head.

I jumped off, letting Yogi go with the lead rope trailing on the ground, confident that either a misplaced hoof or the first patch of grass would act as an anchor. Swift found a tasty anchor of her own, and contentedly stood munching while I tended to her bags. It's always a fair stretch for vertically-challenged me, to adjust the bags once up on Swift's back. Not finding a root or stone to stand on, I was struggling to reach.

I was also struggling to figure out what it was I'd done wrong this morning, but concluded it was a symptom of being near a rest day (and a re-stock). The absence of food this time, and the lighter resulting load, was causing imbalance. I was just putting finishing touches to the re-adjustment when Swift pushed into me with a firm nose-bump of impatience.

"I know my love. You hate your personal space invaded, but I'm nearly done now."

"It's not that this time," she responded, pointing frantically down the trail.

I turned to see where she'd directed, to observe a rounded ginger butt disappearing around the corner...

"Yooooooo-giiiiii!" I yelled, as I tightened the last two straps on the packsaddle, picked up Swift's lead rope, and set off at a fast march after the Bear.

He glanced back as we began to catch him up, but he didn't stop despite requests. I was more amused than concerned however, as this wasn't a new situation to find myself in, and at least he was only walking with determination rather than a trot this time. Sometimes, Yogi can get so focused on the end of the day that he won't stop and won't walk when asked. His gears always get stuck one notch up. This drive is useful on tougher days, but when I'm needing some food, a sip of coffee, to open a gate, or to adjust bags - he treads a fine line of response between gratitude and grumpiness.

Laughing inside whilst trying to look stern, I provided my own anchor with my foot on his trailing rope and gave the command to “Whoa!” It *never* does any harm to reinforce this message, whether he was truly listening or not. I suspected it was my foot rather than voice that caught his attention this time, but either way he paused long enough for me to grab his reins and reunite the team.

Adding to Yogi’s general drive today was the knowledge that we were on familiar ground. We were following the route we took three years ago, with only a short deviation for a small section to come. I knew he had a memory like an elephant and would know exactly where he was, despite only being here once before. I tried to muster up some energy to deal with the rest of the day that was stretching out with persistent Yogi impatience.

I decided to stay on the ground for a while to ease my aching knees, and to postpone a wriggling remount onto a hot-headed horse. Besides, it’s nice sometimes to walk at the same level as your equine companions, with hot sweet breath on your skin and a soft nose bumping your elbow (Yogi) or your neck (Swift).

We proceeded in this manner down through the trees, rounded a corner at Connachat Cottage, and paused for as long as Yogi would allow (which wasn’t long) at the 10-foot granite memorial dedicated by Queen Victoria to her son-in-law Henry Morris. Carved with an ornate Celtic Cross, its fading inscription reads: 'Brief Life! In sport and war so keen, morned by these winds in heath and fir as where the falling breakers stir the pains that crowned thy closing scene.’ This thought-provoking and poetic text suggests either pain at his passing, a painful death, or both.

Liko, as he was known by his family, had persuaded Queen Victoria to allow him to fight in the West African conflicts of the Ashanti War (present-day Ghana) – “not to win glory, but from a sense of duty." He didn't have long to carry out this duty though, as rather than death through injuries sustained in battle, he'd succumbed at the age of thirty-eight to malaria, aboard the HMS *Blonde* off the coast of Sierra Leone.

"I have a sense of duty too, you know," said Yogi proudly.

"Oh, yes?"

"To get the team to the end of the day, in the shortest possible time."

Swift and I sighed in unison.

"We'd better let you get on with it then."

Remembering to avoid the low road this time, to bypass a bridge that was difficult with horses, we turned to the left to take the higher route. Three years ago the Mar Lodge rangers had warned me about this bridge, but forgetting their instructions at the time, I'd led the team towards it. It had been challenging to cross due to its strange construction of wooden slats with gaps, much like a cattle grid. I knew Team Swogi would cross it again if I asked, but it was an avoidable stumble and it's always nice to explore new places.

The rise in the trail brought about a rise in speed that was too fast to match, so I jumped back on board. Yogi only allowed me a brief window of time in which for me to do so. No longer having to watch my own feet, I soaked up the detail of this beautiful little trail winding through the woods with the river running alongside.

The river was running fast, with a rumble and a tumble. Its dark, peaty flow was in sharp contrast to the whipped-up white waters cascading over rocks, and the frothy-cream foam formed on the eddy lines. The roar was impressive, and through the soft earth at our feet was a vibration of shaken land being creatively carved as the waters ran their course. They seemed to be in such a hurry to join the River Dee (and eventually reach the sea), I wanted to say "slow down a little, stay awhile, and savour this stunning scene." Maybe like Yogi, they didn't feel they had a choice, and the drive to complete their journey completely filled their thoughts.

This higher route was only a minor diversion into the unknown, but it had delivered such delights. The experience left me debating the difference between exploring somewhere new or covering familiar ground. The new catches your attention as you soak up, seek out, and detect every unfamiliar feature - the sights, sounds, smells, and the ambiance of the place. The old reassures with the security of association and fosters more of a 'check-in' process, where quick glances replace thorough examination.

This transition into familiarity doesn't necessarily devalue the experience, as a route that's imprinted in your mind can allow your mind some freedom. A path you've travelled a hundred times, provides habitual placement of steps; this allows you to lift your head a little and the liberty, should you choose, to consider more.

As Team Swogi nimbly negotiated a tumble of branches crossing this unknown trail (whilst I was still soaking in the surrounds), my thoughts concluded that perhaps exploring on the back of a horse gives you the best of both worlds.

We left the tumbling tributary behind and took our own trajectory to the River Dee, arriving at the Old Invercauld Bridge, now a footbridge following construction of a new road bridge. The river here was roaring too as it descended a series of stone ledges, but despite its thunder, I could hear the zoom of fast traffic from the road ahead. It was five full days since we'd been near a main road, and both horses pricked their ears at the unusual sound as we reached the apex of the bridge's hump.

Luckily, we wouldn't need to ride along this road. Instead, we could follow a little trail along the river's edge and cross it further down. The path itself was clear and was well-marked underfoot but the trees were overgrown above. The branches waving in the wind hit me across my face several times, as the detail of side-stepping and steering was lost in Yogi's determination.

We crossed the road during a pause in the stream of traffic, trotted up the side road with Swift spurring Yogi on alongside (which was the last thing he needed), then clattered into the small carpark. Managing to slow Team Swogi to a walk, we passed a few vehicles to position ourselves in a grassy corner at the back. I knew from three years ago that there was a handy fence to tie the horses to. I also knew that if I didn't tie them, they'd be off down the trail without me in a blink of an eye.

Satisfied they were securely attached, I made use of the public toilet and returned to discover a man crouching down looking at their legs. This was a surprise, but more so was the fact that both horses were snoozing, enjoying the heat from the sun which had finally decided to join us for a while. At last! A break in Yogi's onwards drive.

As I approached, the man enquired about my ride.

"What are you doing with these guys?" he asked, standing up and pointing at Team Swogi.

"I'm completing a circuit of the Cairngorms over two weeks."

"Isn't that a bit cruel with a horse as lame as that?"

Aghast, I reassessed my team. They'd bounced into the carpark full of beans, even in step, and no signs of discomfort. Had one of them become tangled in the rope and become injured during my brief ablutions absence? Yogi's head was lowered, his eyes were closed, he was standing equally on all four feet, and his bottom lip was decidedly droopy. No sign of distress there. My attention switched to Swift. She too had a lowered head, closed eyes, and was relaxed, resting a hind foot.

I've explained before how agile my lanky lass is and that she doesn't do things by half; well, she applies both these principles to resting too. Why half-rest a hind when you are flexible enough to do more? As far as I could tell, she was snoozing in her usual manner of hip dropped, leg out behind, toe down, and due to her flexibility, the full front of her hoof was parallel to the ground.

Under Scrutiny

"Are you a horse rider too?" I enquired.

"To be honest I don't know much about them," he responded.

"Well then, I can categorically state that Swift is *not* lame and is merely having a sleep."

The look on his face informed me that he really wasn't convinced, so in the spirit of a unified team, Swift switched to resting her other hind leg in the same bendy manner.

"I've got your back if you'll scratch mine," she whispered with a wink of the eye that she'd now half opened.

"Fair enough," said the guy with a shrug as he turned away.

I was left a little flabbergasted by this interaction with a complete stranger, who'd felt the need to critique something he knew nothing about.

I'd only ever been subject to this kind of approach by couch-riding, self-proclaimed 'experts' online, never in the flesh. I tried hard to find the funny side, but a tight coldness had lodged itself firmly in the pit of my stomach. The balance of putting yourself out there, to encourage and hopefully inspire, against the critique you might face from those who don't understand or disagree, is a fine line and sometimes an uncomfortable one to tread.

I'm not sure whether tying a lead rope to a fence has the same effect as connecting an electric car to a plug socket, but both horses were fully recharged after their snooze and were keen to get underway. I let Yogi walk ahead, positioning myself between him and Swift, as in turbo-boost mood it was easier this way. Following his ginger butt, we set off up the old tree-lined driveway towards Invercauld House.

The sun was still out, and the trees were casting a mishmash of shadows across the road. Glancing down to the sizeable baronial mansion below us (with its six-storey tower), there was a new towering figure standing boldly in the grounds. At least I think it was new, as I hadn't noticed it three years ago.

Although the bulbous form stood some distance away, both Yogi and Swift paused for a while, ears pricked to assess, suggesting they hadn't noticed it last time either. The sculpture was a giant, black, curvaceous torso, with a hole in the midriff, and it reminded me of a Henry Moore. Having been dragged round numerous displays of his bronzes as a young child by my dad, I recognised a similarity of style.

Happy that the dark form was staying where it was, Team Swogi continued up the slight rise. I wasn't sure whether I was getting slower, or they were getting faster, but my energy levels were in the red and I knew I'd have to jump back on soon. I also knew there was a cattle grid ahead with a sticky side-gate, so I resolved to survive on foot until then.

Both horses were ahead of me now, pulling me along. We rounded a corner and the reason for their renewed haste became clear. Yogi's twin was in the next field! At least he looked like he could be related, with his identical chestnut coat, white blaze, white socks, and the same love of speed. This handsome chap strutted his stuff with an extravagant trot, a spurt of gallop, and a huge stallion-like call. Team Swogi answered in unison and with equal enthusiasm.

"Isn't he just the best colour," said Yogi with pride.

"Pretty common if you ask me," replied Swift, swishing her shining silver tail over her white-spotted butt. "But he seems like a nice sort."

I'm not sure whether it was his matching appearance, or his sustained excited behaviour, but Team Swogi seemed unusually enthralled. Their shouted conversation continued the hundred metre distance to the sticky gate, throughout gate negotiations, as I mounted, and about another two-hundred metres more. Whatever their exchange was about, I was glad of the slowing distraction it caused and the chance to catch my breath.

We continued up a wide, hard-packed track, winding through trees of various shapes, sizes, and shades of green, and Team Swogi's focus switched back to the task in hand. Swift began jogging up beside Yogi, urging him on in a competition worthy of a racecourse as to who could place their nose first over the line.

"Might this have something to do with my mention of a nice grassy field and a rest day tomorrow, per chance?" I enquired.

Neither offered a response but the glints in their eyes and the smug look on their faces told me all that was required.

Nearing the end of this wooded section, the first glimpses of Braemar appeared as the trees began to thin. I'd be making my way there tomorrow for a restock of supplies, while Yogi and Swift enjoyed a day of relaxation as guests of the Mar Lodge estate. At the rate we were travelling, with known grassy tracks yet to come, we'd reach our rest stop in no time at all.

"I'm thirsty though," said Yogi, pointing at the ditch with his nose.

"Me too," said Swift, licking her lips.

I steered them over to where Yogi had directed, but all I could see was a muddy patch of shallow water which didn't look very appetising. Both horses agreed, so I looked instead for a way down to the River Dee to our left. The ground here was wet and marshy, and each side-channel of the river had a large step down to the water.

"I'm not *that* thirsty yet," said Yogi, assessing the soggy ground and the sinking drink it might be.

Luckily, not far ahead, was a large puddle flooding the width of the track. We paused there and they both drank their fill. As it started to rain, I considered that sometimes riding through inclement weather can deliver the Bear's necessities of life.

Humming *Jungle Book* tunes in my head, we left the trees behind and ventured onwards into the openness of the Upper Dee Valley. The track, now grassy, followed the twists and turns of the river, and a neglected stone wall hanging onto the past did the same beside us. The day was now decidedly wet, but it didn't dampen any enthusiasm as far as Swift and Yogi were concerned.

I didn't have much chance to soak up the scene of fern-filled slopes down to a twinkling river with hills and mountains behind, as my hands were filled by the racecourse competition which appeared to be on the home-straight. At the next slight incline, Yogi set off at a canter and threw a couple of merry bucks into the mix. Swift flicked one of her own, flinging feet up high in a gymnastic display that was worthy of Olympic Gold.

"Hey, hey, hey!" I shouted. "That's enough of that. You can go faster but keep to the horizontal please!"

Team Swogi settled into a gentler rhythmic canter and we ate up the next few kilometres of trail, only slowing where water-washed stones crossed the trail, or for a brief pause to fertilise the land. We quickly arrived at the crossing of the River Quoich (a tributary of the River Dee) to find that the road bridge between us and the other side was closed. Closed for good reason it appeared, as it now only reached half-way across the watery divide.

I knew that this area had suffered from flood-damage during Storm Frank in 2015 but was surprised at the extent, and that two years later repairs still hadn't been made. With his mind on the rest day ahead, Yogi didn't hesitate at the request to ford the river below the bridge today. He completely ignored the loose stones under hoof, the roar of the white water beside us, and the incredible width I was asking him to wade. What a difference a day makes!

The fast pace of the day and the horse management it had entailed had completely sapped my strength, and the last thing I needed was the thing before me – a difficult gate to undo. It was a high wooden deer gate, wrapped in fencing wire, and although I could see it was unlocked and only fastened with a clip, the clip was a long way down. I approached with the latch to our left (Yogi's favoured side) and dangled myself out of the saddle to reach it. Thankfully Yogi stood stock still for this process and I opened it with ease. Closing the gate was another matter altogether...

Now on the 'finish-line' side of the gate, Yogi had a bee in his bonnet about getting there and the buzz was drowning out our communication. It was tricky finding just the right angle for my hand through the wire to reattach the clip, whilst again dangling out of the saddle, but this time on a horse with fidgety feet. Several circles later and somehow managing not to fall off (or fall out with each other), it finally fell into place.

We collected Swift from her nearby grass search and joined the tarmac road along the north side of the river. It was only a couple of kilometres to Mar Lodge, and with easy riding and an absence of traffic we promptly arrived at the old stable block. The building was a traditional courtyard, with a cobbled stone interior and an archway entrance under a modest bell tower. No longer used to house equines, it instead contains the ranger's office and

'Base Camp', a well-appointed (group bookings only) bunkhouse.

Feeling incredibly weary, I steered Team Swogi under the arch in search of a ranger to show me where to camp, and in anticipation of collecting my pre-positioned restock box that Dave had dropped off sometime during my travels. The hoof-steps echoed off the stone walls and I could imagine the clatter of a horse-drawn carriage doing the same in times gone by. The courtyard then would have been busy with grooms and stable lads ready to see to the horses but appeared empty now.

Not finding anyone to greet us, I dismounted and made some clatter of my own by knocking on the office door. Yogi tried a different approach to attract attention and peered in through the window, leaving hot breath on the glass. My knocks remained unanswered and trying the handle, I discovered the door to be firmly locked. Joining Yogi at the window, the room was dark and devoid of staff, but I could see my box give an enticing wave from where it rested - on a table at the back of the room.

Disappointed that the delights it held would have to wait until later, I waved back and promised to release it as soon as I possibly could. The luxuries within the box were a secondary concern though, as I first needed to find the field and set up camp before my energy dial dropped to empty. I was just about to leave, to see if I could find my own way, when another door opened further into the courtyard. The man behind it wasn't one of the rangers but another employee of the estate, and although he didn't have the key to the office, he directed me to the field. He also sincerely promised to tell the rangers of my arrival when they returned.

Dragging my feet, I retreated under the archway and made the long walk down the driveway to where we'd been told to go. Last time here, corrals for those staying with horses were set up quite close to the lodge. This time, however, we were in the furthest field. With energy in short supply by this stage of the day, it felt inconvenient to say the least, but I knew Team Swogi would appreciate the serene slumbers that the increased solitude would induce.

The large field was further away but I was pleased to find a tap for easy access to water. It also came equipped with a handy tie-rail, and after a day of chasing mine and Yogi's tail at top speed, I was grateful to be able to root the horses to one spot. The fence line also eased construction of a fairly large corral, and Team Swogi were soon tucked up in their rugs and tucking into long grass with snorts of contentment. I meanwhile flopped down on the pile of kit and temporarily closed my eyes.

Struggling up from here ten minutes later, feeling like a zombie, my section of camp seemed to take a long time to assemble. Finally, though, the tent was up, the tarp constructed, and the stove was on the go. The cup of tea and the remains of my rations (which were now of meagre portions) had a small restorative effect. However, with 'seven o' clock' feeling like eleven, I decided to turn in. After today's powerwalk, I'd need a powernap of at least twelve straight hours to recover.

I'd just begun the squeeze into my one-man tent, with the bodily contortion this entailed, when I heard a vehicle approaching. Bottom first, and with as much elegance as my achy joints could muster, I extracted myself to go and meet the driver. The driver was one of the rangers, who greeted me with a cheery "Hello!" and presentation of my restock box.

"Thank you so much for the free delivery service," I said after human and horse introductions were complete.

"You're welcome. Do you have everything you need?"

"I do for tonight, but I'll probably walk into Braemar tomorrow for a few extra items."

"Would you like a lift?" she asked.

"Oh *YES PLEASE!"* I replied with much appreciation.

Sometimes a small offer of help is all that it takes to raise your spirits, as in my tired and achy state this evening, I'd been dreading the six kilometre walk to town in the morning. Glancing inside the box after the ranger left, my spirits were raised again, although this time in a completely different way.

Sitting inside on top of clean clothes was a surprise bottle of spicy rum, some Coke, and a little smiley label that concluded with Dave's signature and three large kisses. *Maybe,* I thought, *I could stay up just a little bit longer, to toast my incredible horses, good support crews, and a loving husband back home.*

Two Bobs and a Bender

Day 12: Rest Day Mar Lodge (Distance 4km, Ascent 120m) into Braemar

Waking in the cosy comforts of my warm sleeping bag and tiny tent, my eyelids felt heavy despite the length of sleep. I rubbed my eyes and lingered, enjoying the snug confines. The light filtering through the flysheet wasn't that bright, I couldn't detect any wind, and the air felt damp. Without opening my tent, I sensed our rest day would be a little overcast.

Yawning and stretching, and I do confess snoozing a little between pages of my book, I was glad of the easy agenda today. My lift into the village wasn't until ten o'clock and I didn't intend to stray too far before then. I couldn't hear much from the horses, no munching, footfall, or snorts, so I presumed they too were having a bit of a lie-in.

My mind strayed from my book, contemplating our journey so far, and more importantly, the two days left to come. Tomorrow we'd be back to unfamiliar turf with a great pass through the Cairngorms to complete – the Lairig an Laoigh, followed by the wide expanse of the Bynack Moore. I knew this pass had been completed by many horses before, but it was described as 'challenging' and up high on the plateau we'd be at the weather's mercy.

Trepidation was at an all time high as I considered this to be the most committing part of our circular route, even more so than the Minigaig pass of day two. Hopefully, finding some phone reception in town later today, I'd be checking the weather forecast with interest and concern. *Although, if I don't get my lazy butt out of bed,* I thought, *I'll be missing my lift there if I'm not careful*!

Rising slowly, I tip-toed around the tent so as not to wake Team Swogi who were fast asleep on the far side of the corral and made a leisurely breakfast. It's not usual to follow porridge with pudding, but rules can bend on the trail where treats are infrequently found. I watched Yogi slowly rise with a grunt. He yawned, bowed down with front legs straight for a stretch, then shook himself from head to tail. He ambled over for a chat, and Swift soon followed. Giving in to requests for a bending of their rules and bonus treats too, I made up an extra feed as Dave had supplied plenty within the box.

I was just finishing the chocolate orange and a second cup of tea, when the ranger's car appeared at the gate to the field – ten minutes early. Grabbing my jacket, I stuffed my wallet, phone, and charger hastily into my pockets and as I zipped up the tent, I asked Team Swogi if there was anything they wanted from town.

"Carrots," said Swift.

"A whole bag each," agreed Yogi.

"I'll see what I can do and see you later then. Be good while I'm away."

The last part of my sentence was more of a warning than a request, but then the promise of carrots for good behaviour might be bribery enough. I jogged the short distance across the grass to the gate, climbed over it, and seated myself in the passenger side of the ranger's car.

"Thank you so much for running me into town," I said.

"That's okay, I was heading in anyways. No problem at all."

As we chatted about day-to-day things on the short distance to Braemar, it felt strange to see the scenery pass by the window at such a rate. Yogi might be fast, but I'd become accustomed to a slower pace of life. Tired as

I was, I wasn't looking forward to the return to civilisation at the end of my adventure. A little dip into it today, however, would be welcomed for the luxuries it contained.

"Where would you like dropped?" I was asked as we reached the outskirts.

"At the best café in town please," I replied.

I offered more thanks, and a wave goodbye, then entered the Gordon's Tea Room and was soon settled at a table with a lovely cup of coffee and a plug socket to recharge my phone. I tapped into the Wi-Fi, sent some messages home, then checked the weather forecast for the rest of the day and more importantly tomorrow. The report suggested that both days would be much the same - overcast, reasonably dry, and with only moderate wind.

This was a relief, but I hoped the cloud base would stay high enough to offer the full extent of the views from the top of the pass. We'd be climbing over eight hundred metres first thing in the morning, and it would be a shame to have the scenery obscured. Coffee complete, I wandered next door to the corner shop to restock perishables (such as cheese and meats) and made sure to pick up two bags of carrots for you-know-who.

I felt it would be rude to leave the village before lunchtime, so I ambled up the street full of tourists to pause on the bridge for a while. The bridge spanned the River Clunie, which tumbles down a narrow channel above the bridge and a series of small drops below, before stilling in a wide, flat pool just around the corner.

This was another river I'd kayaked several times, at first in a wobbling and nervous manner, led by coaches from my local canoe club. In later years, it was me doing the leading - and the whooping and looping when playing in the last drop before the pool. Happy memories of kayaking companions emerging from the river, endorphin-rich, shivering, and hungry, filled my mind.

Today wouldn't be the first day I'd be seeking a good hearty feed in this village.

Braemar, split by this river, used to be two separate hamlets on either side (Auchendryne on the west and Castleton on the east) and used to be known as Cinn Drochaid (Bridge End). Around 1059, a bridge was built to connect the banks and the two rival estates of Invercauld and Mar. A medieval wooden fortress and later the stone Kindrochit Castle (now in ruin) was constructed to protect this prime location where important hill passes from all points of the compass converge.

The village has had royal connections long before Queen Victoria made Balmoral Castle her favourite holiday destination only fifteen kilometres away. In early history, it's reported that the first ruler of Scotland (King Kenneth Macalpin) frequented this area for sport and, like a plaque on a winner's trophy, the hill behind the village still holds his name - Creag Choinnich, or Kenneth's Crag.

In the 11th century, King Malcolm Canmore took sports to the next level by introducing an event to test acts of strength, endurance, and speed, in order to identify his finest soldiers. These traditions continue in the annual Braemar Gathering (known simply as The Games), taking place on the first Saturday of September, and habitually attended by the royal family.

If this wasn't enough to put Braemar on the map of every tourist bus travelling north, then the Earl of Mar sealed this fate in 1715. Raising his standard on the site where the Invercauld Hotel now stands, he started the Jacobite Uprising known simply as 'The Fifteen'. It was one of several attempts to restore James VII of the House of Stuart to the throne of Great Britain. It was more successful than the later and last famous crushing defeat at Culloden, but The Fifteen still ended in retreat.

In a cemetery beside Braemar Castle (built in the 17th century) can be found the grave of Peter Grant (known as Auld Dubrach) – the last of the Jacobite soldiers. He died in 1824 at an astonishing age for the time, of one-hundred-and-ten. His inscription reads, 'The old, loyal Jacobite was at peace, he had kept faith and those whom he thought were his rightful Monarchs all of his life, a hero and a man of honour to the last.'

Surviving the Culloden slaughter, he was taken prisoner to Carlisle to await sentence (commonly death), but he somehow managed to escape and make his way back to Scotland. He had to live many years in hiding but was able to evade recapture, despite the price on his head. He married, had six children, and if his life-story sounds very familiar – it was perhaps the inspiration for a popular book and television series (*Outlander*).

This may be questionable, but another author, Robert Louis Stevenson, certainly found inspiration in Braemar. Whilst on holiday in the village, the concept of *Treasure Island* was born – focussed on a map of an imaginary island drawn with his stepson. It is said that he penned sixteen chapters here, confined inside by the usual inclement Scottish weather, and that some of his characters in the book were based on those observed in the village.

The weather wasn't all that inclement today, but it couldn't be described as hot, so I set off back to the tea room for a warming spot of lunch. After finding the good hearty feed I was seeking (and a sneaky pint of real ale), I felt restored enough to walk back to Mar Lodge via the lower slopes of Morrone - a hill to the south-west. This route would take me away from the possibility of thumbing a lift on the valley road below, but it was a route I wanted to explore - not only for its viewpoint across the valley but for future horse adventures.

Leaving the outskirts of the village, I passed a picturesque duck pond with happy ducks quacking away, no doubt kept well fed by a steady stream of tourists. The track climbed a gradual ascent, and I was soon surrounded by trees that were heavily draped in lichen and which rose from a dense blanket of juniper below.

Reaching the top of my small climb, the viewpoint was marked by a conical stone cairn set within a clearing. Erected by the Deeside Field Club, it had a bronze view indicator on top, listing all the peaks and the angles at which to find them. The bronze, aged by the weather, was oxidized to a blue-green sheen, but the text of the mountain names was clear. So too was the inscription by George Stephen below them.

'Upon this vantage ground I fain would stand
The prospect with delight my spirit fills
How often in glowing rapture have I scanned
The waving outline of the distant hills.'

The text was clear, but the distant hills weren't waving that distinctly today, as I was straining to make out the individual peaks smothered by thick shrouds of clouds. My struggles may not have been due to weather alone though, as rumours suggest that the cairn had been constructed seventeen metres lower than designed. True or not, the cairn's position still afforded an impressive panorama even on a dreary day.

Setting off on a winding trail through the Morrone Birkwood (a Special Area of Conservation, managed by Scottish Natural Heritage), I appreciated the change in texture compared to the swaths of forestry plantations I usually frequent. The birks (or birches) here were the less common downy variety, a little smaller and with darker bark, than the well-known silver. Adding to this uncommon scene was an abundance of juniper, one of only three conifers native to Scotland and not usually seen in such accumulation.

The Morrone Birkwood is said to be the largest and most diverse surviving example of a sub-alpine birch-juniper woodland in Britain. Pollen samples taken from the peaty soils suggest that the birch, juniper, moss, and wildflowers that exist today remain much the same as the flora present at end of the last Ice Age, more than 10,000 years ago.

Savouring the same views and feeling the same ambiance as many whose feet had stepped this way before, I emerged from the Birkwood to an open heathered moorland. The peaty track wound through more modern vegetation (marshy and low growing) then disappeared into a forestry plantation a little way ahead. Holding onto thoughts from the past and shared sensations with those long gone, I mused that this more modern view - although not present at the end of the Ice Age - probably hadn't changed much over the last hundred years.

The ground was firm underfoot until passing a pond with soggy reaches that spilled out over the trail. Picking my way carefully in an effort to keep my feet dry, I spotted a circular item lying on the peat. I picked it up, rubbed off the dark brown soil, and discovered I was holding an old half-crown. *Well, this little treasure wasn't going to help my mind return to the present, was it?*

Worn and weathered, I couldn't make out the date of the coin. I was, however, fairly certain that it displayed King George VI on one side, so this narrowed it down to somewhere between 1936 and 1952. Turning it over, I could see the outline of a shield - depicting the coats of arms of England, Scotland, and Northern Ireland. This side was well-worn too, and given the oxidized state, I suspected it was of a later minting made with cupro-nickel rather than silver.

My treasure might not be worth much now, but it was an important feature of times gone by. First issued as far back as 1549 and not withdrawn from circulation until 1970, it was a sizeable coin at thirty-two millimetres across, and considered a respectable tip. According to *Etiquette and Entertaining: To Help You on Your Social Way*, by Lady Troubridge (1939), it would be an appropriate amount to bestow to a maid – "This treasure, on whom so much devolves, should receive half-a-crown for a week-end, though she deserves more" or a footman who "carried up the breakfast-trays for the lady visitor."

I could imagine, out here on the heath, this particular coin being presented to a young stable-lad for leading a pony as it carried a stag down off the hill. I felt sad that the pocket he'd placed it in had obviously had a hole. Worth two shillings and sixpence, which in today's money had the buying power of around five to ten pounds, it was an amount not to be sniffed at. The poor young lad, at the bottom of the ladder, had missed out on a good chunk of his daily wage.

Placing it in a pocket of my own (double checking for holes), I continued my walk towards the gate that marked the boundary of the An Car forestry plantation. The wide grassy track and the regular-spaced trees to either side felt more familiar as I descended the slope back down to the road. With only two kilometres remaining to get back to camp, I paused for a while in the lay-by opposite to take in the view across the valley.

As the River Dee had snaked its way across the glen over the years, it had created a flat expanse of fertile soil. As a result, the grass was a vivid bright green compared to the heather patch at my feet and the craggy hills on the other side. Only a few trees had dared to take root in this ever-changing land, their dark, scattered figures accepting the risk of being swept from their feet during the next flood.

"Are you looking for a ride?" an American tourist asked, interrupting the view and my thoughts.

"Depends - which way are you heading?" I replied with a smile.

The American couple had also been enjoying the view, sat in their car with a picnic, and were now leaving to head up to a favourite picnic spot of Queen Victoria - the Linn of Dee. Situated at the head of the glen, the river at the Linn squeezes through a rocky gorge and the impressive rush of water is a popular tourist destination.

I explained that with only two kilometres to go I'd happily walk, but they wouldn't hear of it at all since they were heading in my direction. Accepting the lift and sitting in the back of the car, I listened to the couple's tales of where they'd toured so far: "Edinberg, Glain Coe, the Eye-el of Skye, and now Bal-morr-aahl." They were "off to Aae-bir-deeen next" and hearing I lived in the north-east, wondered if I knew their cousin who worked in the oil industry there...

Giggling a little, but thanking them kindly for the ride, I offloaded at the Victoria Bridge having offered a few top tips of things not to miss on their onward travels. This meeting had stirred a few memories of my own American travels, and their assumption that everyone wants to be saved from walking took me back to a time in Flagstaff.

Staying there briefly prior to taking part in a kayaking expedition down the Grand Canyon, I was on a tack finding mission and only had one afternoon spare. Western riding equipment is hard to source in the UK and even harder to find in Swift's kind of size. Many failed attempts online had me seize the opportunity of visiting American tack shops while I was there, to see if I could find a bridle and breast collar in size 'LL' (lanky and large). My long-suffering husband was tasked to help me in my quest.

The first shop (or rather *store)* was on the east side of town and didn't have what I needed, so I politely asked for directions to another, over on the west. After listening to a series of instructions based on the view from a car, I sought clarification as to how these might appear from on foot. At first, I thought it was a language barrier that had caused the storeman's gift of the gab to dry up, but his next question - asked in horror - cleared the matter up a little...

"You guys aren't gonna *wawk* there are you?"

"It's only three kilometres, and we don't have our horses with us," I replied, hoping that some humour might lift his jaw off the floor.

"But don't you have a truck? I'm not sure how you'd get there on foot."

He watched us leave the store, joined by the other assistants who were all shaking their heads in disbelief. I don't think they truly believed that we didn't have *some* sort of motorised transport to take us the *huge* distance across town. Returning on foot to the hotel later with a bag full of Swift-sized tack, and not meeting anyone else on the sidewalks, it appeared that around there at least - American's don't walk!

Ambling over the bridge, through the gate to the field and across the grass, I was met by the staring twin gaze of hopeful horses. I duly fed some well-deserved carrots to Swift and Yogi and settled down by my tent for a brew. They settled down too and my slurps of tea were soon accompanied by contented snores. The back of the field was peaceful, nothing but the bleats of distant sheep and the occasional tweet from a bird, and Team Swogi's slumbers deepened.

Yogi was lying curled up with his chin resting on the grass. His eyes were closed, his ears twitching, and his head bobbed to the side like a student trying to stay awake during a post-lunch lecture. I willed him to let go completely and flop onto his side like Swift, who was currently lying flat out. Her eyes were flickering, her lips were drawn back, she was uttering the odd grunt, and her legs were twitching rhythmically as she dreamed of winning the Grand National.

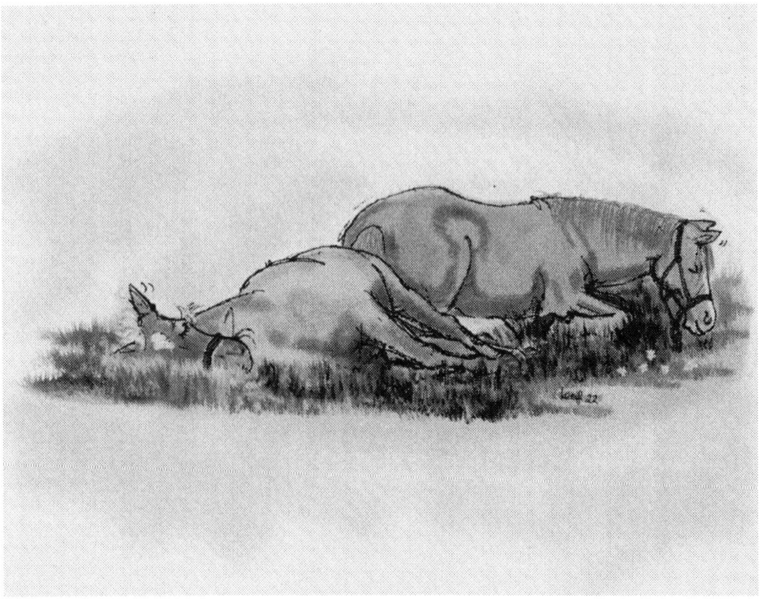

Grand National Dreams

Horses don't sleep all that much, around six hours within twenty-four, and the majority of this is done standing up thanks to a soft tissue 'stay apparatus' that locks their legs. This complex arrangement of muscles, tendons, and ligaments stabilizes their legs and calls for a minimal amount of energy while they slip into a light sleep. A heavier or REM sleep is only achieved lying down as all their muscles (including the stay apparatus) need to relax. According to studies, horses require a minimum of thirty minutes of REM sleep a day.

Swift often achieves this quota or more, but Yogi, as far as I could tell (having spent many twenty-four-hour periods in his company), rarely does. He's far too alert most of the time, assessing surroundings for the dangers that he feels are his responsibility to deal with.

Watching his head bobs become more extreme, he finally flopped onto his side with a fart – *really* letting go - and I stifled a giggle so as not to wake him. I love that life on the trail means that I could offload his burden by taking my turn 'on watch' and I also love that he seems to trust me to do so.

Half an hour later, his REM quota achieved, Yogi was back on his feet and was complaining that he'd run out of grass. Catering to another of his daily needs, I moved the corral slightly to allow access to fresh ground. Needless to say, this caused much excitement and the resulting bucks and squeals confirmed that the afternoon nap period was well and truly over.

Feeling refreshed myself after the little sit down and the cup of tea, I turned my attention to repacking my bags for the final two days. Taking fresh clothes out of the supply box, I swapped them for discarded smelly ones, counted out rations of food, then poured as much spicy rum as I could into my hip flasks. For the second time this trip, the flasks wouldn't contain my usual tipple of whisky, but the rum would make a nice change from ginger mead.

Satisfied that everything was in order and in its right place, I closed the lid on the box and carried it up to the ranger's office – where it would await collection by the next passing friend. Whilst up at the buildings, I mooched around the outside of St Ninians Chapel, built in 1898 for use as a private chapel by Alexander Duff (1st Duke of Fife) and his family.

Set in a walled enclosure, the chapel was designed by the same architect as Crathie Church, frequented by the royal family when based at Balmoral Castle. It's a small, rectangular building and the walls formed of large pink granite blocks are topped neatly by bright red tiles. Three small, stained-glass windows are set into a side wall and another in the end gable. I couldn't imagine they let much light in so the interior, despite the cold from the stones, should have a cosy feel.

I didn't try the door to find this out however, as I suspected it was locked and I became distracted by the noisy arrival of a helicopter on the far side of the lodge. I'd thought I'd heard one earlier in the day as I'd dashed across the grass to the ranger's car but had assumed it was just passing by. This second visit had my mind whirling. Was it a VIP visitor to the lodge? Oh, how the other half live! Perhaps Mountain Rescue tending to a poor injured soul? I hoped nobody was seriously hurt. Maybe a deer count, for management of the estate or a cull to aid rewilding?

The National Trust for Scotland (NTS) who own the Mar Lodge Estate had in the past used helicopters to reduce deer populations to a level the land could naturally support. The return of rare species and the woodland regeneration that resulted is commendable, but thinking back to the beautiful herd I'd observed at Glen Prosen, I shuddered and sincerely hoped the helicopter wasn't here for deer.

I returned to camp to cook dinner and used up the last of the luxuries that wouldn't survive saddle-bag travel. After a large feed at lunchtime and another tonight, I was feeling rather stuffed. Team Swogi looked stuffed too, having had an extra feed and ample grass for the day, but they appeared to be in denial.

"I've still got room for more carrots," said Yogi.

"Me too!" said Swift, leaning over the fence.

"OK then, you can have a couple more," I relented.

The extra sugar wouldn't do any harm, not even for Yogi's Cushing's, as they'd been working hard each day and had an energetic day ahead tomorrow.

To distract from worries of the route we'd take, and to ease my fullness of tum, I slipped my hip flask in my pocket and wandered back down to the river for a gentle evening stroll. The clouds that had been present all day had lifted a little, and down on the bank at the base of the bridge, the sun's golden rays slipped through the ornate rails. It was too early to set yet, and it seemed determined to shine at least once today before being displaced by the darkness of night.

Sitting for a while, I leant back on the comfy rock I'd found and let the river's tinkle, the taste of rum, and the sun's rays on my face transport me back to the banks of the Brahmaputra – a river in North-East India. 'River Rum' was the tipple of choice for this three-week kayaking excursion nine years ago and sipping it around a campfire on a sandy beach each night was part of the 'debrief' and part of the fun.

The mighty Siang (as it's known by the locals) is described by many as one of the world's largest rivers, it is also one of the most inaccessible. Draining the Himalayas, the waters flow through Tibet to Arunachal Pradesh in India and onwards to Bangladesh. Passing though remote villages dotted with tribal settlements, weaving through deep gorges amidst jungle-clad hills, its upper reaches cross disputed land on which China still holds a territorial claim. It's no normal river. The speed of the flow, the power, and the six metre waves are hard to handle, and at times just hard to believe.

The Siang could never be described as a 'tinkle'. The roar of its call was relentless, and waking through the night on its shores, the thought of the huge rapids you'd paddle the next day were never far away. The flavours I was savouring - not of the rum, but the whole river expedition - didn't feel a million miles away from those experienced whilst dobbineering. Living outside for days on end, equipment packed with a minimalist approach, and the constant concern of what was yet to come mixed with the exhilaration of what you'd already achieved.

Feeling content, I drew myself away from the water and back to grass, where Team Swogi trotted over for night-time cuddles. Soaking in their solid, reassuring presence and feeling the calm they exude wash over me, I concluded that horses might be more work and take longer to get ready in the morning, but my kayak has never evoked such inner peace.

The Runaway Train

Day 13: Mar Lodge to Loch an Eilein (Distance 45km, Ascent 1078m)

Leaving Mar Lodge took longer than expected, considering there was an easy corral to deconstruct in the confines of a field with a tie-rail to facilitate the process. I'd forgotten how long it takes to clear up after my equine friends. A poo pick isn't always required in the wilds, but it was here, and it took three wheelbarrows full. Adding to the time was the nuisance of packing up in the rain and the care this requires to keep everything as dry as possible.

This rain wasn't in the forecast I'd seen yesterday, nor detailed in the mountain weather report blue-tacked to the office window up at the rangers' station. It wasn't raining heavily but it was heavy rain. Each individual chubby droplet was visible as it fell, bouncing with a patter from every leaf, stone, or flesh it hit. I hoped this blip in the weather would drip away as the day unfolded, otherwise it was going to be a gloomy pass through the hills.

Our initial climb would take us to over eight-hundred-and-thirty metres where we'd stay for nearly eight kilometres whilst crossing the remote plateau. Crossing in summer, the rain should only cause discomfort and not disorientation, but I couldn't help but spare a thought for the Abernethy soldiers who lost their way in the wintered pass in 1804.

During leave from their station in Edinburgh, they decided to walk home using Glen Derry but became disorientated in a storm. Floundering in the snow, they wandered off the pass into the peat hags and five out of seven of the party perished. One of the demised was not found for eighteen months, discovered with his head severed from his trunk and his flesh torn. No mention of whether this was due to man, beast, or weather is recounted in folklore though.

Trying to think of more cheerful and dry thoughts, I steered Yogi's soggy ears and mane towards the pass that ran alongside the River Lui, and as the track climbed, I looked down over the old Canadian Campsite – now smothered by a forestry plantation. Between the River Dee and the Lui Water that feeds it, this corner of land was occupied by Canadian Lumberjacks during World War II. They felled around seven hundred acres of trees from the surrounding hills, much of it used as pit-props for trench construction on the western front.

Use of the old site for camping and caravanning by the public was tolerated into the 1970's and many used it on a semi-permanent basis to access the hills and glens. This came to a sudden end when the area was fenced off and ironically planted for trees. More ironic still (and if rumours are correct), the plantation viewed from the sky is the shape of a maple leaf.

The track was sandy underfoot, and since it was uphill, Yogi needed no encouragement or guidance, so I took the opportunity to add another layer. There was a chill in the air, and I'd now cooled down after my wheelbarrow exertions. I murmured gratitude to my steady horse and the saddle's handy pommel to hang things from, as both assisted the jacket shuffle without any unplanned stages in the process.

Emerging from the far end of the 'Maple Wood', the view down Glen Lui opened up. The trees no longer hid the vista of the highest Cairngorm mountains, but the low clouds were managing that all on their own. I knew the pointed summit of Derry Cairngorm was in there somewhere, with Ben Macdui not far away and Cairn Toul off to the left, but the tops couldn't be seen today. The glen, heather covered and bare, with the gravel edges of the river meandering through it, was clear; but as the open moorland reached up to the grey crags above, they plunged into a wispy wrap of mist.

The track, now level with the glen's floor, widened and followed the river's course. A helicopter, possibly the same one as at Mar Lodge yesterday, also followed the river's course, but on the far side of the glen. It was black in colour and reasonably small, so certainly not for medical evacuations – more likely privately owned or hired. I pondered on the purpose of its continued presence whilst Yogi and Swift followed its progress with their left ears. As the chopper moved ahead, their left ears swivelled forward to join their right ones and all four became focussed on the next interruption in the otherwise tranquil glen.

This was a small group of Duke of Edinburgh walkers who were dreary, dripping, and drookit in their drudge towards us. Backpacks decorated with rustling and colourful covers, maps in map cases flapping around necks, and feet placed in plastic bags before boots. Despite their damp discomfort, they were still expressing a noisy motivational chatter which cut through the heavy drops of rain in more ways than one.

"Waaahhh!" cried Yogi, as the group approached. "What have they got on their backs, and what are those flapping things?"

"Whatever they are, they're rustling in a highly irregular way!" exclaimed Swift, somewhat alarmed.

Yogi had by now jumped onto the heather at the side of the track and was dancing on the spot. Swift held her ground, although with her neck stretched in full giraffe-alert mode, I suspected it wouldn't be long before she followed suit.

"Can you possibly stand still for a moment?" I shouted out as politely as I could whilst being jostled around by a silly bouncing-bear.

My request aimed primarily to the group, seemed a reasonable appeal for Yogi to consider too.

"No problem at all," the leader of the party cheerfully responded, bringing the rest of the group to a halt.

I let Team Swogi have a good look at the 'scary' rucksacks and flapping maps as we side-stepped and jigged around them, and I tried to express my thanks to the group whilst still on the move.

"Gorgeous horses," the last girl in the line declared.

I was grateful for their understanding and in particular this parting comment, which had suddenly altered Team Swogi's view of Duke of Edinburgh groups in general. This was just as well, as I could see several more making their way towards us further down the glen. In parties of around six each, I could see three separate clusters of brightness, flapping, and rustling heading in our direction.

"Please pull yourselves together," I pleaded. "I don't want any dramatics and certainly don't need to be jigging the full length of this glen."

"They aren't as bad as I thought," said Yogi. "They called me gorgeous," he continued, smugly.

"They said we *both* were actually," huffed a slightly disgruntled Swift.

"Well, obviously I agree. I think you are both gorgeous, both clever, and both extremely brave when it comes to walking past scary objects with absolute calm..."

A bit of flattery, optimism, and neuro-linguistic programming is always worth a try.

The first of the three groups politely stood still at the side of the track with no need for me to ask, and I managed to steer Team Swogi in a more direct and less sideways manner past them. Again, positive comments were made about the 'beautiful' and 'stunning' appearance of my companions. This increased confidence, and by the third strange-looking crowd, nose-snuffles and neck-pats were granted, and those brightly coloured backpacks were tentatively frisked for any spare food that might be fit for a horse. Unsuccessful on the food front but not deflated, Team Swogi continued with a spring in their step - their hearts warmed, and poise bolstered by the numerous compliments received.

Glen Lui's beauty and the relatively short south-eastern approach to the Cairngorms has always made it a popular and busy place, but I couldn't believe that in one hour, I'd just met more people than I'd seen in the previous twelve days of travel. I wondered how busy we might find the area around Bob Scott's Bothy and Glen Derry Lodge when we arrived there shortly.

On the approach, the glen's cover of heather gave way to a new plantation of trees to the right and a sprinkling of older Scots pines to the left marking the path down to the bothy. I decided to follow these trees and divert off the main trail for a while. I'd heard much about this popular and historic shelter but had never paid a visit and there was no time like the present.

Paying a visit in times gone by would have raised a fee of one shilling and six pence, to receive shelter for the night in a wooden hut situated further along the glen at Luibeg Cottage. This was across the river and was where Bob Scott (the bothy's namesake) lived from 1947-1973 as the Mar Lodge Estate gamekeeper. A shelter was in use near this location since the 1940's, but was burnt down in 1986 following frustrations between walkers and the new keeper. The replacement bothy (after renewed understanding with the estate and built further down the glen), suffered a similar flaming end in 2003 - but by accident this time.

The third-time-lucky edition that I was admiring now (managed by the MBA) looked more fireproof with stone cladding around the base. Situated in a beautiful stand of pines, down by the river's curve and under the shadow of the surrounding mountains, it looked a fabulous place to plan a future overnight stop.

"The grass is delicious," agreed Swift.

"The butt-scratching potential looks good too," stated Yogi as he rubbed his nose across the Scots pine's bark to assess its scratch-ability.

I jumped off and left Team Swogi to explore both grass and bark as I explored the dim depths of the bothy's interior. As always, in the best bothies, the fire was at its core. Several basic tables and chairs were scattered within, and a large sleeping platform filled the far end. The bothy was empty of people, but it had the feel of a busy place and despite the lack of physical evidence (as it was tidy and swept clean) I could sense a recent occupancy.

Outside, as Yogi and Swift confirmed their approval, I vowed to come back to stay the night – although noted that this should be a mid-week and out-of-season visit, to avoid substantial crowds. The fulfilment of this promise, however, might depend on how the next part of our journey went, as we were about to swing north up Glen Derry and face the challenge of the climb to the edge of the Cairngorm massif. Using a fallen tree as a mounting block, I jumped back up on Yogi and followed the thin sandy trail along the river's edge towards Derry Lodge.

The chunky raindrops splashed in a deep pool beside us, disturbing the crystal-clear reflections of the trees.

The riverbed, strewn with moss-covered rocks and holding the leaves' images on its surface, oozed a green glow. As it twisted to the left ahead towards the mountains, both banks seemingly converged at the vanishing point of the bend. The reflections and colours were astounding, even on a grey day, and I could only imagine the enhancement a brighter day might bring. I promptly added 'sunny' to my requirements of my mid-week, out-of-season promised return.

The thin trail widened again as we left the river behind and emerged from our detour at the forlorn and forgotten buildings of Derry Lodge. Once an impressive Victorian hunting lodge built on the site of an 18th century shieling, it was used to accommodate shooting parties for meals and for overnight stays - then later as housing for gillies and other estate workers. In 1942 the lodge was requisitioned by the army to accommodate training troops instead, but was relinquished after two years and left in a sorry state.

The Cairngorm Club leased it for a while as a mountain base for walking and climbing activities (and no doubt a few social meets too), but the expense of maintenance and repairs became untenable. From 1967 it has remained empty. Back in its heyday, I could imagine how proud the lodge felt to host Queen Victoria when she paused there in 1859 after climbing Ben Macdui by pony, and I was sad to see it boarded-up and neglected now.

"That's an impressive climb," said Yogi in awe.

"Sounds like cruelty to me," said Swift, with a shudder at the thought of being asked to carry anyone to the top of the highest mountain in the Cairngorms - irrespective of whether they were royalty or not.

Passing the lodge, we also passed the Mountain Rescue Hut – a strong, dark, wooden building evolved from the first aid station, first positioned here in 1938.

Behind it, we had a choice to make as the path forked with options of travel on either side of the Derry Burn. Our route turning north would shadow the river that descended from the mountains along the length of Glen Derry; we just had to decide whether to do that on the right or left bank.

Consulting my map as well as my equine companions, the track on the left appeared wider for a couple of kilometres, and neither horse had objections to fording the burn today. Yet again, a wooden bridge spanned the water, but was only suitable for human transit.

"There's a theme running here," said Yogi, stepping into the shallow but pebbled waters.

"I do enjoy a good sploosh-splash," answered a distracted Swift, as she paused halfway to stir up the water with her right fore.

Eventually reaching the other side the trail wove through remnants of ancient Caledonian forest, the tall Scots pine widely spaced and dotted up the glen. At the base of their trunks was a thick blanket of grass, scattered heather, and the light-green oval leaves of blaeberry shrubs, their berries not yet ripe. It was a beautiful glen with a lovely, serene feel, and I was instantly reminded of my favourite Glen Feshie - in its upper reaches where it turns to the left at the toll tree.

Sometimes a place can cause you to catch your breath a little and I was feeling this now; not as intense as I'd felt once before, but noticeable, nonetheless. The term 'breath-taking' is often applied to a scenic setting, but until you've physically struggled to breathe in a place, I don't think this expression is fully understood. I've travelled to some amazing places in the world and would have thought that the depths of the Grand Canyon, or the sight of the Taj Mahal in pink pastels of morning light, would have instigated such a reaction.

However, I was never moved to such deep emotion until one time on familiar turf in Glen Feshie.

Travelling with Team Swogi and rounding the corner at the head of the glen on an early summer's morn, I was suddenly hit with an astonishing sensation that literally left me unable to take my next breath. The track we were on wove through the river several times, as both the river and track were squeezed together by dramatic, sheer rocky cliffs on either side. There was the rich smell of mature pine basking in the sun, mixed with the fresh sweet smell of young trees only starting out in life.

Sparkling leaves of silver birch highlighted by the blazing sun danced in the stiff breeze. Their leaves waved like celebration bunting as we passed by. The birch seemed to approve of our passage and our appreciation of their gaiety - noticed despite the minor part they played within the magnificent splendour.

It was more than just the sights and smells taking my breath away though. There was a sensation of deep connection as the rhythm of the horse's feet seemed to progress in-time and in-tune with the land - at a gentle and steady pace. Within this connection was an acknowledgement of risk and a feeling of exposure should anything go wrong in this remote glen. Self-reliance, skills, and knowledge (of hills and horses) were the only back up if that wrong should take place. I felt elated, grounded, part of nature, at one with my companions, and - once I'd got my breath back – powerful, enchanted, and utterly content.

The enchantment of today's glen washed over us as we progressed up the side of the rocky stream. The magic spread to the skies, drying the heavy raindrops and lifting the clouds a little. The clouds still clung to the tops, but they looked like they too would vanish as we climbed our way towards them. Old trees lined the trail, their corridor effect and their sense of guiding duty not diminished by the passing of time. We ducked under their branches and negotiated a maze of roots as the trail steadily rose in an undulating way.

Suddenly, when weaving through the final set of trees, the helicopter reappeared right over our head towing a large white bag on a length of rope below it. Serenity shattered the thrum of the rotors drew closer and the downdraft gently rustled the tops of the trees. Hovering off to the right less than one hundred metres away, its beat changed to thwop-thwop-thwop and the noise filled the air.

Thankfully, other than slightly raised heads and ears that were rotating as much as the helicopter's blades, Swift and Yogi appeared unconcerned and continued along the trail. Drowned-out by the disturbance, my reassuring words went unnoticed, as did our team's progression by the pilot as they again flew overhead back up the glen – minus the heavy white bag.

"That looked like the bag you deliver our hay in back at home," said Yogi, hopefully.

"It looked pretty heavy. Maybe it's a carrot delivery from one of our fans," said Swift, with a dreamy look in her eyes.

"I think the chopper mystery has been solved," I said, a little nervously. "They are obviously rebuilding the trail on the other side of the river, so it seems that the choice of left was right."

My nervousness was due to the fact that the pilot appeared not to have noticed us, despite my wearing of a hi vis waistcoat. We might have more encounters to come, and I hoped that none were closer than this one.

Chopper avoidance was put aside for a while as we reached the next crossing of the Derry Burn. When choosing the left bank, I had noticed we'd have to cross the water again, but was hopeful that this time the bridge marked on the map might be suitable for hooves. Looking at the rickety scaffolding-type creation before us, and the large step down the bank into the water, all hope vanished. Three circles later, and a couple of minor rears (Yogi never objects with more than twenty centimetres at a time), I feared I was going to have to get my feet wet.

"Oh, for goodness' sake," shouted Swift. "I'm not going through all that again. Stand aside you silly Bear and I'll show you how."

She barged Yogi out of the way with her shoulder (from his objecting stance on the edge of the river's bank) and plopped down into the water with a large splash.

"Oh!" said Yogi. "I get it now." And promptly followed suit.

Swift continued ahead, jumped up the bank on the far side, and nimbly negotiated the boggy ground that led back to the solid trail. It felt strange for me to be the one towed on the end of a lead rope for a change. It was also unusual for Swift to take the lead so strongly. Maybe my complex gal had finally located her confidence, and *maybe,* I thought, *I should ride her for tomorrow's final day*.

Switching back to the correct running order for now however, with the glen more open and the clouds lifted, we were offered a stunning view of the steep slopes of Carn Crom and Derry Cairngorm that bordered the western edge of the glen. Ahead to the left of the trail stood a solitary dead tree. Either a ballet dancer in pirouette or a dragon set for flight, its trunk and branches were sculpted by the weather to form a striking pose. The figure flamboyantly waved their limbs to invite us in and urged us to admire the dramatic scene beyond.

Up ahead to the right, on the crags of Coire an Fhir Bhogha, I could see a handful of men busy filling large white bags with rocks. Having lifted one of these bags, the helicopter was again on a direct course towards us. They were passing us higher this time and the horses didn't seem to mind, but I could see a potential problem beginning to unfold. By the time we reached the section of trail directly under the rock collection point, the chopper was likely to be back for its next load, and as far as I could tell – the pilot still hadn't seen us.

Although Team Swogi had coped thus far with the air irritation, I suspected a hover this close would be a step too far. Given the trail was thin and had a steep drop to the left, this combination was unlikely to offer a favourable outcome. I couldn't increase our speed though, as the trail was starting to increase its challenge with loose rocks littering its surface. As we steadily picked our way along, I reached into a saddle bag to wrap Yogi's cantle bags in a bright yellow rain cover and to place a similarly bright pink cover over my hat.

Feeling appropriately dressed for an eighties disco, I hoped the pilot would see us now – without the need to resort to pulling my glitter ball out of a bag.

"I knew you'd packed some non-essentials," grumbled Swift from behind.

I wasn't sure if it was our new neon attire that did the trick, or whether the men on the side of the hill were in radio communication with the pilot, but as the chopper approached again it suddenly banked off to hold position, hovering on the far side of the glen. *Phew!* I pushed Team Swogi on as fast as I dared, then when judged to be far enough away, waved the pink hat cover in thanks and as a signal for them to move on in.

Leaving the deafening noise behind and continuing our climb, we soon reached the next of the day's challenges – the crossing of the Glas Allt Mor. Tumbling in eagerness to add its waters to the Derry Burn, the riverbed consisted of a haphazard jumble of large, loose boulders. Perhaps due to a recent flood, there didn't seem to be an obvious nor safe place to cross for walkers, let alone horses.

I jumped off and led Team Swogi down the rough, heathered slopes for sixty metres or so to reach the confluence and cross there. The climb back up was tough and tortuous – the steepness mixing with knee-high heather, patches of bog, and hidden holes. I was gasping for breath and covered in sweat by the time we rejoined the trail. As usual, Yogi wasn't offering any respite time, as the trail ahead proceeded in an uphill manner.

"Come on," he said, "We've not reached the top yet!"

He wasn't wrong, as here the boulder-strewn trail began to steepen and I was amazed at how the horses were coping - maintaining a good pace through the jumble without so much as a minor stumble. It was an ascent full of twists and turns, but despite the wet ground between the stones, was solid enough and safer than other options I'd tried through the Cairngorms - like boggy Glen Gelder or tricky Glen Tilt.

The trail forked, with the left route taking a turn up to a grand amphitheatre formed by the Etchachan rocky ridges. The Hutchison Memorial Hut, dwarfed by the mass, was taking centre stage. Continuing north, we climbed more steeply still into the Lairig an Laoigh, 'The Pass of the Calves.'

One of two great passes through the main mountain range, the Pass of the Calves is lower in elevation than the Lairig Ghru to its west, but both were main routes when droving was at its peak. The Lairig an Laoigh, considered the easier of the two (particularly for youngstock) would have seen thousands of cattle passing through every year until about 1873. It's hard to imagine with the loose stones and roughness under foot that it was ever considered an easier option. However, until this way of droving life died out, local people had been paid to clear the boulders to the side each year.

"Shame they're not doing that now," moaned Swift, as she heaved herself up the last rocky rise to the saddle of the pass.

"Would you like a little break?" I asked.

Standing on the granite-gravel mound, I admired the long views north and south as Team Swogi picked their way between the boulders to find their favourite spiky grass. The bright green made it easy to find in amongst the pinks and greys of weathered rock. Deer grass (tricophorum cespitosum) isn't particularly favoured by deer, so I'm not sure why it's named so. I am certain, however, that it's either sweet-tasting or contains essential minerals for hard-working horses as Team Swogi are always determined to eat it.

The view to the north stretched down over Dubh Lochan to the Bynack Moore beyond, and the distance still to travel was daunting. Glancing back to the south, however, our progress thus far was equally extensive, and offered some much-needed encouragement. The long, rocky trail snaked and thinned into the distant glen before becoming indiscernible into the depths of where we'd started. I could understand why Dr. E. A. Baker, in his book *The Highlands with Rope and Rucksack,* explained the feel of the Cairngorm range as so: "The chief impression is, not of towering heights, but of unfathomable depths."

I stayed on foot to descend to the north, and was glad that I had, as the track became rougher still with increased areas of soft, wet ground along the side of the loch. We made a twisting and turning approach, avoiding the worst of the bog, to the Ath nam Fiann crossing, or as its more commonly known - 'The Fords of Avon.' Both these names are a newer designation than the original 'Uisge Ban nan Clachan Sleamhuinn' (meaning white water of the slippery stones).

The first renaming ceremony was apparently bestowed by Fionn, the leader of the Fianna bands of mythical hunter-warriors described in Irish, Scots, and Manx folklore. Accompanied by his wife whilst hunting in this glen, they'd tried to cross the river in spate. Slipping on a stone, his wife had been swept downstream and drowned.

Possibly overcome by grief and not seeing sense, rather than leave the original name as a warning to others, he marked her passing by calling the river Ath-Fhinn (meaning Fionn's Ford). Over time this name had evolved to the one more commonly used today, as the river runs from the Loch of Avon.

"They definitely should have left the name as it was," griped Yogi, as he slid and slipped his way through the water.

"And I can't feel any ford here," agreed Swift, as she stumbled over the random rocks scattered across the river's bed.

I'd jumped back on to keep my feet dry, but was now hanging on for dear life, as Yogi in a mild panic - rather than choose the easiest route - had set off in a direct beeline for the far bank. His feet were flailing in four different directions and I threw myself forward, grabbing hold of his mane, as he launched himself up the other side onto the safety of solid ground. Swift followed in keen pursuit, not stopping for her usual midstream play.

Safely at the top of the bank, I gave both manes a good scratch in appreciation of my amazing duo, then let them munch some grass surrounding the tiny stone mountain refuge hut as we all paused to recover. This hut differs from a bothy, in that it's tiny and would only be sought out for use in a real emergency situation. After a suitable break, we continued our climb on a track that was now more solid. Still littered with boulders, the pink gravel core became interspersed with large drainage channels which we stumbled over or avoided by nipping through the heather at the side.

At the top of the rise it finally levelled out, and the large expanse of moorland unfolded before us. The area of emptiness was vast, both ahead and to the right. The steep ridge of Bynack More to the left was the only reassuring handrail. The trail, well defined against the dark peat and heather, worked its way across the moor's reaches, then rose again before disappearing over a final brow.

A heavily woven blanket of stillness covered the sky; noncommittal, neither threatening rain nor promising sun. The silence was deafening. Little moved in this wild and empty landscape except for the humble vegetation, clinging low to the ground and ruffled slightly by the breeze. Our presence, only a pinprick within this vast expanse, felt trivial yet significant at the same time, as it was otherwise devoid of wildlife - any life - from this world or the next.

Scottish bogland is like no other; its dark peaty soils are perilous and of a deceiving nature. The ground may look like grass or mud but can disappear up to eight metres deep at the slightest pressure from unsuspecting feet. A network of watery channels weave through it, with unstable edges that give way into bottomless depths. Not confined to flat lowlands, the treachery can be found on slopes or peaks too - and it breathes, swelling and contracting depending on the weather.

Navigation of the maze is achieved by following a tightrope of certain plants that indicate harder ground: heather, bog myrtle, sundew, blaeberry, or at a push, reeds. Beware the white of bog-cotton, and the bright green of sphagnum moss or sedges - displaying their vivid warning signs of sinking places.

It's intimidating and threatening, particularly in bad weather; yet looking at the large mass beside me, I felt drawn into its challenge. To pitch one's ground-reading skills against the harshness of the land – no path to follow, except the one you create. I could imagine the absorption of the task, feeling my way through the maze, in tune and knowing just where to tread.

"Oi! Snap out of it will you," cried Yogi, with a shudder from nose to tail. "You'll give me nightmares!"

"The only mare you need around here is me," said Swift, trembling slightly too. "You know I can read your mind, and *that* was a terrifying thought."

"Sorry my loves," I apologised, returning my focus to the trail.

Our movement, the only motion for miles, was watched over carefully by the tall, strong figures of the Barns of Bynack. Perched on the edge of the Bynack Ridge, these large granite tors (of up to fifteen metres in height) seemed to monitor with menace all who passed below. I was reminded of the black, bulbous statue at Invercauld House, and decided that all man-made art is a humble imitation of nature's own exquisite creations.

At the end of the plateau, and still subject to the tor's scrutiny, we started to climb for the final rise of the day.

It was one of those hills that had a continual false peak, where you feel like you'll never find the top.

"Is this Nirvana?" asked Yogi.

"Well, it's certainly not *my* idea of paradise," said Swift.

Looking back across the moor, the River Avon was no longer in sight. As I remembered the Dubh Lochan, the Lairig an Laoigh, and the Derry Glen before that, the range of how far we'd come felt remarkable. Out in the open with the calling of the horizon, there presents a different appreciation of scale than that felt from travel through woodland, where you are unable to see around the last bend. Team Swogi appeared unfazed by the distant horizon or the landscape, content that the way ahead was well-marked, solid under hoof, and lined with tufts of deer grass.

As we finally reached the top, the view down to Abernethy and Glen More revealed a relief of familiar places. In about four kilometres time, we'd meet trails ridden regularly back when we'd lived in the area. The horses hadn't joined the dots of our travels yet and that might not happen until morning, as I'd identified a lovely spot for an overnight camp next to the River Nethy only two kilometres more.

The descent was steep, so I jumped off. It was good to give Yogi a break and riding steep downhill on a horse is never overly comfortable. As we made our way down the hill, I wound down from the tension of the pass and towards the end of the day. Being so close to the finish line, I broke my rule and pulled a Mars Bar out of the saddle bag to munch it on the move. I also fed the two remaining carrots to my noble steeds.

The ground to either side of the trail consisted of heathered wetlands. Patches of fluffy bog-cotton danced in the breeze and puddles of dark, peaty waters were scattered here and there. The only breaks in the dulcet tones were provided by dots of gorse, still in yellow flower and clinging to the side of the trail. Meall a' Bhuchaille (The Hill of the Herdsman) filled the view ahead, with our camp spot hidden in the dip before it.

Rounding a corner, we approached the River Nethy with another too-thin bridge to cross. I jumped back on, then steered Team Swogi to the left to ford instead.

"Oh! It's deeper than I thought," said Yogi, at the halfway point.

He put on a spurt of speed, frantically splashed through the water, and jumped up the other side. My pleas of "Wait for Swift!" went unheeded. Swift was still engrossed in her 'sploosh-splash' in the middle of the river, and once soaked and satisfied - to my dismay - I watched her turn back the way she'd come. She popped up the bank and promptly got stuck into some tasty green grass.

"Hey, Swift, please come over here!" I shouted.

"No thanks, I'm happy just where I am."

I swear I saw a glint of mischief in her eyes and concluded her return to the other bank was solely for her own amusement. With one of those impish eyes, she was watching, curious as to what I'd do next.

"Right then, Yogi, we'll have to go back and get her."

"No way – that was deep, besides, that's back the way we came, and I'm programmed for forwards only."

This statement proved to be true, as no amount of trying could get Yogi back towards the river. *Sigh!* I jumped off, walked back over the bridge, and resigned myself to wet feet as I led Swift through the river.

"You were right, it was deeper than it looked," I said to Yogi, as I inspected my jodphurs that were now wet to mid-thigh. *Still,* I thought, *at least we are all together again and are at camp now.*

On this side of the river, there was a small grassy patch – room enough for me to pitch my tent and for two hungry horses to graze overnight. So long, that is, as I made the corral cover most of the grass, and I set-up on a small area at the side. As I moseyed around the patch, building the corral in my mind and working out which of the three birch trees I'd use for the left boundary, a Duke of Edinburgh group arrived.

In a collective 'thank goodness for that' manner, they dropped their rucksacks to the ground with a thump and started to unpack. It didn't take long to establish that they'd planned this for their camp too, and with another group due to arrive imminently, there wouldn't be enough room for us all. Feeling very weary (and a little disappointed), I gave way to youth and those on foot, put my soggy boots back in the stirrups, and set off to find an alternative.

Initially, as expected, there were rumblings in the ranks about the enforced exodus from camp and the sweet grass it contained. Also, as expected, the rumbles and grumbles mostly came from the Spotty-bum at the back. Yogi had by now begun to recognise his surroundings, and with ears pricked and head held high, he was on a mission to find the new end of the day. Certain that this would be found at one of the carparks we used to park in when riding here on regular day trips, he was seeking the familiar form of the horse lorry.

"It's parked at Loch Morlich, isn't it?" he guessed, as he point-blank refused to turn right at the junction in the trail. The right turn would have taken us to Ryvoan Bothy, another potential camp with grass outside but which is also often busy with bikers and hikers. I, therefore, didn't argue too much at Yogi's choice to head down the glen into Glenmore – as I was sure we'd find a grassy spot somewhere.

We'd now joined the 'Thieves Road' (Rathad-nam-Mearleach), which can be traced all the way from Lochaber in the west. This long road, used by the

Lochaber reivers during forays into Strathspey and Moray, was the scene of many a pursuit and skirmish as landowners tried to drive the thieves off and recover their stock. By the light of the moon, the thieves would ride these familiar tracks to lift cattle in huge numbers at great cost to the landlords and farmers. In 1747, it was estimated that the total loss per annum in monetary terms from reiving was around £37,000. Not just the worth of the cattle, but the cost of paying watchmen and when that failed – a protection money alternative.

Yogi was on his own pursuit (of the lorry) on familiar tracks too, but thankfully we weren't riding in moonlight just yet. We were now at An Lochan Uaine (more commonly known as the Green Lochan), one of four such named within the Cairngorm range. The first on Cairn Toul (the prettiest), the second on Ben Macdui (the highest), the third on Derry Cairngorm (the smallest), and this one in the Ryvoan Pass which is reputed to be the greenest of them all. Nestled between steep slopes on either side of the pass, its deep emerald waters are said to exist because the fairies wash their clothes there.

The green waters are often static in the highest of winds, so it's not difficult to imagine magic in and around the loch. However, it's also believed that the fairy story was invented by those manning the nearby illicit whisky still. Fairies of the past were feared as dangerous, powerful, and sometimes cruel beings compared to their dainty and helpful image portrayed today. I assumed the distillers hoped their tales of spiteful sprites would dissuade prying eyes from witnessing *their own* wayward behaviour.

Whoever was causing mischief back then, they were doing so again now, as Team Swogi had bees in their bonnets and ants in their pants, and just wouldn't stand still. Despite the long way travelled over rough terrain so far today, we set off at a trot towards Glenmore Lodge. I was working hard with voice, seat, and in last resort hands, to keep to a compromised pace. If Team Swogi had their way, we'd gallop to where they thought the lorry was parked!

I didn't have to tell the team to turn as we clattered to the left just before the lodge to wind our way through the trees. At top speed, we rounded a rise, and just before a sharp bend, I was afforded a quick glance at a scattering of small headstones set into a grassy area to the side of the trail. Here was the burial ground of the favourite horses and much-loved dogs of the Denniston Family – a family of shipbuilders from Glasgow who'd once kept the original Glenmore Lodge (now the Youth Hostel) as a hunting lodge. Seven granite headstones, dating from the early 20th century, once placed with loving care were now forgotten and overgrown.

We turned right to follow the course of the Ruigh-euanchan river as it dropped down towards Loch Morlich. The steady beat of Team Swogi's feet increased in pace and I struggled to stay onboard this runaway train. Scenery flew by at an alarming rate as they raced the waters beside us.

"Not far now," shouted Yogi in triumph.

"We'll see the lorry soon," agreed Swift.

"I was thinking of camping at the Hayfields," I said hopefully and a little out of breath, as we emerged at the road that led to the Cairngorm Ski Centre.

Here was a grassy slope, a rare patch of open ground in amongst the cover of the Glenmore Forest. Perhaps remnant meadows of Rieunachan Lodge whose ruins lay at the far edge of the field. It was often used by holiday makers in the winter for sledging and learning to ski, or in the summer for kite flying and grass skiing. I steered the horses to the far-right corner, but I could tell that they wouldn't settle. The adjacent carpark was full of cars and campervans and given that it was weekend and dinner time, several BBQs were on the go. Team Swogi were attracting a lot of attention from adults and children alike.

There was too much traffic, of both the human and the vehicular type, and I knew that I wouldn't settle either. I'd be on high alert all night, worrying that the horses (i.e. Swift) might push down the free-standing corral, then wander onto the road – or alternatively, would set off without me on their staunch search for the lorry. An area with additional corral support was required tonight, to form a sturdy barrier against their strong onward drive.

The Runaway Train

As if to underline my point, after only a few mouthfuls of grass, Team Swogi set off towards the trail that continued to the Loch Morlich carpark. I'd camped along this trail once before, on a small patch of grass in amongst some trees. This sheltered position wouldn't offer much respite from midges, but the trees would provide four solid corners for the fence. The previous stay had been with Yvonne and her two ponies at the time - Katy and Skye. I hoped the memory of that night might fill Yogi and Swift's brains more than the thoughts of transport home.

"Told you it was parked at Loch Morlich carpark," said Yogi smugly to Swift.

"Nice to be offered that snack break at the Hayfields, but seems little point since we'll soon be home," replied Swift, urging him into a trot.

As we flew along the twists and turns of the trail that followed the river's curves, the runaway train threatened to derail at several of the bends. I had to deploy the foot brake, the handbrake, an air brake, and an anchor thrown off the back to come to a brief halt at the place we'd camped before. I was dismayed to find that there was no grass here now – just hip-height ferns.

"Why have we stopped here?" asked Swift, with fidgety feet.

"The lorry's just around the next corner," said Yogi, as he snatched the reins from my hand and restarted of his own accord.

I knew that just around the corner, two members of the party were going to be bitterly disappointed and that I'd have a battle on my hands. Loch Morlich carpark was to the right, and I'd be asking, pleading – well, okay - insisting on a turn to the left. The only other place I could think of to camp was down by the River Druidh in another six kilometres. It was now six-thirty and we'd already travelled thirty-four kilometres over nine hours; but battles aside, at the current speed, this extra distance should take about an hour.

Circling at the end of the bridge that crossed the river, I began to wonder if we'd get to the new camp spot by night fall. Scotland's long evening light in summer was being put fully to the test – as was my patience. I felt bad asking Team Swogi to go further after the long day we'd already had, but couldn't see any other option. My guilt at pushing them on was probably lessening the effects of my insistence to turn left, as it wasn't being delivered with full heart and soul. However, there was only heathered or ferned ground here, not suitable for the overnight appetites of two hungry horses.

"Look Yogi, the lorry is absolutely NOT in Loch Morlich carpark," I explained for at least the sixth time. "We need to go over this bridge."

"Oh!" said Swift. "Do you think its parked at Loch an Eilein then?" she suggested.

"Loch an Eilein?" asked Yogi. "That's this way." He set off with renewed resolve, and Team Swogi's hoofbeats on the wooden planks reverberated through the still evening air.

The wide track around the back of Loch Morlich was even and soft, so didn't offer any ease in pace. We passed cyclists out enjoying the mild, dry evening - at speed and without so much as a glance from my focussed companions. I shouted apologies to numerous walkers who were surprised and scattered as we rapidly approached from behind. The ground to the right was a mixture of dark heather and bright green fern, with a few young trees hiding the view of the loch. From time to time a squeeze of sight was offered of the steel-grey waters.

At the end of the loch, without hesitation and no guidance from me, both Yogi and Swift turned to the left towards Rothiemurchus Lodge, a self-catering military hostel nestled within the huge forest. The name of Rothiemurchus (The Fort of Murchas) dates to the 8th century and the area is understood to have been inhabited since Pictish times. The forest consists of around ten million trees with some believed to be over three-hundred years old. I doubt the original forest in the Iron Age would have looked much different to the way it does now, and a sense of antiquity hangs from every branch.

Another sense of time was developing in the remains of the evening light, as the west facing slopes of the Cairngorms to our left were modelling a pink glow. The cheeks of its peaks blushed, embarrassed by the sun's soft caress. My stomach was watching the clock too, the rumbling alarm sounding out its dinner time reminder. I was glad we only had another two kilometres to go, as not only did I need some food, but I was feeling quite exhausted. I decided that whoever else was camped at Aultdrue – they would just have to make space for the corral and tent because I was all spent.

The Scottish midge is never respectful of one's personal space, however, and none moved over an inch at Aultdrue to allow us room to breathe. Yogi and Swift were pacing around the corral with tails swishing, feet stamping, and snorts of disapproval aimed in my direction. I was desperately trying to heat a hot chocolate on my stove but even with the potlid on, the top few centimetres of liquid was a black mass of additional protein I didn't really need. I was rapidly gathering swollen blotches that itched furiously on any exposed skin and was wondering what on earth to do now.

The corral, built with trees for support along one side, was sizeable, and I'd stretched it out as far as I could into open ground. I'd hoped a breeze there would help relieve the horse's torture, but the evening had descended into absolute stillness. Swift and Yogi were both being driven insane by the thickest cloud of biting beasties I'd ever seen during my twenty years of life in Scotland. It was a blood-sucking, miniature-vampire plague of biblical and unbearable proportions. Adding to Team Swogi's agitation was the call of the familiar trail, as they hadn't found the lorry yet.

Going against the lesson learnt at Old Blair, I still hadn't removed hoof boots, and neither had I pitched my tent. There was this feeling in my gut that staying here wouldn't go well. Yogi and Swift would pace all night – that was for sure, and Swift would test the far reaches of the corral as soon as I looked away, so an all-night watch would be required. I couldn't ignore the irony of that upon the Thieves Road but didn't relish the prospect of this historical re-enactment.

As I sipped my lumpy hot chocolate, I tried not to wretch and tried to summarise my thoughts into a sensible decision. It was now eight o'clock, with fifteen kilometres to our planned finish tomorrow, back at the Uath Lochans. We had been going for nearly eleven hours, and it would take another three to four to complete the Cairngorm circuit. If we continued now, our movement would dispel the midge torture, we'd finish in the dark and then have an hour and a half to drive home. The alternative was to stay here, have no sleep and then two exhausted, hungry, and possibly tucked up horses in the morning from pacing all night.

The horses briefly paused in that pacing to look at me. I knew what they were thinking, and they knew that I knew. The problem was twofold, however. I wasn't sure if I had enough energy left, and I also wasn't sure if Mike had placed the lorry back at the lochans yet. To rule out one of these uncertainties (which might provide motivation to influence the other), I switched on my phone, found that I had enough signal, and gave him a call.

"The upshot is..." I explained to Team Swogi. "The lorry isn't in position yet and Mike is running his bar – he's already had a drink, so isn't able to drive. He does send his apologies though."

Swift and Yogi paced to the far side of the corral in disgust and stood at the corner closest to the onwards trail.

"Go on Swift, just knock it down, I know you've done it before," urged Yogi.

"The electric's on, but my rug might soften the hit," whispered Swift, as she reached her long neck over the wire to measure up the task.

"You can do it, I'm right behind you."

Yogi, terrified as always of the electric tape, was standing with his eyes squeezed tightly shut, waiting for Swift to bravely do the deed.

"I might have another plan," I offered.

"Well get on with it then," ordered Swift, angrily swishing her tail as she set off around the corral at a trot, breaking through the swarms.

Friendships, and the support they offer, often help to push through dark unease on the trail. I hoped this one, on this occasion, might push some dark unease and some dark clouds of flies firmly aside. Grabbing my phone and braving the face recognition software from under my midge net for the second time, I called Yvonne. Having set the scene, Yvonne, with much sympathy and total understanding of the hellish conditions that midges create, immediately offered aid. She agreed to meet me with her trailer at Loch an Eilein just five kilometres away, in about an hour.

"The timings should match," she said. "Of my drive and your travels - to have us arrive at roughly the same time."

Spurred into action with supplementary midge motivation, I packed up in record time, although there was still room for improvement on this personal best. The process undoubtedly would have been quicker if I hadn't had to follow two agitated horses around the corral as I attempted to tack up. I didn't correct this impatient behaviour though, nor their repeated attempts of escape to the trail as I deconstructed the fence.

I did, however, have to remind them both about personal space rules. Desperate as they were to scratch the itchy bumps on their heads, they'd used me as a scratching post, and each had pushed me to the ground with frenzied fervour. I could see and feel their downright distress as midges aren't fickle about where their meal comes from, and I wasn't escaping the torment either, so I had corrected this break of rules gently.

During medieval times, it's said that one form of Scottish torture was to stake a victim out naked, left to the mercy of the ferocious midge's thirst. They are not known for any sort of compassion or merciful manners though, and swarms can inflict about three-thousand bites an hour. We wouldn't be the first to flee their forays. In 1872, Queen Victoria abandoned a Highland picnic after being "half-devoured" and during World War II, soldiers training in the Highlands branded midges a worse enemy than Hitler himself.

Underway as soon as we could (and not a second more), we forded the River Druidh in fading light and set off to the west. At a wooden signpost that was too low down for me to read, Yogi branched left, not stopping to read what it said. I slowed him slightly while I looked at the map, to double check his sense of direction. Taking advantage of the pause in proceedings, Swift rubbed her head roughly up and down my leg. How horses can remember a trail from four years ago, but not rules about personal space re-enforced four minutes ago, remains a mystery to me; but I established that Yogi was correct with his left turn choice.

The dusky trail through the trees was silent and still, the last of the sun spreading between branches with final shards of golden light. It continued its descent, hiding behind the trunks as it gradually went to ground. Our united rhythm, ingrained after almost two weeks on the trail and the long day today, was reassuring in the fading light. It created a trance-like state of perpetual motion, and I didn't want it to end. I'd never ridden my horses off into the sunset before, but cliched as it was, and as tired as I felt, I was thoroughly enjoying the experience.

A cooling forest at night has a different mood; the air is crisper, the sounds are softened, and shadows distort familiar forms. Approaching the witching hour, this vibe was surprisingly absent of threat. The forest felt tranquil, freed from the daytime disturbance of man, and allowed to breathe a little deeper. The wavering call of an owl seemed to announce a definitive end to the day's activities and the coming of the night.

Heeding his hoot, and with just enough light to make our way, we rounded the shores of Loch an Eilein (Loch of the Island). The island in question was situated about four hundred metres away, too far to see in the dark. Possibly an artificial island (or crannog) constructed as a place of refuge from thieves and fighting clans, it remained a bolt hole for many throughout time. It holds the ruins of a 14th century castle – built by Alexander Stewart (the Wolf of Badenoch) – and was a site of conflict for all its owners over the years, finally falling out of use in the late 18th century.

In the dark, shadowed woods, the silver glimmer of the loch's surface stood out, and the gentle lapping of its waters at the edge were soothing. All of us were at ease, acquainted with the features of this familiar trail, and moving as one. As we rounded the final corner to the carpark, still maintaining a similar fast pace to earlier in the day, it was an abrupt arrival from the depths of the trees into the clearing.

"There it is!" Yogi shouted.

"That's not our lorry though," said Swift, her voice full of disappointment and dismay.

"It will do though. Look, Yvonne's brought us carrots!"

"Thoroughly deserved," I said, with tears in my eyes as a feeling of admiration, appreciation, and awe of my two faithful companions washed over me.

"It's time to go home," I whispered, with disappointment and dismay in my voice too.

Across the Finish Line

The early arrival of our last night on the trail brought our Cairngorm circumnavigation to a rather terse end. The midge attack removed a fair amount of blood as well as the opportunity to ease into a contemplative finish. The savouring of final steps, the anticipation of homecoming, and the loosening of connections to wilderness had been stolen by the swarm. Back at home, with lorry collected and cup of tea in hand, I was sitting in the field with Yogi standing over me dozing while Swift gently nibbled my feet. As I relished their company, I caught up on the missed period of reflection.

The warp of time is strange – it can seem like a blink of an eye or stretch out in slow motion, depending on what you are doing with the minutes, hours, or days. On one hand, it seemed like two minutes from the start of our adventure at Uath Lochans. On the other, each day dawdled with vivid images of every moment replaying in my mind.

Time on the trail is measured by alternative means to those at home: the change in the length of the day, or the growth and demise of vegetation as leaves unfurl then wither and turn to dust. The change of season and the time of day are more apparent when living outside, but in passing through unchanged lands once travelled by others in the long-ago past, you are free to use their eyes to jump through the years. Meanwhile at home, time appears to stand still – paused for your return.

They say that 'home is where the heart is', but my heart is often torn. Horseback, nomadic existence offers unity, balance, release, and a feeling of contentment.

However, I'm also happy at home in amongst routine, comforts, and loved ones. I believe that Yogi and Swift feel a similar conflict, as they too seem satisfied in either situation. When on the trail, we all feel the draw of home; and when home, the wild places continue to call.

These wild places offer restoration. They reset, alter perspective, then send you on your way; humbled, refreshed, and with renewed appreciation. Scotland, with its remote lands, mountains of all shapes and sizes, layers of past, and an abundance of wildlife, is beautifully untamed. It is full of ways through the hills rarely travelled, where resilience, solitude, and connection can be found. I consider myself extremely fortunate to live here.

I felt restored and rebooted in a variety of ways. Mentally, I'd shaken off the stresses and strains of everyday life for a while and had a renewed resolve to return to it all. Setting out on this adventure, I'd needed a 'more normal challenge' and achieving a positive outcome had been good for my soul. I was, however, surprised to feel physical benefits too, especially given my recent hospital stay. I was exhausted - that I couldn't deny – particularly given the extremely long final day, but it felt like 'normal' tiredness. The kind you'd expect after a physical two weeks living outside.

This wasn't the Lyme fatigue I was so familiar with - the kind that was mind-numbing, that left you staggering and shaking after simply taking a shower. I felt stronger, with less aches and pains (so let's just put aside for a moment that my heart was still misbehaving). This wasn't the first time I'd felt relief from symptoms due to a wandering interlude. I'd enjoyed periods of better health following my 'riding made easy' excursions over the last three years too.

I'm intrigued to know what factors are at play that make a period of continual movement improve health.

Was it the physicality, the pushing yourself gently on a daily basis, with just the correct level of muscular challenge? Was it a lack of indulgence – living sparsely – your body thriving on leanness? Perhaps a lack of everyday stress and the body's resulting chemical response? The avoidance of toxins, yet undiscovered in urban living? Or does the mind cure the body by being in a better place?

I'm not the only one to ask these questions. Raynor Winn in *Landlines* has similar enquiry when her husband's corticobasal degeneration improved against the odds after walking long-distance routes. Much about Lyme is left unknown due to a lack of research, a lack of funding, a lack of recognition, and an apparent lack of interest, but perhaps there is a bigger picture (encompassing the root cause of this and other conditions) that is being overlooked.

The horses appear to benefit too, not just physical improvements in strength and fitness, but in their state of mind. Travelling around thirty kilometres a day is the natural routine of horses in the wild, and decision-making surrounding hazards and necessities would exercise their brains. Maybe Yogi and Swift have a requirement for challenge beyond the safe environment of home, and their need is just as strong as mine.

Returning home with more confidence, increased self-esteem, and improved resilience - all three of us are able to cope better with the daily trials of life. Facing difficulties has individual benefits, but facing these with others creates a very close bond. The trust formed and the cohesion established is indescribable. Moving as one, totally in tune with two opinionated and formidable creatures, fills your heart to the brim and nourishes your soul.

Horses are gentle, forgiving, and sensitive, but at the same time they are powerful and perceptive. True connection with these magnificent beings takes time, honesty, and a disclosure of one's flaws. Thankfully, they are patient and wise tutors. Receiving an invitation to join their herd is an absolute honour and I am so very grateful that my two heart-horses have welcomed me into their midst.

Epilogue

The test to see if Yogi and I were back on track had drawn to a successful conclusion. His Cushing's diagnosis certainly hadn't held him back and I'd muddled through. I went on to be diagnosed with Lyme carditis and the month-long course of intravenous antibiotics to treat it calmed any irregularities and eased other symptoms such as fatigue and brain-fog. It remains a wavering journey though, one that I suspect will stay with me for life.

I've continued to seek challenge and have benefited health-wise from further long-distance rides. Maybe one day I will 'ride off into the sunset' for real and return completely cured. Perhaps hope can change an outcome if it is felt strongly enough. In my first book *From East to West by Saddle is Best,* I described a hope to one-day undertake a one-thousand-mile journey "with Team Swogi by my side." Little did I know that eighteen months later, this dream would come to fruition.

In May 2022, I set off from Ullapool with my faithful equine companions and wove a winding route through the Highlands. Exploring the mountains and glens of the place I love most, we finished at Spey Bay, close to home, three months later. It was probably the hardest thing I've ever done. The weather throughout the summer was unsettled, and we all had to dig deep to cope with huge storms, bitterly cold high passes, heat waves, and of course the infamous Scottish midge. We didn't retreat from their onslaught this time.

It was also probably the most incredible experience to date. The warmth and generosity of people we met along the way offset the cold of the weather and restored faith in humankind. Travelling with horses (particularly on my own) appears to open hearts and doors. We might not use horses for work in the UK anymore, but the nostalgia and the connection with these amazing creatures who give so much to their humans still remains.

Our relationship and teamwork strengthened further – despite this having been developed over similar (but shorter) excursions over the last ten years. Already, I thought, at a point where it could improve no more – I was proved wrong. Their trust in me absolutely astounds me: crossing high bridges, raging rivers, cattle grids with only a flimsy 'horse-safe' covering, squeezing through gaps in fences, deep river fords, tunnels under canals, negotiating flights of steps, dealing with traffic, stampeding herds of cows, *very* low flying jets, handling mountainous terrain, and staying in unfamiliar places.

This depth of trust and understanding only evolves after moving and living together for a protracted period. It seems the further you travel together, the more layers and depths are revealed. Swift led the way on numerous days, with remarkable confidence and ease. Yogi's dependable drive carried us over the finish line. I'm in awe of them both, they gave me their absolute all in their characterful and individual ways. To say that I'm extremely proud of my equine friends seems entirely inadequate.

Returning home, we were invited (and delighted) to join the Long Riders Guild – "an international fraternity of mounted men and women who have chosen to saddle up their horse(s) to complete a life-changing, one-thousand-mile continuous journey." Maybe one day, I'll write about this adventure too.

When I nervously set out in 2010, to stay overnight in the hills for the very first time with my horses (and my good friend Yvonne), I never imagined where it might lead. The experience gained and the unity evolved over the many years of shorter journeys were more than apparent this summer. This preparation was essential to the journey's success. It just goes to show that it's prudent to take small steps at a time – aiming within reach but dreaming big.

With such a huge dream now ticked off the bucket list, I'm sure I can be forgiven for asking myself "Well what now?" but I'm relaxed about the answer to this pertinent question. Inspired by a quote from Nan Shepherd in her book *Living Mountain,* "Often the mountain gives itself most completely when I have no destination." I am curious about a nomadic existence with no set timescale and no defined end, and I think this is where my aspirations now lie.

Team Swogi and I will attempt a more flexible style, to see what secrets a land reveals when approached with less purpose. As J.R.R. Tolkien famously said, "Not all who wander are lost."

Exploring the Place I Love Most

Poetry Corner

The Dog who loved his Cheese

No dog, you can't have my cheese
No matter how nice you say please
Self-made to look thin
The drool down your chin
But I'll ask you politely to leave

No dog, you can't have my cheese
No matter how nice you say please
Your tail a mad wag
Your tongue all a sag
I'll ask you more sternly to leave

No dog, you can't have my cheese
No matter how nice you say please
Ears perfect in fold
You just won't be told
I really insist now, you leave

No dog, you can't have my cheese
No matter how nice you say please
Your head with a tilt-on
For a piece of my Stilton
Go on now, get out, just leave

No dog, you can't have my cheese
No matter how nice you say please
Your paw on my knee
To gnaw on my Brie
What chance do I have that you'll leave?

OK dog you CAN have my cheese
Considering how nice you said please
I am so mesmerised
By those big sad eyes
How much would you like in reprieve?

Printed in Great Britain
by Amazon

14815984R00169